Beyond Decent Work

International Labour Studies

Edited by Klaus Dörre and Stephan Lessenich

Volume 14

Felix Hauf, Dr. phil., is a research associate at the Department of Political Science at Goethe University Frankfurt.

Felix Hauf

Beyond Decent Work

The Cultural Political Economy of Labour Struggles
in Indonesia

Campus Verlag
Frankfurt/New York

ISBN 978-3-593-50644-9 Print
ISBN 978-3-593-43489-6 E-Book (PDF)

Cover design: Campus Verlag GmbH, Frankfurt-on-Main
Printing office and bookbinder: CPI buchbücher.de, Birkach
Printed on acid free paper.
Printed in Germany

www.campus.de
www.press.uchicago.edu

Contents

Acknowledgements

This book would not have been possible without cooperation and support from many individuals, groups and organisations. First and foremost, I want to thank all the Indonesian workers, unionists, activists and academics whose testimonies form the empirical basis of my analysis. As they remain anonymous throughout the book, they cannot be named here, unfortunately. I want to thank Uta Ruppert and Claes Belfrage for their invaluable supervision and critical input as well as Veronica Schild for good advice. Claes has been more than a supervisor; he has become a friend and mentor. Bob Jessop and Ngai-Ling Sum were indispensable for my work, both theoretically and personally. Thanks are due to Anita Fischer and Daniel Keil for reading, criticising and commenting on my work as well as Anja Engelhorn, Samia Dinkelaker and Tobias Cepok for helping me getting access to the field. Special thanks go to Melanie Schreiber for supporting me in every respect, for her patience on the private side of life and for so much more. Last but not least, I want to thank the *Freunde und Förderer der Goethe-Universität* as well as the *Deutscher Akademischer Austauschdienst* for financially supporting my fieldtrips to Indonesia.

Figures

Tables

Abbreviations

ABGTeks	*Asosiasi Buruh Garmen dan Tekstil* (Association of Garment and Textile Workers)
ABM	*Aliansi Buruh Menggugat* (Alliance for Workers' Demands)
ACILS	American Center for International Labor Solidarity
AFL-CIO	American Federation of Labor and Congress of Industrial Organizations
AFW	Asia Floor Wage
APINDO	*Asosiasi Pengusaha Indonesia* (Indonesian Employers' Association)
ASEAN	Association of Southeast Asian Nations
BFC	Better Factories Cambodia
BTI	*Barisan Tani Indonesia* (Peasants' Front of Indonesia)
BWI	Better Work Indonesia
CBA	Collective Bargaining Agreement
CCC	Clean Clothes Campaign
CDA	Critical Discourse Analysis
CGT	Critical Grounded Theory
CoC	Code of Conduct
CPE	Cultural Political Economy
CSR	Corporate Social Responsibility
DRA	Dialectical-Relational Approach
EOI	Export-Oriented Industrialisation
FBSI	*Federasi Buruh Seluruh Indonesia* (All-Indonesia Labour Federation)
FES	Friedrich-Ebert-Stiftung
FNPBI	*Front Nasional Perjuangan Buruh Indonesia* (National Front of Indonesian Labour Struggle)

FoA Protocol	Freedom of Association Protocol
FSBKU	*Federasi Serikat Buruh Karya Utama*
	(Federation of Main Plant Labour Unions)
FSP-BUMN	*Federasi Serikat Pekerja - Badan Usaha Milik Negara*
	(Federation of State-Owned Enterprise Workers' Unions)
GARTEKS	*Federasi Serikat Buruh - Garmen dan Tekstil*
(FSB-GARTEKS)	(Federation of Garment and Textile Labour Unions)
GASBINDO	*Gabungan Serikat Buruh Islam Indonesia*
	(Amalgamated Indonesian Islamic Labour Union)
GCC	Global Commodity Chain
GMAC	Garment Manufacturers' Association in Cambodia
GPN	Global Production Network
GVC	Global Value Chain
GSBI	*Gabungan Serikat Buruh Independen*
	(Federation of Independent Labour Unions)
ICFTU	International Confederation of Free Trade Unions
IFC	International Finance Corporation
ILO	International Labour Organisation
IMF	International Monetary Fund
ISI	Import Substitution Industrialisation
ITGLWF	International Textile, Garment and Leather Workers' Federation
ITUC	International Trade Union Confederation
KASBI	*Kongres Aliansi Serikat Buruh Indonesia*
	(Congress of the Indonesian Labour Union Alliance)
KHL	*Kebutuhan Hidup Layak*
	(Decent Living Needs)
KORPRI	*Korps Pegawai Republik Indonesia*
	(Public Employees' Corps of the Republic of Indonesia)
KPKB	*Kelompok Perempuan untuk Keadilan Buruh*
	(Women's Group for Workers' Justice)
KPRI	*Konfederasi Pergerakan Rakyat Indonesia*
	(Indonesian People's Movement Confederation)
KSBSI	*Konfederasi Serikat Buruh Sejahtera Indonesia*
	(Confederation of Indonesian Prosperity Labour Unions)

KSN	*Konfederasi Serikat Nasional*
	(National Union Confederation)
KSPI	*Konfederasi Serikat Pekerja Indonesia*
	(Confederation of Indonesian Trade Unions)
KSPSI	*Konfederasi Serikat Pekerja Seluruh Indonesia*
	(Confederation of All-Indonesian Trade Unions)
LBH	*Lembaga Bantuan Hukum*
	(Legal Aid Institute)
LIPS	*Lembaga Informasi Perburuhan Sedane*
	(Sedane Labour Resource Centre)
MFA	Multi-Fibre Agreement
NGO	Non-Governmental Organisation
PERBUPAS	*Perkumpulan Buruh Pabrik Sepatu*
	(Association of Footwear Factory Workers)
PFA	Play Fair Alliance
PKI	*Partai Komunis Indonesia*
	(Communist Party of Indonesia)
PKU	*Paguyuban Karya Utama*
	(Main Plant Circle of Friends)
PRD	*Partai Rakyat Demokratik*
	(Democratic People's Party)
PRP	*Perhimpunan Rakyat Pekerja*
	(Working People's Alliance)
PT	*Perseroan Terbatas*
	(Private Limited Company)
SARBUMUSI	*Serikat Buruh Muslimin Indonesia*
	Indonesian Muslim Labour Union
SBGTS	*Serikat Buruh Garmen Tekstil dan Sepatu*
	(Garment Textile and Footwear Labour Union)
SBKU	*Serikat Buruh Karya Utama*
	(Main Plant Labour Unions)
SBSI	*Serikat Buruh Sejahtera Indonesia*
	(Indonesian Prosperity Labour Union)
SISBIKUM	*Saluran Informasi Sosial dan Bimbingan Hukum*
	(Channel for Social Information and Legal Guidance)
SOBSI	*Sentral Organisasi Buruh Seluruh Indonesia*
	(All-Indonesia Central Workers' Organisation)

SPN	*Serikat Pekerja Nasional*
	(National Trade Union)
SPP	*Serikat Pertani Pasundan*
	(Peasants' Union of Pasundan)
SPSI	*Serikat Pekerja Seluruh Indonesia*
	(All-Indonesia Trade Union)
SPTP	*Serikat Pekerja Tingkat Perusahan*
	(Enterprise-Level Trade Union)
SRA	Strategic-Relational Approach
TATA	Trade Agreement on Textile and Apparel
TURC	Trade Union Rights Centre
TNC	Transnational Corporation
TSK	*Federasi Serikat Pekerja - Tekstil Sandang dan Kulit*
(FSP-TSK)	(Federation of Textile Garment and Leather Trade Unions)
ULN	*Upah Layak Nasional*
	(National Decent Wage)
UMK	*Upah Minimum Kabupaten/Kota*
	(District/City-Level Minimum Wage)
UMP	*Upah Minimum Provinsi*
	(Provincial Minimum Wage)
UMSP	*Upah Minimum Sektoral Provinsi*
	(Provincial Sectoral Minimum Wage)
UMSK	*Upah Minimum Kabupaten/Kota*
	(District/City-Level Sectoral Minimum Wage)
UN	United Nations
US	United States (of America)
WCL	World Confederation of Labour
WTO	World Trade Organisation

1. Introduction

Indonesia is one of the Asian countries industrial production has been shifted to after the crisis of Atlantic Fordism. While European and North-American countries—the former "industrial nations"—are transforming themselves into "knowledge-based economies", world market production of industrial goods is now located in countries like China, India and Indonesia. Whereas export production has fuelled rapid economic growth and rising national income, it was underpinned by poverty wages and inhumane working conditions in those world market factories that became to be known as the new "sweatshops". Multinational corporations like Nike and Adidas began shifting their production sites to Indonesia in the 1980s looking for cheap labour (Merk 2011b). In fact, it was Nike in Indonesia that sparked the anti-sweatshop movement in the 1990s after reports about massive human rights abuses in factories producing shoes for Nike had surfaced. The subsequent global campaign against Nike can be considered one of the constitutive moments of the emergence of the broader movement against neoliberal globalisation. Civil society organisations managed to effectively damage the public image of Nike through the tactic of "naming and shaming" (Bartley and Child 2014). Image, today, is a core asset for companies like Nike—selling not only shoes, but a sportive lifestyle of freedom and youth. This image and the picture of young women producing these shoes under hellish conditions were a bad match. Growing consumer pressure endangered Nike's profits. It was only in reaction to these movements that Nike felt the need to introduce one of the first "voluntary codes of conduct" of a transnational corporation (Merk 2011b). Clearly, Indonesia is a critical case when it comes to discussions of workers' rights in the age of globalisation.

Today, Corporate Social Responsibility (CSR) is a general feature of the global economy; every global player has a CSR programme. While these programmes are supposed to demonstrate to consumers that the companies are taking responsibility for working conditions along their supply chains, they have been widely criticised for largely failing to deliver on the promise of substantially improving them (Burckhardt 2011). Mere company-side codes of conduct and CSR policies are widely seen as "blue-washing" (John 2011), because they are geared towards improving public image without fundamentally changing their business model in order to enable social improvements. CSR initiatives are voluntary, usually unilateral and not legally binding. Company codes of conduct that have been criticised as mere "window dressing" are increasingly replaced or amended by industry-wide codes, multi-stakeholder initiatives and global framework agreements. Many companies seek to improve the credibility of their codes of conduct by linking them to the core labour standards of the International Labour Organisation (ILO). These are the most commonly acknowledged reference points for the content of codes of conduct—prohibition of child labour, prohibition of forced labour, non-discrimination, freedom of association and the right to collective bargaining (ILO 1998). The ILO as the only tripartite organisation of the United Nations (UN) framework representing governments, trade unions and employer associations is one of the central nodes of a global multilevel governance network of public and private labour regulation.

Since 1999, the ILO is organising its activities around the notion of "decent work" (ILO 1999). The decent work agenda is the result of a major revision process within the ILO, developed as a response to the challenges of neoliberal globalisation. Global restructuring processes of deregulation, liberalisation and privatisation transformed the world of work in profound ways, requiring the ILO to adopt a completely new strategic framework for its institutional action (Vosko 2002, 2004). On the one hand, this framework recognises the need to extend labour rights and social protection to groups of workers outside the "standard employment relationship" or at the margins of formal employment systems. The proliferation of informal, precarious, non-standard work or "downgraded labour" (Castells and Portes 1989) has been a central feature of neoliberal global restructuring. The new ILO convention *Decent Work for Domestic Workers* (ILO 2011a) is an example of the commitment to work towards incorporating marginalised and vulnerable groups of workers in the "informal sector"—mostly women—into the framework of international labour regulation (Schwenken 2012). This move can be seen as a progressive step towards representing the interests of the majority of workers worldwide, rather than protecting the relatively high standards of European and North-American standard employees—mostly men—at the expense of informalised workers. On the other hand, this move also means that the previously existing body of international labour standards has been weakened, because only the most fundamental labour rights have been defined as the core labour standards that the ILO aims to implement around the globe as part of the decent work agenda (Standing 2008).

From a scholarly perspective stressing the progressive potential of "decent work", the ILO's agenda may be seen as an element of an emerging post-neoliberal framework of labour regulation (on the notion of post-neoliberalism cf. Brand and Sekler 2009). This perspective is underpinned by the hope that the world economic and financial crisis starting in 2008 may have signalled the end of the neoliberal period and opened up political space to re-regulate the global economy, shift power away from financial markets and reignite productive growth generating new jobs. By now, these hopes have been largely disappointed (Scherrer 2011). Austerity policies in Europe show rather that the crisis has been used by political and economic elites to embark on a further round of "roll-out neoliberalism" (Peck and Tickell 2002) flanked by new social policy discourses (Graefe 2006).

1.1 Research Question and Hypothesis

The following question arises: What is "decent work" in this context? Is decent work a discourse that challenges the hegemony of neoliberalism by mobilising counter-hegemonic forces such as progressive trade unions, social movements and activist non-governmental organisations (NGOs)? Is it a flanking mechanism for neoliberalism, adding legitimacy to the neoliberal framework through a largely symbolic appeal to social policy without fundamentally changing underlying power structures and, thus, reproducing neoliberal hegemony?

My hypothesis is that it can be both, depending on the context, on who is making use of the decent work discourse in what kinds of practices, for which ends and how. What is new about decent work, it can be argued, is less its actual content in terms of hard law labour regulation than its discursive form that symbolically proclaims the right to decent work for all.

Decent work by itself does not codify any new legally binding agreements and subsequent possibilities of sanctions. Rather, it uses moral persuasion and voluntariness to promote compliance with existing conventions (Vosko 2002). What is more important, it creates a new normative framework or discursive order not only for the ILO itself but also for other social actors working on the field of (transnational) labour rights or struggling to improve the working and living conditions of workers worldwide. The domestic workers convention is an example of how a specific network of social movements and institutional actors appropriated the decent work discourse in order to extend existing labour rights to vulnerable groups of workers who have been previously excluded from these rights. Decent work proclaims the "right to labour rights" that can be used by different actors on various scales and sites to claim those rights. On the one hand, decent work can thus be seen as a typically neoliberal soft law instrument lacking force. On the other hand, decent work can be regarded as an "economic imaginary" (Jessop 2004), which symbolically proclaims the right to decent work for all and, thus, opens up new avenues for social actors to struggle for better working and living conditions. If, for instance, emerging unions or union-like organisations within the informal sector, women's organisations and other NGOs are using decent work in order to locally appropriate basic economic and social rights, the platform itself can become a vehicle of counter-hegemonic, post-neoliberal politics.

So the initial question can be reformulated: Does the decent work discourse help trade unions, labour NGOs and social movements in their political strategies and everyday practices to struggle for better living and working conditions? In such cases, how do they make use or appropriate the discourse? In other cases, how does decent work relate to alternative discourses, strategies and practices of unions, movements and NGOs? This book aims to contribute to answering these questions, not in the abstract, but by looking at concrete case studies of decent work strategies in Indonesia, with a special focus on the garment, textile and shoes industry.

1.2 Theoretical and Methodological Framework

In order to critically analyse the nature of decent work, I conceptualise it as an "economic imaginary" (Jessop 2004). This notion refers to "the semiotic moment of a network of social practices in a given social field, institutional order, or wider social formation" (Jessop and Oosterlynck 2008, 1157–1158). It is a key concept of Cultural Political Economy (CPE) as put forward by Bob Jessop and Ngai-Ling Sum (2001, 2006, 2010, 2012; Sum and Jessop 2013). CPE is a framework under construction combining different conceptual perspectives including regulation theory and discourse theory. I elaborate the theoretical framework of CPE in Chapter 2. CPE aims at "making the cultural turn [within political economy] without falling into soft economic sociology" (Jessop and Oosterlynck 2008), that is, integrating poststructuralist insights about the constructed and contingent nature of discourse into an account of political economy that retains a materialist understanding of the specific contradictions and crisis tendencies of the capitalist mode of production. CPE, therefore, differentiates between *semiotic* and *material* dimensions of social relations and puts the interplay between the two at the centre of analysis, aiming at both the interpretation of discourses and the explanation of interdependencies in the "real world" (Fairclough et al. 2004, 24). The underlying ontology and epistemology of CPE is rooted in critical realism, as was the regulation approach before (Jessop 2002). CPE, however, puts more emphasis on "semiosis" defined as all forms of the social production of meaning. The discursive production of meaning is understood as historically contingent but not as free-play of signs and symbols as more radical approaches to social constructivism would have it. Rather, it has to correspond to the material world in an "organic" way in order not to appear as "arbitrary, rationalistic and willed" (Jessop 2010, 345); in other words, it must meaningfully relate to the "decisive nucleus of economic activity" (Gramsci 1971, 373) within social relations. Discourses are embedded and enacted within specific practices, projects and strategies of particular actors with particular interests, rather than being the disembodied circulation of differences without subjective agency.

Researching economic imaginaries, therefore, requires more than discourse analysis alone. Methodologically, discourse analysis tends to focus on the discourse itself by looking at discursive artefacts such as a corpus of texts. Critical Discourse Analysis moves beyond the dimension of the discursive and looks at the material and historical context of discourses (Fairclough 2005), but the non-discursive context is included as an *explanans,* not as an *explanandum.* This research project is interested in how specific actors are using a certain discourse practically; it can thus not rely on Critical Discourse Analysis alone. If the research interest is primarily located on the discursive level, the research object "can be studied productively with the tools of semiotic analysis (especially, for CPE, those of critical discourse analysis)" (Jessop and Sum 2012, 86). However, "the 'imaginary' refers not only to semiosis but also to its material supports and this requires a broader toolkit" (ibid.). In my case, it requires ethnographic fieldwork in Indonesia; it requires interviewing trade unionists and NGO activists in order to gain insight into their political strategies and everyday practices. Therefore, the broader methodological toolkit for this project has to include tools and techniques for generating and evaluating ethnographic data as well as for using empirical findings to reconstruct existing theory. Claes Belfrage and I have proposed Critical Grounded Theory (CGT) as one possible way to introduce grounded theory's strengths in empirical and ethnographic work into a research framework that, like CPE, is critical and particularly theoretical in nature (Belfrage and Hauf 2015). In Chapter 3, I elaborate CGT as the methodological framework for this study.

1.3 Historical and Empirical Analysis

Before analysing the empirical data, I provide a brief outline of the historical context of my research topic in Chapters 4 and 5. First, it is necessary to recount the history of neoliberalism from a labour perspective as a response to the crisis of Fordism that was geared towards restoring capital's profitability and underpinned by the weakening of the organised labour movement (Albo 2009). Global restructuring processes like the internationalisation of production, the liberalisation of international trade, the deregulation of financial markets and the neoliberal roll-back of the welfare state have contributed to the present international division of labour. Transnational supply chains have emerged, in which women workers in the Global South are relegated to the lowest echelons of a global labour market hierarchy deeply divided along gender, ethnic and citizenship lines. Labour-intensive industries such as garments and clothing were the first to be relocated from industrialised to developing countries and it was primarily young women that were drawn into the new world market factories, often located in "export processing zones" where labour rights were suspended and unionising activities suppressed. What became to be known as the "feminisation of labour" (Standing 1989, 1999)—rising women's participation in the labour market as well as proliferation of precarious, unprotected, low-wage (formerly typically female) work—was underpinned by the assumption that women workers are not only cheaper, but also more docile and less likely to unionise (Salzinger 2004).

This global perspective is necessary to provide some background knowledge about the larger macro processes pertinent to the local context of my research. By the same token, I secondly and also very briefly outline the history of international labour regulation from the beginning of the ILO, passing through its cold war phase and focussing its development from the crisis of Atlantic Fordism to neoliberal globalisation, in order to contextualise the decent work agenda within the history of the ILO. In Chapter 5, I spotlight the history of organised labour in Indonesia from the militant mass organisations of the independence period and the violent repression under Suharto to the reigniting of an independent, democratic labour movement in the *Reformasi* era. Then, the current situation of organised labour in Indonesia is illuminated. I look at strategic priorities of trade unions and the recent upswing in militant labour activism, leading in some cases to substantial wage hikes. I argue that mass demonstrations, large-scale strikes and other "traditional" (albeit from today's vantage point "radical") working class strategies are more effective in terms of raising wages than "social dialogue" strategies promoted by the ILO. These moderate strategies are useful in contexts of institutionalised national class compromises (as in central Fordism) and they presuppose a certain balance of power between capital and labour. In a neoliberal context of transnational (buyer-driven) supply chains, however, workers lack *economic* bargaining power in isolated negotiations with the employers. Given the huge power imbalance, "social dialogue" strategies are here disadvantageous to workers. The radical strategies, directed to the state and especially local governments, are sources for *political* union power, serving as a substitute for economic power in this particular context.

Chapters 6 and 7 are the centrepiece of my empirical analysis. I compare two different approaches towards decent work in Indonesia's garment, textile and shoes industry in terms of how the decent work discourse is being put into practice and how the meaning of decent work varies in different contexts: a) the Better Work Indonesia project of the ILO and the International Finance Corporation (IFC) exemplifying a top-down "decent work from above" imaginary primarily addressing employers and their needs to demonstrate Corporate Social Responsibility and b) the Play Fair Alliance as a regional multi-stakeholder initiative typical for a more deliberative, bottom-up "decent work from below" imaginary addressing all stakeholders and facilitating social dialogue among them. These two approaches are juxtaposed as contested economic imaginaries of decent work and c) complemented by an analysis of labour unions and social movements in Indonesia envisaging alternative imaginaries beyond "decent work" such as "alternative economies", taking the Indonesian People's Movement Confederation (KPRI) as a case study. The final Chapter 8 summarises the results and ends with some concluding remarks about the paradoxes of decent work.

2. From Regulation Theory to Cultural Political Economy

This chapter[1] is dedicated to the general theoretical approach of this study—Cultural Political Economy (CPE). First, I introduce basic concepts from Regulation Theory that serve as theoretical foundations of CPE's general view of capitalist accumulation, social regulation and their embedded contradictions and crisis tendencies. Second, the most important concepts of CPE itself are discussed, including semiosis and structuration, discourse and dispositive, economic imaginary as well as hegemony, sub- and counter-hegemony.

2.1 Regulation Theory

Before turning to Cultural Political Economy, it is necessary to remember the historical and academic context of its emergence. CPE can be seen as an answer to the crisis of and as a successor to Regulation Theory. At least the variety that is of interest here, the critical CPE strand as developed by Bob Jessop, Ngai-Ling Sum and others (cf. Sum and Jessop 2013), clearly grew out of discussions about regulation and state theory and how to perform the cultural turn within a critical political economy framework that, like Regulation Theory, has freed itself from a dogmatic relationship with traditional or orthodox Marxism while retaining the key concepts of the Marxian critique of political economy (Nadel 2002, 28). I introduce the concepts of accumulation regimes, modes of regulation, social and institutional forms before discussing state and hegemony and some conceptual shortcomings.

---

1 This chapter is partly based on Hauf (2013) and Hauf (2006). Section 2.2, in turn, partly flowed into Hauf (2015) and Belfrage and Hauf (2015).

2.1.1 Accumulation and Regulation

Regimes of accumulation

The regulation approach has developed concepts for analysing stability and change or structures and dynamics of those societies in which the capitalist mode of production prevails. It allows for dividing the development of the capitalist world system into different periods and for analysing the accumulation of capital in its historic-concrete forms. Marx had analysed the accumulation of capital in its most abstract form—as the "automatic expansion" (Marx 1890, 169) of value. In the three books of *Capital*, his project is a presentation and critique of the capitalist mode of production in its "ideal average" (Marx 1894, 839). This kind of presentation may determine in the abstract the fundamental forms of capitalist societalisation (*Vergesellschaftung*) such as value, commodity, money, capital and accumulation, which are characteristic for all phases of capitalist development. It is necessary to retain a Marxian understanding of these categories, for CPE indeed, in order to remember basic facts about the specific materiality and contradictions of capitalism, regardless of their historic-concrete forms. To summarise while simplifying, capitalist production in general is production for profits, not needs; capital can only exist within the constantly renewed movement of its own accumulation; accumulation therefore is limitless, but always endangered by its own crisis tendencies, which are based on capitalism's internal contradictions and barriers. This abstract knowledge is however insufficient for concrete analyses of historically specific conjunctures or of different modes of accumulation varying from country to country or between historical periods. Therefore, Regulation Theory has developed the concept of accumulation regimes to signify the historically specific mode of capitalist production that secures a more or less coherent correspondence between social norms of production and social norms of consumption, thereby rendering the self-expanding movement of capital relatively stable over a certain period of time (Hirsch 1995, 49).

The notion of accumulation regimes was developed against the backdrop of the contradictory experiences of the 20th century. On the one hand, the world economic crisis of the 1930s seemed to have confirmed the Marxian theory of crisis, according to which the accumulation of capital is structurally and necessarily endangered by its own expansive dynamic and periodically enters into crisis. On the other hand, the aftermath of that crisis had witnessed the outbreak of World War II and the Shoah, but not of a social revolution marking the end of the capitalist mode of production. On the contrary, a regime of accumulation was established during the post-war period that combined mass production and mass consumption with hitherto unprecedented stability. Hirsch explains:

"High gains in productivity, for the first time in the history of capitalism, made continuous raises of wage incomes and a certain degree of mass prosperity not only compatible with the profitability of capital, but even made them its foundation" (Hirsch 1995, 76, my translation).

This accumulation regime is called "Fordism" in regulationist terms—a notion that was borrowed from Antonio Gramsci (Lipietz 1992, 36). This so-called golden age of capitalism produced the appearance as if the contradictions and crisis dynamics of capitalism were immobilised and the combination of growth and prosperity was permanent, but the economic crisis of the 1970s strikingly made capitalism's contradictions and antagonisms re-surface (Hirsch 2005, 83). The analysis of this crisis of Fordism initially provided the focus of early Regulation Theory and continues to play an important role in current debates around the crisis of neoliberalism.

The central question of Regulation Theory revolves around the contradictions of capitalist social relations, their structural crisis tendencies and their ability to reproduce themselves in spatially and temporally very different forms despite these contradictions and crisis tendencies. The starting point is an inherent improbability of capitalist reproduction.

Modes of regulation

The concept of regulation was developed to replace Althusser's notion of reproduction that was criticised for being devoid of a dialectic understanding of capitalism's contradictions and crisis tendencies. Regulation captures the ways in which a contradictory social relation reproduces itself *despite and through* its contradictions: "Thus the notion of regulation can only be understood within a particular schema: relation-reproduction-contradiction-crisis", as Lipietz (1988, 11) argues. Contradictions have to be processed; antagonisms and conflicts of interests have to be pacified or resolved (temporally and tendencially) in order to secure periods of relatively stable and crisis-free capital accumulation. The concept of regulation aims at the paradox that, on the one hand, people in capitalist economies are producing commodities independent and isolated from one another without having a regulating centre from which to coordinate individual plans consciously. On the other hand, there is no Smithian "invisible hand" securing that atomised market transactions would regulate themselves. Regulation means that the disparate actions of individuals and the antagonistic interests of social classes are made compatible with the conditions of capital accumulation through a multi-dimensional and decentral process that simultaneously ensures social cohesion (Hirsch 1995, 50).

This is the result of diverse and complex practices of social actors respectively pursuing their own strategies and interests but, nevertheless, contributing to successful regulation through forging and institutionalising certain (class) comprises. The process of regulation is mediated through manifold social struggles. Its historically specific form—a particular mode of regulation—is dependent on social balances of power and therefore open-ended and contingent as a matter of principle. Lipietz explains: "Regimes of accumulation and modes of regulation are 'chance discoveries' made in the course of human struggle" (1987, 15). Regulation Theory has redefined the role of social compromises and balances of power as well as the relationship between necessity and chance. It has stressed the open-endedness and contingency of historic developments while retaining a Marxian understanding of the "hard core" of capitalism with respect to its necessary contradictions, antagonisms and crisis tendencies. It therefore potentially provides a possibility for overcoming deterministic and economistic thinking, which was dominant within orthodox Marxism, without giving up the idea of a comprehensive critical theory of society (Nadel 2002, 28). I return to the question of how this potential was realised in the section on CPE below.

A mode of regulation refers to "the totality of institutional forms, networks and explicit or implicit norms assuring the compatibility of behaviors within the framework of a regime of accumulation in conformity with the state of social relations and hence with their conflictual character" (Lipietz 1988, 24). Regulation Theory asks about the historically and spatially specific forms, in which the structural contradictions of capitalism are being processed in the concrete. With the conceptual coupling of regimes of accumulation and modes of regulation, it aims to tackle the classical problem of structure and agency. These terms capture structural constraints and economic contradictions as well as political, cultural and ideological everyday practices giving rise to them and the concrete institutional forms, in which they are being incorporated and processed. Structure and agency are thus conceptualised as a contradictory or *dialectical* unity. Of course, modes of regulation and regimes of accumulation must not be misread as separate spheres similar to the separation of economics and politics in mainstream economic theory. Rather, they represent two different analytical perspectives on the same contradictory phenomenon— the problem of the reproduction of society as a whole.

2.1.2 Social Forms and Institutional Forms

The contradictory articulation or mediation of accumulation and regulation is expressed in more concrete terms in the concept of institutional forms. These are analytical categories that enable a theoretical access to social reality differentiating between different levels and aspects thereof but, more importantly, aiming to analyse their interdependent and contradictory coaction within societal reproduction. The notion does not refer to simple empirical evidences or concretely isolated institutions, even though they play a significant role within institutional forms.

Joachim Hirsch distinguishes (abstract) social forms from (intermediate) institutional forms. Social forms are the physical guises in which people experience their own social relations in alienated, fetishised ways: "Under capitalism, people cannot freely choose their mutual relationships, nor can they master their social existence through immediate action. Rather, their social coherence expresses itself in reified social forms externally turning against them" (Hirsch 2005, 22, my translation). A basic social form we find in Marx is the value-form, including the different forms it acquires during the process of accumulation—commodity, money and capital. According to Marx, the value-form at once expresses and disguises the social relations of independent commodity producers, because they do not produce their social coherence in a conscious and coordinated manner, but via the market-mediated exchange of commodities. Money as the general equivalent and the "immediate form of existence" (Heinrich 2001, 159) of value, in which the social relation of value acquires a physical form, is the precondition for the exchange of equivalent commodities. Within the production process as a unity of labour process and process of creating value (Marx 1890, 201), money takes the form of capital that can only preserve and expand itself within the continually renewed accumulation process. Although the logic of capital is self-referential, it is contingent upon the conformity of people's actions. Regulation Theory aims to analyse how people are reproducing the basic social forms of capitalism through their everyday practices. Thus, it looks at how different ways of living are subjected to social norms and routines. Institutional forms are seen as more concrete codifications or instantiations of the abstract social forms and occupy the intermediate level between structure and agency. Their particular shape is an outcome of social struggles, balances of power and institutional compromises (Lipietz 1985, 113). Traditionally, the Regulation School has known five institutional forms: the wage relation, money, articulations of space, competition and the state. Here, I only cover the most important one for this study— the wage relation. Hegemony and the state are discussed in the next section.

The wage relation

For many regulation theorists, the wage relation is the most important institutional form since it is here that the fundamental contradiction between capital and labour is being processed in a historically specific way. The hegemonic form of producing value and appropriating surplus-value, specific to a particular time and space, is being institutionalised within the wage relation through social struggles and building compromises (Boyer and Saillard 2002, 39). Regulation Theory has always stressed consumption as the other side and a necessary part of production, because value and surplus-value have to be realised in circulation, that is, the commodities have to be sold. Commodity prices and wages, therefore, have to be aligned in a certain ratio accordingly. However, this presents a contradiction "the unity of which is resolved through struggle: excessive wages and insufficient accumulation, or excessive profits and insufficient demand. This is the fundamental problem of the regulation of the wage relation" (Lipietz 1988, 21). The struggle over the length of the working day and over the amount of wages is a central moment of class struggle, which determines the social distribution of the surplus product. Class struggle also determines the social definition of what counts as necessary for the reproduction of labour power (the survival of workers). The value of labour power, just as any other commodity, is determined by the amount of labour time socially necessary for its reproduction, but what is seen as a necessary need or want varies from time to time and from country to country. Again, it is contingent upon social struggles and balances of power and, thus, "there enters into the determination of the value of labour-power a historical and moral element" (Marx 1890, 185, Moore and Aveling's translation).

Marx argued on the assumption of subsistence wages. I argue below that there are accumulation regimes that capitalise on wages below subsistence level, secretly relying on women's unpaid reproductive and subsistence work. Paying wages to workers that are below the value of labour-power constitutes a form of "over-exploitation" above and beyond the "normal" rate of exploitation. "Exploitation" here does not contain a moral element. It describes how the consumption of labour power in production creates value, the amount of which is higher than the value of labour power itself and how the difference is appropriated by capital as surplus value or profit. Because of the reservoir of unpaid reproductive and subsistence work—mostly performed by women—"the opportunities for capital to appropriate surplus labour are massively expanded" (Bennholdt-Thomsen cited in Feministische Autorinnengruppe 2013, 108, my translation). Boyer summarises the elements of the wage relation as follows:

"the type of means of production; the social and technical division of labor; the ways in which workers are attracted and retained by the firm; the direct and indirect determinants of wage income; and lastly the workers' way of life, which is more or less linked to the acquisition of commodities or the use of collective services outside the market" (Boyer 1990, 38).

It is clear that the wage relation is comprised of components that are usually classified as either economic, political or cultural and, thus, plays a central role in the historically specific articulation or mediation of accumulation and regulation. The classic example is the ideal-typical wage relation of Atlantic Fordism, which organised a class compromise between capital's and labour's representations of interests (business associations and labour unions), mediated by the Keynesian welfare state, that secured rising wages through collective bargaining agreements (CBAs) and social security measures, thereby stabilising mass consumption and capital accumulation. I return to the question of how this plays out in the context of Indonesia, which of course is very different from Western Europe or North America, below (see Chapter 5).

State and hegemony

The form of the state, or forms of statehood, is an institutional form that performs a number of tasks and functions for capital accumulation and social regulation. It delimits the territory of the national state, institutionalises monetary regimes and codifies the wage relation (Lipietz 1985, 112). According to the German school of Regulation Theory, the state is the institutional centre of regulation, because "the physical coercive force is a basis for the maintenance of class relations, their social forms and institutional expressions and because social compromises can only be bindingly stipulated there" (Hirsch 2005, 91, my translation). There is no economic space that could be meaningfully conceptualised independent from politics and the state. The political and the economic are rather mutually interrelated, mediating each other in contradictory ways. They are not separate entities, but relate to each other dialectically in a contradictory separation that, at the same time, constitutes a particular connection: "This separation is only the specific form that the constitutive presence of the political within the relations of production takes under capitalism" (Poulantzas 2002, 47, my translation).

Hirsch and others have amended French Regulation Theory by referring to Nicos Poulantzas' materialist state theory and Antonio Gramsci's theory of hegemony. Here, the state is conceptualised as the political form of capitalism analogous to the value form, that is, as a basic and reified social form of capitalist societies. Just like value appears in the money form, but disguises its social origin in the social relations between independent commodity producers, so does the political form at once express and disguise the social relations between competing individuals, but appears to them as an external, alien, powerful object—as the state (Hirsch 1995, 17–18). Competition on the market requires individuals to recognise each other's private property and to refrain from appropriation by means of violence. The state's monopoly on the use of force necessitates its formal separation from all social classes and groups (Hirsch 2005, 23; Lipietz 1985, 112). This separation is simultaneously the basis for the state's presence in the relations of production in guaranteeing private property. The state is socially necessary for the social cohesion of a society of atomised market actors: "the state is the form that polity acquires under the social conditions that prevail within capitalism" (Hirsch 2005, 26, my translation).

It is important to note that the existence of the state is not explained by its function for the reproduction of capitalist relations of production. Rather, historically there is a co-evolution of the capitalist mode of production and the bourgeois state. The state is constitutively related to the capital relation, but it is not simply the instrument of capital. Poulantzas coined the term "relative autonomy" (Poulantzas 2002, 158) for this type of relationship. It means that different societal spheres or domains are at once separate and yet inseparably related to each other, present in and inscribed into one another. It describes a contradictory separation/connection (Hirsch 1995, 22) or, in other words, a relation of dialectical intermediation. Poulantzas criticised both the orthodox Marxist view of the state as a neutral instrument in the hands of the ruling classes without any autonomy and the bourgeois conception that the state is an autonomous subject representing the general will. He argues that the state is "a relation, more precisely [...] the material condensation of a relation of forces between classes and class fractions, expressing itself within the state always in specific forms" (Poulantzas 2002, 159, my translation). Hirsch distinguishes the abstract level of the state as a social form from the more concrete and complex level of particular forms of statehood, which are embedded in the respective net of a given mode of regulation and contingent upon social struggles and balances of powers or relations of forces. For example, the Keynesian welfare state of Atlantic Fordism was the primary locus of the class compromise securing accumulation through mass consumption. Hirsch calls this form of statehood "security state" in a doubled sense, as a welfare state and as a bureaucratic state of control and surveillance (Hirsch 1995, 79). After Fordism, in contrast, a new form of statehood emerges that is primarily geared towards optimising the conditions for a globalising and flexibilising capital to invest and accumulate. This new type is termed the "internationalised competition state" (Hirsch 2005, 145). This is an important argument for understanding the complex relationships of states and markets in the neoliberal era of globalisation, including what has been referred to as the "race to the bottom" (Ehmke et al. 2009, 26) in labour rights and social standards as states seek to attract foreign investors looking for cheap labour (see Chapter 4.1.2).

Closely connected to Regulation Theory's approach to the state is the discussion of hegemony. This notion is borrowed from Gramsci who conceptualised it as a capitalist form of domination that rests upon a certain combination of coercion and consensus: "In general the state acquires hegemony itself, a hegemony armed with coercion" (Lipietz 1988, 14). Thus, the state is not only the expression and condensation of relations of social forces, but also the terrain in which these relations are organised. The state here is understood in its inclusive sense, referring to Gramsci's concept of the "integral state", composed of the state in the narrow sense (political society) as well as the field of civil society. The state in the narrow sense commands the repressive and administrative apparatuses exercising the state's monopoly on legitimate force. The civil society has hegemony apparatuses at its disposal, securing ideological-cultural leadership for the ruling classes and consensus on the side of the subaltern classes or, in other words, securing recognition of the state's legitimacy (Gramsci 1992, 815–816). Public institutions like schools are hegemony apparatuses, but also institutions usually defined as private such as the church or the press. This is similar to Althusser's distinction of repressive and ideological state apparatuses (Althusser 1977). Repressive state apparatuses (police, military, etc.) serve to uphold a certain order by means of force. Ideological state apparatuses (including the family) reproduce labour power as a commodity ideologically and culturally. Poulantzas adds the notion of economic state apparatuses that intervene into the production process in order to secure the reproduction of the conditions of production. He stresses that presenting the terrain of the state in these terms can only serve descriptive purposes, because these are analytical distinctions that cannot be made between empirically observable institutions.

The concept of hegemony is central to Regulation Theory for a number of reasons. It enables us to analyse how a dominant group or class fraction may be successful in representing their particular interests as universal, or at least in privileging their interests vis-à-vis the interests of other groups, when certain imaginations, attitudes or habits become hegemonic (Lipietz 1985, 111). It also illuminates the interrelatedness of the macro structures of capitalism and the micro practices of people's everyday lives, how hegemonic ways of life emerge that reproduce and stabilise the capitalist mode of production. It thus helps to make sense of the problem of structure and agency. According to Thomas Sablowski, Regulation Theory claims to understand social relations and institutional forms as congealed and stabilised forms of praxis, thus liquefying the structural domain with reference to agency, but it failed to show how these forms of praxis come about to be condensed into a mode of regulation (Sablowski 1994, 144). This gap could be filled by referring to Gramsci's theory of hegemony, because it has broken with Marxist economism and given concepts such as consensus, compromise and relations of forces a much greater weight—concepts that are equally important for state theory, Regulation Theory and CPE.

2.1.3 The Improbability Question

The key question of Regulation Theory is the "improbability question": why do subjects act in ways that reproduce certain fundamental structures of capitalism despite their inherent antagonisms and contradictions. This question cannot be answered adequately without referring to the specific materiality of capitalist relations, the objectification and naturalisation of social relations captured in the notion of "social forms" that displace these historically specific relations from the individuals' horizon of action and gives them the appearance of transhistoric, natural forms of all human societies. Marx (1890, 85ff.) demonstrated how this naturalisation works in his theory of the fetishism of commodities. The value form is a social relation historically specific to capitalism that emanates from the routinised practice of private commodity production and market exchange. Consequently, the value form is historically contingent and potentially subject to change. In the consciousness of those whose praxis is producing and reproducing this relation, however, it appears to be a natural quality of all modes of production, because the social relations specific to capitalism become reified and fetishised. Within Regulation Theory, this complex has been called the "'stroboscope' phenomenon" (Lipietz 1988, 13). Although the process of reproduction can only work through the everyday actions of individuals, it appears to them as if it was a quasi-automatic, "autopoietic" process. A specific social praxis constitutes a contradictory, dialectical complex of social relations, "objective forms of thought" (Marx 1890, 90) and individual practices. This complex appears to be an automatic process although it is mediated through peoples' everyday activities. Capital is not an automaton; rather, as a fetishised or reified form of social relations, it is indeed beyond the will or the doing of individuals. It is this materiality, the "hard core" of capitalist relations, that falls out of view when one gives up the dialectical conception of structure and agency and replaces structure with discourse entirely when moving from Regulation Theory to Cultural Political Economy.

Figure 1: The Basic Categories of Regulation Theory

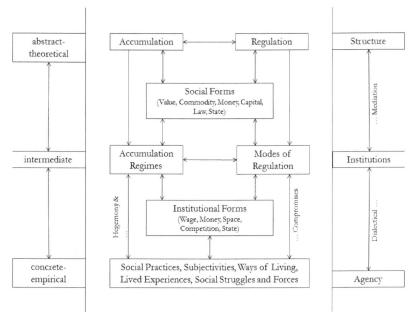

Source: Hauf 2006, 30

Regulation Theory can be understood as a contribution to renewing materialist critiques of society by overcoming economism, determinism and structuralism. As a "rebel child" of Althusser's structural Marxism, it can be seen as a "post-structuralism" of its very own kind. Regulation theorists stress the idea of Marx that people make their own history, that people produce and reproduce the very social relations under which they are dominated and exploited. In answering the central "improbability" question, however, most regulationist studies tended to explain subjective agency by structural requirements instead of focussing the processes of structuration through agency despite the common talk of the dialectic of structure and agency. Different scholars have, thus, criticised a conceptual surplus of objectivity and a deficit of subjectivity (Sablowski 1994, 155; Scherrer 1995, 462). This is one of the shortcomings of the regulation approach that have sparked the development of CPE.

Another critique was articulated by feminist scholars (Ruddick 1992, Dackweiler 1995, Jenson 1997). If Regulation Theory is to be a critical theory of society, then critically accounting for gender relations and gendered forms of power, domination and exploitation should be an integral part of the approach. Indeed, many regulationists have acknowledged the role of gender relations and mentioned them at certain points, but failed to systematically include them in their studies. Lars Kohlmorgen (2004) has attempted to systematically extend Regulation Theory and include the analysis of gender relations on all conceptual levels, from the most abstract level of capital accumulation and social reproduction as such, to the intermediate level of accumulation regimes, modes of regulation and institutional forms, to the concrete level of ways of living, power balances and social struggles. Kohlmorgen has opened up Regulation Theory for feminist interrogations of gendered divisions of labour, the interrelations between class and gender as well as the relevance of modern gender relations for the reproduction of capitalist social relations. The central feature of his theoretical extension is the introduction of a new institutional form: the household and family form, which is conceptualised to express the general norm of the gendered division of labour and the hegemonic family model (Kohlmorgen 2004, 59).

Another important shortcoming was the way Regulation Theory has treated ideational, discursive or symbolic dimensions of social relations "that are not exhausted by the notion of ideology in Marxian approaches" (Knapp 2010, 235, my translation). Regulationists have always stressed the role of cultural norms in routinising subjective agency, but the "cultural" itself, how it is constituted and how it becomes articulated with material practices, has been left under-theorised. This is one of the reasons for the emergence of CPE.

2.2 Cultural Political Economy

Regulation Theory has always stressed the meaning of cultural norms and values for stabilising accumulation regimes and modes of regulation. Only the transition to CPE, however, provides a conceptual framework for analysing how such norms and values are discursively constructed. Regulation Theory can broach the issue of how everyday practices of individuals are subjected to a routine and made compatible with the requirements of capital accumulation. CPE can start one step before and analyse how normative orders emerge discursively, which discourses become hegemonic, how certain norms and values become articulated with the interests of relevant social actors and how they may become condensed in institutions. Jessop and Sum do not give up the idea of the dialectic of structure and agency, rather, they shift the focus from how actions are normalised through structures and institutions to how norms and institutions are structured by actions. Regulation Theory's own standard to capture the mediating movement between social structures and subjective practices is, thus, better met by CPE.

Cultural Political Economy can therefore be a chance for reformulating the conceptual framework and the research programme of the Regulation Approach, in a way as the *Aufhebung* of Regulation Theory, while overcoming the objectivity-surplus and the economy-centeredness of many regulationist studies. The constitutive role of cultural-symbolic forms, discursive orders and economic imaginaries giving sense and meaning to material practices can be accounted for adequately without leaving the framework of historical materialism in favour of a radical postmodernism. CPE can be, furthermore, a chance for integrating feminist approaches into political economy in a new and more fruitful way. Integration here should not be understood as a form of incorporation that includes feminist concepts as add-ons into the conceptual framework, which remains otherwise untouched, but integration in the sense of a trans- or post-disciplinary research perspective. Possibly then, integration should not lead to the attempt to build up an all-encompassing "grand" or "master" theory that incorporates and subsumes all other theories that have something interesting and critical to say about society. CPE as a paradigm that describes itself as "pre-disciplinary in inspiration, trans-disciplinary in practice and post-disciplinary in its aspiration" (Sum and Jessop 2013, ix) should, rather, compile a theoretical toolbox from which to choose different concepts and combine them as they become relevant for particular analyses of specific research objects. CPE might combine feminist and regulationist concepts in the context of constellative analyses of concrete circumstances, confront them and relate them to one another, let them learn from each other, without attempting to fuse them together to a holistic grand theory.

In this section, the central concepts of Cultural Political Economy are introduced. I start with CPE's specific interpretation of the notions of semiosis and structuration, discourse and dispositive, discuss economic and political imaginaries and reflect on how hegemony (including sub- and counter-hegemony) is used within the CPE framework.

2.2.1 Semiosis and Structuration

Jessop and Sum suggest the term "semiosis" in order to grasp all forms of the social production of sense and meaning (Jessop 2009a, 20). On this abstract level, they prefer this term to the concept of discourse because the latter can have various meanings in different contexts, but sometimes use them interchangeably. Discourse can (1) be used in the general sense of the social production of meaning systems and symbolic orders (semiosis); it can (2) denote the specific language of a certain social field (e.g. political discourse), or (3) refer to a certain aspect of the discursive construction of social reality (e.g. the neoliberal discourse of globalisation), as Norman Fairclough (2009, 162–163) puts it. CPE systematically allows for discursive or semiotic dimensions and analyses them in their interrelations with non-discursive dimensions. It understands economic categories as inherently semiotic and (at least to some extent) discursively constructed, but it does not neglect their structural and material dimensions. It takes up and critically re-articulates concepts and notions of Regulation Theory. Regulation, for instance, is then understood as a process that operates partly discursively and constitutes the objects of regulation through the very process of regulation (Jessop 2004, 163). CPE reformulates the basic question of Regulation Theory of how capitalist social relations are being reproduced and transformed by referring to discourse theory and evolutionary economics.

The existential necessity of complexity reduction

In CPE, semiosis is seen as one of two necessary moments of complexity reduction, the other being structuration (Sum and Jessop 2013, 149). In order for social agents to be able to "go on" in the world, they must translate the inordinate complexity of the "real world" into a set of calculable and manageable aspects of that world. While critical realism—the underlying philosophy of both Regulation Theory and CPE—posits that the "real world" pre-exists any effort by human subjects to make sense and meaning of it, it also acknowledges that these human subjects can only access the real through their sense- and meaning-making efforts. Their lived experience of the real is shaped by an imaginary relation to it that reduces complexity and makes it calculable. The two moments of complexity reduction translate the "actually existing economy" (the chaotic sum of all economic activities) into an "imagined economy" (a discursively and structurally circumscribed subset of these activities) (Jessop and Sum 2012, 87). Sum and Jessop explain:

"Semiosis and structuration are both necessary for social agents to 'go on' in the world and each involves specific forms of enforced selection and selectivities. Semiosis is a dynamic source of sense and meaning. Structuration sets limits to compossible combinations of social relations and thereby contributes, as far as CPE research interests are concerned, to the institution of specific political economies. Together these two modes of complexity reduction tend through time to transform relatively meaningless and unstructured complexity into relatively meaningful and structured complexity" (Sum and Jessop 2013, 148).

Semiosis and structuration serve as the two ontological foundations of CPE. Semiosis is foundational to the social world, because it gives sense and meaning to it, without which it would remain incomprehensible for its inhabitants and could not be said to be social. Structuration is foundational, because it is necessary to transform the endless variety of *possible* elements of an unstructured complexity into a "requisite variety" of *compossible* moments that, when composed or articulated, may form a relatively stable and coherent structure (Sum and Jessop 2013, 24). The notion of compossibility goes back to Leipniz who used it in his metaphysical "best of all possible worlds" argument. According to Leibniz, there are an infinite number of *possible* worlds in the mind of God. A possible world is composed of *compossible* elements not contradicting each other and God chooses the best of all possible worlds to be realised as the actual world we live in: "Not all possibles are compossible. Thus, the universe is only a certain collection of compossibles and the actual universe is the collection of all existing possibles, that is to say, those which form the richest composite" (Leibniz cited in Rutherford 1998, 182).

According to Sum and Jessop, structuration "is a form of enforced selection that sets limits to compossible combinations of relations among relations within specific time-space envelopes" (Sum and Jessop 2013, 4). At a given point in time and in a specific space, social interactions are structured in the sense that infinite possibilities for individual actions are limited by their compossibility when combined or articulated. Social structures thus reduce complexity by providing a set of compossible possibilities and excluding alternative possibilities. Semiosis is also a form of enforced selection that filters out certain meanings out of the infinite number of possible meanings of a given sign, discourse or imaginary. Through processes of variation, selection and retention (see below), meaning may become sedimented and acquire an appearance of stability and fixity, but sedimentation can never be fully completed since discourses can never achieve full closure. Excluded meanings may re-enter the discursive arena, challenge sedimented meanings and re-politicise taken-for-granted "truths". Similarly, the stability of structured complexity is improbable over time, because the contradictions and crisis tendencies internal to the economic structures of capitalism can only ever be partially and temporarily "fixed" or processed. Sooner or later, a given arrangement to deal with these contradictions, to make them calculable and manageable (a given mode of regulation), will be de-stabilised and thrown into crisis. This aspect of structuration closely resembles the regulationist view on structural or institutional forms (see above) that temporarily and incompletely process the contradictions inherent in capitalism's basic social forms. CPE extends the "improbability question" to matters of sense- and meaning-making: How does semiosis contribute to the improbable reproduction of capitalist social relations, what role does it play in structuration and in moments of crisis?

The following graph summarises Sum and Jessop's conceptualisation of structuration and semiosis as the two fundamental forms of complexity reduction as well as their respective improbability in the long run.

Figure 2: The Improbability of Complexity Reduction via Enforced Selection

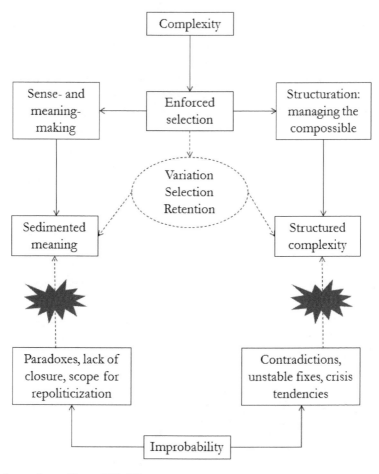

Source: Sum and Jessop 2013, 192

2.2.2 Discourse and Dispositive

Taking the cultural turn within political economy without falling into "soft economic sociology" (Jessop and Oosterlynck 2008) requires carefully navigating between what Jessop and Sum call the "structuralist Scylla" and the "constructivist Charybdis" (Sum and Jessop 2013, 148). They want to avoid simply replacing structural Marxism with radical constructivism, especially because they argue that otherwise the internal contradictions and crisis tendencies of capitalism, rooted in the specific materiality of its social relations, would fall out of view. Therefore, CPE only integrates theories of discourse, language and semiosis that meet a number of criteria, making them compatible with its philosophical roots in critical realism (see Chapter 3.3). CPE thus excludes discourse theories that are "1. universalist and/or transhistorical in character, seeking to develop universal laws of language and language use; 2. structuralist in their denial of authorship, agency, or subjectivity; 3. methodologically individualist in their explanation of language development; 4. reductionist in seeking to reduce the world to language or semiosis" (Sum and Jessop 2013, 98).

In incorporating discourse theories into political economy, Jessop and Sum differentiate a "general theory", which they reject, from "grand theories" (ibid.) of semiosis, which they affirm given that they meet the criteria just mentioned. Especially, they have to distinguish semiosis (sense- and meaning-making) from structuration (the making of social structures) instead of collapsing structures into discourses completely. For their own development of semiotic concepts, Jessop and Sum work through three of these grand theories: Peter Ives's "vernacular materialism", German "historical semantics" and Foucault's analytics of discourse, power/ knowledge and dispositive.

Ives (2004) has analysed Gramsci's theory of language in order to critique the "vulgar materialist" interpretation of the base-superstructure-metaphor, where the cultural and political superstructure is misconstrued as an epiphenomenal reflection of the economic base. For Gramsci, language is material and as such "is very much a substantial part of social reality" (Ives 2004, 13). In the German tradition of historical semantics, Jessop and Sum refer to Reinhart Koselleck's conceptual history (*Begriffsgeschichte*) and to Niklas Luhmann's theory of communication and evolution. Koselleck (and others) explored how certain "basic concepts in history" (*geschichtliche Grundbegriffe*) such as domination, democracy, economy, ideology or capitalism changed in mutual co-determination with changes in the economic and political structures of 18th and 19th century Germany. Conceptual changes are not thought of as simply reflecting structural changes or *vice versa*, rather, "concepts are both indicators of and factors in political life. Put metaphorically, concepts are like joints linking language and the extra-linguistic world" (Koselleck cited in Sum and

Jessop 2013, 108). Conceptual history therefore has to be combined with social history in order to study their mutually constitutive development. Luhmann's approach to historical semantics, presented as similar to Koselleck's, is invoked in order to stress the co-evolution of semiosis and structuration (Sum and Jessop 2013, 134–135).

Foucault's analysis of discourse

Foucault is one of the many sources of the theoretical innovations of CPE vis-à-vis Regulation Theory as far as they can be interpreted as reflecting a more thorough reading of Foucault and re-evaluating Foucauldian concepts like discourse, dispositive, technologies of power, truth regimes and power/knowledge-relations. Jessop and Sum argue that "what Foucault offers us [...] is a study of how meanings are produced and circulated in a discursive economy. [...] Foucault's analysis of discourse insists on its materiality and its specific spatio-temporal location" (Sum and Jessop 2013, 111). The starting point for Foucault is the chaotic sum total of all actual statements—similarly CPE will take the sum total of all economic activities as its starting point. A "discourse" then refers to a multitude of statements belonging to the same "discursive formation", which is defined as a more or less structured and regularised set of statements. The relative unity and regularity within discursive formations is secured through "rules of formation" (Foucault 1972, 38) that limit the scope of what can and cannot be said within that formation.

Foucault is interested in the formation of objects, the formation of concepts and the formation of subjects in and through discursive formations. Famously, he wrote in the *Archaeology of Knowledge* that discourses should not be treated as "groups of signs (signifying elements referring to contents or representations) but as practices that systematically form the objects of which they speak" (Foucault 1972, 49). This phrasing has invited numerous misleading interpretations on the side of radical constructivists. Taking the production of a flute as an example, this is at once a discursive practice (the semiotic aspect of action) and a non-discursive practice (the material aspect of action). Producing a flute materially, carving out the wood in ways that will allow sonic waves to transmit music, requires a concept of the flute in the imagination of the producer. Without this concept, without a discourse that delimits what a flute is and is not, she would not be able to produce it.[2] In this way, the discourse forms the flute as an object of knowledge. However, of course, the flute as a material object is not the product of the discourse itself; rather, it is the product of human action—the actual material production of the flute. Foucault did not abandon the distinction between the discourse and its material referent as did some of his followers. In the *Archaeology of Knowledge*, arguably his most structuralist work, he is simply interested in the discourse itself, in making it "emerge in its own complexity" and therefore he wishes to "dispense with 'things'" (Foucault 1972, 47). However, he also writes: "a history of the referent is no doubt possible; and I have no wish at the outset to exclude any effort to uncover and free these 'prediscursive' experiences from the tyranny of the text" (ibid.). In later works, he turned more explicitly to the complex interplay of discursive and non-discursive practices, especially with reference to the notion of the dispositive (see below).

Integrating Foucault into CPE requires a materialist reading of his writings, overcoming the temptation of following the prevailing tendency in the social sciences of seeing his concept of power as replacing Marxian theories of society. Rather, as Sonja Buckel notes, it should be interpreted as "a critical continuation of the 'critique of political economy' under the conditions of the 'crisis of Marxism'" (Buckel 2007, 165, my translation). The Marxism of his time was dominated by structuralism on the one hand and by the specific current of the Third International and Stalinism on the other, plagued by economism and historical determinism and distorted to a mechanistic, reductionist conception of history and society that served to legitimise the system of social domination in the Soviet Union. It is thus not surprising that Foucault found little inspiration in most of his Marxist contemporaries. However, his analyses of discourse and power/knowledge start from the materiality and historicity of discursive practices, rather than from an abstract system of language as in linguistic structuralism (Lemke 1997, 44–45). Therefore, Foucault can be read as belonging to the historical-materialist tradition in the sense of Gramsci's philosophy of praxis. Poulantzas argues that "some of his analyses are not only

---

2 Compare the famous quote from Marx's Capital: "A spider conducts operations that resemble those of a weaver, and a bee puts to shame many an architect in the construction of her cells. But what distinguishes the worst architect from the best of bees is this, that the architect raises his structure in imagination before he erects it in reality" (Marx 1890, 193, Moore and Aveling's translation).

compatible with Marxism, but can only be understood starting from it" (Poulantzas 1978, 60, my translation).

Foucault and Poulantzas

The relation of Foucault and Poulantzas is complicated. Both share a critical stance towards structural Marxism and both seek to move beyond Althusser in their social analyses, albeit in very different ways. Nevertheless, it has been argued that Foucault and Poulantzas engaged in a "secret dialogue" in their late writings on state power and governmentality, the secrecy of which came from Foucault (Buckel 2007, 167). Jessop has analysed this dialogue in his *State Theory* and discovered some borrowings of Poulantzas from Foucault, a number of convergences between them, various criticisms of Foucault by Poulantzas and some hidden parallels (Jessop 1990, 220–247). He concludes that both commit complementary fallacies—Poulantzas in overestimating the unity of a social formation on the macro level and Foucault in overestimating the diversity of potential power relations at the micro level (Jessop 1990, 240). The total unity of a society, however, is impossible, because "there is always a surplus of meaning and a surplus of social elements, relations and practices which are excluded from a given totalization [...] project" (ibid.). Likewise, the scope for change and polyvalence of micro power relations is always limited in relation to any given societal project. Thus, the fallacies of Foucault and Poulantzas complement each other and reflect their respective entry points on the macro or the micro level of power and a lack of mediation between them.

Jessop also concludes that Poulantzas and Foucault seem to agree that the overall unity of a system of domination must be explained in terms of a certain strategic codification of power relations (Jessop 1990, 235). Taking Foucault's writings on governmentality closer into account, he argues that Foucault moved closer to theoretical positions on the micro-macro continuum similar to Poulantzas in acknowledging that the interweaving of different power relations on the micro level "delineate general conditions of domination and this domination is organised into a more-or-less coherent and unitary strategic form" (Foucault 1980, 142) on the macro level. Out of the chaotic totality of micro practices of power, a "general line of force" emerges on the macro level that is the complex resultant of the interaction between the institutional structure of the state and the clash of specific strategies and tactics. This "general line of force" is unintentional in the sense that it is not the result of a plan, a choice or decision of any individual or collective subject, but it is intentional in the sense that it is connected to specific objectives and interests (Jessop 1990, 235). This point is taken up by CPE's somewhat belated reception of Foucault's notion of the dispositive.

Discourse and dispositive

Crucial for CPE's concern with the interaction of micro and macro levels as well as semiotic and extra-semiotic dimensions of social relations is Foucault's notion of the dispositive. In an interview, he defined this concept as "a thoroughly heterogeneous ensemble consisting of discourses, institutions, architectural forms, regulatory decisions, laws, administrative measures, scientific statements, philosophical, moral and philanthropic propositions—in short, the said as much as the unsaid. Such are the elements of the apparatus [dispositive]. The apparatus [dispositive] itself is the system of relations that can be established between these elements" (Foucault 1980, 194).

Joachim Becker (2009) proposed to use the term "dispositive of regulation" instead of "mode of regulation" in order to capture both the material and the discursive dimensions and move away from the presupposed stability entrenched in the latter. CPE aims at a similar kind of post-structuralist re-interpretation of Regulation Theory and, lately, has adopted the concept of dispositives for the further elaboration of its theoretical agenda. For Jessop and Sum, a dispositive comprises a strategic response to a discursively constituted problem with the result of a "general strategic line that no one willed but that emerges from the clash of different strategies and tactics and that is, even at best, incomplete and provisional and, of course, subject to resistance that threatens to escape its routinization and confinement within the dispositive" (Sum and Jessop 2013, 113).

Jessop and Sum also review the English and German literature on discourse and dispositive analysis as method (Fairclough 2009, Wodak/Meyer 2009, Jäger and Jäger 2000, Bührmann and Schneider 2007). I return to the methodological aspects of these literatures in Chapter 3. Here, I only discuss their sometimes differing concepts of discourse and dispositive that have fed into the elaboration of CPE. First, Jessop and Sum refer to the works of Siegfried and Margarete Jäger and others as the

Duisburg School of discourse analysis, which "puts discourse in its place in two ways: it refers it back to human thinking and consciousness and, via the activities of individual and collective subjects, forward to the (re)making of reality" (Sum and Jessop 2013, 115). Discourse here is understood as an institutionalised way of talking, regulating action and thereby exerting power. A dispositive, then, is the synthesis of discursive and non-discursive practices as well as materialisations, i.e. the material products of human action.

Siegfried Jäger, in adopting and adapting the dispositive concept, notes an inconsistency in Foucault. He argues that, ultimately, Foucault fails to convincingly demonstrate how discursive and non-discursive practices, how discourse and reality are interrelated *in the concrete* (Jäger 2001, 75). What is it that bands discursive practices, non-discursive practices and materialisations together to form a dispositive? According to Foucault, it is the dispositive's "dominant strategic function" of "responding to an *urgent need*" (Foucault 1980, 195, emphasis in the original). The elements of the dispositive are held together by nothing else than serving a common purpose—warding off dangers of a current or permanent state of emergency—such as "the assimilation of a floating population found to be burdensome for an essentially mercantilist economy" (ibid.). Another inner band cannot be found in Foucault. However, as Jäger argues, "this band exists in the form of human-sensual *activity* or *labour* mediating subject and object, social worlds and objective realities, thus through the non-discursive practices" (Jäger 2001, 77, my translation, emphasis in the original). Because Foucault does not see the mediation of subject and object, of society and discourse through human activity/labour, he ultimately fails to uncover the "more" of discourses that "renders them irreducible to the language and to speech" (Foucault 1972, 49), which he wishes to reveal and describe. Jäger proposes to move beyond Foucault's concept of the dispositive by referring to Leontjew's activity theory, placing "the subject as that link [...] that links discourses to reality" (Jäger 2001, 82). This critical-realist reinterpretation of Foucault makes the Duisburg School of discourse and dispositive analysis compatible with CPE.

Critical Discourse Analysis as theory

Next, Jessop and Sum review the literature on Critical Discourse Analysis (CDA). Although Jäger has termed his approach *Kritische Diskursanalyse* as well, they understand CDA to be a distinct school comprised of authors such as Norman Fairclough, Teun van Dijk and Ruth Wodak (Sum and Jessop 2013, 124). What distinguishes CDA from more linguistic forms of discourse analysis is its commitment to study discourses in both their discursive and non-discursive contexts: "CDA aims to go beyond description to offer explanation and critique and, in particular, to show how language is linked to ideology and power" (Sum and Jessop 2013, 125). Although CDA pays due attention to the social and historical context of discourses, it tends towards linguistic analyses. Thus, Jessop and Sum largely regard it as a supplement to critical political economy that can be integrated into CPE when combined with "substantive theoretical work on what critical realists would call the real mechanisms" (Sum and Jessop 2013, 126). Otherwise, it would fail to show how discourse is related to power and domination and would have to restrict itself to analysing discursive practices rather than being able to analyse the interplay of discursive and non-discursive practices. The approaches to CDA that Jessop and Sum deem fit for appropriation and integration into CPE, albeit not without serious reworking, are the Duisburg School (see above), the "dialectical-relational approach" of Fairclough and the so-called Essex School of discourse analysis established by Ernesto Laclau and Chantal Mouffe (ibid.).

Fairclough terms his version of CDA the "dialectical-relational approach" (DRA), because he views semiosis "as an element of the social process which is *dialectically* related to others" (Fairclough 2009, 163, emphasis in the original). Dialectics here refers to a contradictory relationship of mutual co-constitution and intermediation between entities or dimensions that are at once separate and inseparable and thus form a contradictory unit of diverse determinations. The use of the term "dialectics" already indicates that the DRA is less disinclined to work with both Marxian and Foucauldian concepts than other versions of discourse analysis. It is also clearly critical-realist in the way it differentiates between social structures, practices and events. Social practices are seen as mediating between the abstract level of general social structures and the concrete level of particular social events, actions or strategies. Again, we find a dialectical relation of structure and agency and, within each level, a second dialectical relation between the semiotic and the extra-semiotic (Fairclough 2009, 164). The latter is specified through three interrelated concepts that indicate how semiosis—in line with CPE defined as sense- and meaning-making—relates to other elements of the social world— discourse, genre and style. "Discourse" refers to a particular way of construing, representing or interpreting aspects of that world (e.g. the neoliberal discourse on globalisation). "Genre" refers to a particular way of acting and interacting based on discourse (e.g. global meetings of business and political elites such as the World Economic Forum in Davos). "Style" refers to a particular identity or "way of being" based on discourse (e.g. the "Davos man").

Crucial for CPE is the notion of "orders of discourse" which are defined as particular configurations of these three categories: "An order of discourse is a social structuring of semiotic difference, a particular social ordering of relationships between different ways of meaning-making— different genres, discourses and styles" (ibid.). Also, Fairclough's way of conceptualising how discourses may become practical realities under certain conditions has fed into CPE's understanding of the variation, selection and retention of economic imaginaries (see below). Discourses "may be *enacted* as new ways of (inter)acting, they may be *inculcated* as new ways of being (identities) and they may be physically *materialized*" (Fairclough 2009, 165, emphasis in the original) as new objectifications. The problem of materialisation or objectification of discourses is especially important for CPE.

The difficult relationship to Laclau and Mouffe

Another concept that captures this problem is "sedimentation" of meaning, taken up by Jessop and Sum (2013, 133) although borrowed from Laclau and Mouffe, whom they criticise for their "discourse imperialism" but, nevertheless, find useful for their own theoretical endeavour, especially the concepts of sedimentation, suture and nodal points. A short excursus on CPE's relation to these post-Marxist theorists may be apposite to illuminate some of Jessop and Sum's arguments as to how to perform and not to perform the cultural turn in political economy.

In *Hegemony and Socialist Strategy*, Laclau and Mouffe set out to "decon- struct Marxism" (Laclau and Mouffe 1985). Not unfamiliar to regulation theorists, their reaction to the crisis of Marxism aims to overcome economism and determinism, albeit with a very different strategy of argumentation—and with important differences in ontology and epistemology. Their deconstruction follows the traces of the emergence of the hegemony concept. Gramsci's theory of hegemony challenged economism and highlighted the role of intellectual and moral leadership. Laclau and Mouffe are especially interested in Gramscian concepts such as "articulation", "collective will", "integral state" and "historical bloc". The term "hegemony" already appeared in Russian Marxism in the context of a class alliance of workers and peasants, whose class identities were thought of as objectively rooted in the relations of production and giving rise to objective class interests that have to be represented politically. Gramsci reconceptualised "hegemony" as "articulation", that is, as the "result of political construction and struggle" (Laclau and Mouffe 1985, 65). Instead of assuming a fixed unity among political actors based on pre-given class identities and interests, Gramsci (according to Laclau and Mouffe) replaced the principle of representation with that of articulation. Thus, he went beyond the idea of class alliances held together by a coincidence of necessary interests. Rather, the hegemonic connections between the diverse elements (classes, interests, identities) are entirely a political product of contingent articulations:

"Intellectual and moral leadership constitutes, according to Gramsci, a higher synthesis, a 'collective will', which, through ideology, becomes the organic cement unifying a 'historical bloc'" (Laclau and Mouffe 1985, 67).

Although Gramsci has opened up the possibility to think hegemony as articulation, Laclau and Mouffe nevertheless accuse him of holding on to a hidden essentialist core, the fundamental class, which reinstates the determination through the economy in the last instance, thus overcoming economism and essentialism only incompletely. Their post-Marxism aims to complete this unfulfilled task.

Unfortunately, this theoretical move results in what Terry Eagleton (1993, 244–245) has called the radical-constructivist "exaggeration" of an actually legitimate critique—their critique of economism leads them to lose sight of the economy as an external, indeed material, referent. The reason for this is an ontological one. Radical constructivism is predicated on de Saussure's semiotic theory that defines a sign as twofold—signified and signifier. The signifier is that which carries meaning (e.g. the word "table"), the signified is that which this meaning refers to (e.g. the concept "table"), but there is a third element that both of these must refer to—the material referent (e.g. an actual wooden thing we refer to as a "table"). The "forgetting of the referent" (ibid.) leads to what Jessop and Sum call "discourse imperialism" (Sum and Jessop 2013, 180)—the complete conflation of discourses and material practices. Indeed, Laclau contended that in his work "the discursive is not, therefore, being conceived as a level nor even a dimension of the social, but rather as being co-extensive with the social as such" (Laclau 1980, 87). Non-discursive aspects of social reality are ignored, the referent is forgotten and the ideas of materiality and causality are given up. Sum and Jessop argue: "Although this equation of the social and discourse is a foundational ontological claim, it is presented as anti-foundational and anti-essentialist" (2013, 132). They conclude that Laclau and Mouffe have one-sidedly appropriated post-structuralist theories that deal with semiosis and failed to appropriate parallel theories that shed new light on questions of structuration (Sum and Jessop 2013, 133). CPE is, in contrast, interested in the relations between semiosis *and* structuration. To analyse these relations, despite their critique, they find some concepts and arguments of Laclau and Mouffe useful: the "sedimentation" of meaning that contributes to the naturalisation and institutionalisation of social relations, a "suture" that temporarily binds diverse elements and relations together as well as "nodal points" that serve as privileged reference points for hegemonic articulations (ibid.).

The non-fixity of sense and meaning, their always partial and temporary fixation in hegemonic articulations, the sedimentation of meaning that makes it taken-for-granted although it is the product of political praxis and the possibility to re-politicise discourses through the entry of new meanings have all left their marks on the basic concepts of CPE. It is possible to interpret these ideas in line with critical realism, that is, without the exaggeration of radical constructivism. Jessop and Sum's reading of Laclau and Mouffe, despite important differences in ontology and epistemology, has fed into CPE's understanding of "imaginaries" and their evolutionary development through the moments of variation, selection and retention.

2.2.3 Economic Imaginaries

"An imaginary is a semiotic ensemble (or meaning system) without tightly defined boundaries that frames individual subjects" lived experience of an inordinately complex world and/or guides collective calculation about that world. Without imaginaries, individuals cannot 'go on' in the world and collective actors (such as organizations) could not relate to their environments, make decisions, or engage in strategic action" (Sum and Jessop 2013, 165).

The notion of the "imaginary" refers to the semiotic moment of complexity reduction, but not as such or in and of itself but in relation to its structural moment. CPE not only asks about the structural and institutional forms, in which social practices are subjected to norms and routines, but also about the symbolic-cultural forms, discourses and imaginaries that flow into the constitution of such institutional forms. Fordism and the Keynesian welfare state, for instance, entailed not only institutional arrangements and material compromises, but also discourses and ideas of a social market economy that were equally important in stabilising the formation. Economic imaginaries are initially more discursive in nature, but they may materialise and be condensed to institutional forms, thereby enabling and constraining actions and shaping the world materially. Jessop defines the concept as follows:

"An economic imaginary is a semiotic order, i.e., a specific configuration of genres, discourses and styles and, as such, constitutes the semiotic moment of a network of social practices in a given social field, institutional order, or wider social formation" (Jessop and Oosterlynck 2008, 1157–1158).

An example of an economic imaginary he provides is the "knowledge-based economy", a master narrative that has the potential of becoming a hegemonic discourse shaping economic strategies on various scales as well as steering hegemonic and state projects (Jessop 2004, 168). The knowledge-based economy, thus, has good prospects of being translated from an economic imaginary to a hegemonic discourse that shapes material reality (ibid., 169). In order for economic and political imaginaries to be able to shape the world in this sense, they must not be "arbitrary, rationalistic and willed", rather, "if they are to become organic, these imaginaries must have a significant, albeit necessarily partial, correspondence to real material interdependencies in the actually existing economy" (Gramsci's "decisive economic nucleus", Jessop and Sum 2012, 87; Jessop and Sum 2006, 362). Only then will they be able to gather support from different actors or social forces, resonate with their interests across different sites and scales, guide social practices and effect social change or continuity. This means that there are limits to what can be discursively construed. Not all *construals* are equally plausible and, therefore, likely to be translated from construals to *constructions* (Sum and Jessop 2013, 162).

The evolution of economic imaginaries

Which imaginaries become hegemonic, which are being selected and retained by relevant actors, which become discursively reinforced and finally materially condensed and institutionalised is largely dependent on social balances of power and constellations of interests.

These are the three moments in the evolution of imaginaries Jessop (2009a, 25) identifies: *variation* or proliferation of competing imaginaries, *selection* of a particular discourse and *retention* of some resonant characteristics (e.g. inclusion in an actor's habitus, hexis and personal identity, enactment in organisational routines, integrated into institutional rules, etc.). The moment of retention also involves an economic imaginary's *reinforcement* by procedural devices, serving to privilege an economic imaginary at the expense of competing discourses and practices as well as *recruitment/inculcation* of these discourses by relevant social agents. This evolutionary conception of capitalist social reproduction "highlights the dialectic of path-dependency and path-shaping that emerges from the contingent co-evolution of semiotic *and extra-semiotic* processes" (Jessop 2009b, 340, emphasis in the original).

Figure 3: Variation, Selection and Retention

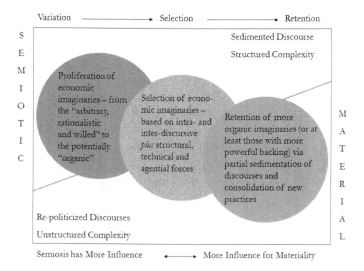

Source: modified from Sum and Jessop 2013, 403

Ngai-Ling Sum adds the moments of *embodiment* and *resistance* to variation, selection and retention. Economic imaginaries may not only be material-ised in institutions, but also within the bodies of those subjects, the social practices of which are being regulated. What is more, hegemonic discourses are only ever partial and unstable, which is why there is always a moment of resistance and space for counter-hegemony that primarily lies within the gaps between discourse and practice (Sum 2006, 20). The human rights discourse is a classic example. It can be unmasked as ideological given the capitalist order of inequality, on the one hand, but it can be used for counter-hegemonic mobilisations and resistance strategies as well, on the other hand. Societal conflicts, thus, are not only fought out using material resources, but they also take place fundamentally on the discursive-symbolic level as a "battle for ideas" (Jessop 2009a, 22). Since the notions of hegemony, sub- and counter-hegemony are central to my empirical analysis below, they deserve some closer attention.

Hegemony, sub- and counter-hegemony

Jessop and Sum describe Gramsci as "a proto- and post-regulation theorist" (Jessop and Sum 2006, 348) and as "a pioneer of cultural political economy" (Sum and Jessop 2013, 72), because he laid some important groundwork for how both approaches treat the interrelatedness of economics, politics and culture. This is most obvious in Gramsci's account of hegemony, the relevance of which for Regulation Theory has already been discussed above (see Chapter 2.1.2). In CPE, the traditional understanding of hegemony as a form of domination based on consensus armoured with coercion is extended to analyse the variation, selection and retention of imaginaries in terms of hegemony, sub- and counter-hegemony:

"Imaginaries exist at different sites and scales of action—from individual agents to world society. Social forces will therefore seek to establish one or another imaginary as the hegemonic or dominant 'frame' in particular contexts and/or to develop complementary sub-hegemonic imaginaries or, again, counter-hegemonic imaginaries that motivate and mobilize resistance" (Sum and Jessop 2013, 165–166).

Sum (2005, 2006) unravels the relationships among hegemony, sub-hegemony and counter-hegemony, referring to neoliberalism as a hegemonic project. The hegemonic codes of neoliberalism include discourses of competitiveness, privatisation, deregulation and free trade. Key actors ("organic intellectuals" in Gramsci's sense) promoting these codes are to be found within international organisations such as the International Monetary Fund (IMF), the World Bank and the World Trade Organisation (WTO) as well as on the different levels of states and governments (national states, supra-national states such as the European Union, local governments). However, in line with Gramsci, hegemony needs to be secured within the (transnational) civil society, which is why non-state actors such as transnational corporations, think tanks, consultancy firms, rating agencies, NGOs, trade unions and so forth play a crucial role. So, hegemonic discourses emerge from a variety of local to global scales and from three "mediating arenas": international organisations, states and civil society (Sum 2006, 11). But from these scales and arenas, sub- and counter-hegemonic discourses may emerge as well.

The ILO, for instance, due to its tripartite structure, while not in opposition to international competition and free trade *per se*, aims to strengthen the "social dimension of globalization" (ILO 2008a) which extends the hegemonic meaning of globalisation but "can be subsumed and contained within the hegemonic codes" (Sum 2005), making the ILO a site for both hegemonic actors (powerful member states, employer organisations) and sub-hegemonic actors (other member states, trade unions). Sub-hegemonic discourses and practices "may strengthen the overall consensus around the hegemonic project" (Sum 2006, 21), when they become appropriated by hegemonic actors and absorbed into hegemonic discourses. The example Sum provides, the remaking of neoliberal hegemony through a "new ethicalism" (Sum 2006, 15) is taken up in Chapter 8. Typical sub-hegemonic actors include service-oriented NGOs providing social services that, while in many cases motivated by humanistic ideals or similar non-market oriented imaginaries, effectively strengthen market rule by serving as "flanking mechanisms" (Graefe 2006) for the neoliberal market regime. Lastly, counter-hegemonic discourses and practices can be defined as those which contribute to the articulation of a counter-hegemonic project that cannot be subsumed and absorbed into the hegemonic project. Typical counter-hegemonic actors include a huge variety of social movements and movement-oriented NGOs, certain types of trade unions or echelons within them, critical intellectuals and producers of counter-culture. These actors operate within their respective local settings as well as on global and regional scales in arenas and networks such as the World and regional Social Forums.

This discussion is important for my empirical analysis of decent work, looking at how decent work may be conceptualised as a sub-hegemonic flanking mechanism for neoliberal globalisation or as a counter-hegemonic imaginary moving beyond the confines of neoliberalism.

Strategic selectivities

In order to study the "production of (counter-)hegemonies" (Sum and Jessop 2013, 203), CPE draws on the "strategic-relational approach" (SRA) to differentiate four modes of strategic selectivities operating in the evolutionary moment of selection: structural, agential, discursive and technological selectivities.

In previous works, Jessop had developed the SRA as a materialist theory of the capitalist state (Jessop 1990, 2007). While the capitalist state is not capitalist in the sense that it only serves capitalist interests (see Chapter 2.1.2), in securing hegemony it still selectively responds to different interests and demands—privileging some while marginalising others. Intervening into Marxist debates about how to conceptualise the state within capitalist societies, the SRA provided a "third way" between two strands seeing either the "capital logic" or "class struggle" as the main driving force of change and continuity in the state system. The first strand emphasised the logic of capital, i.e. Marx's "economic law of motion of modern society" (Marx 1890, 15) on an abstract level of analysis—the state responds politically to imperatives and demands structurally inscribed into the economic structures of capitalism. The second strand emphasised the concrete modalities of class struggle as the "engine of history"—the state is a terrain of class struggle reflecting shifting balances of (class) forces. While each strand one-sidedly emphasised capital-logical over class-theoretical arguments or *vice versa*, Jessop aimed to resolve the problem by combining both perspectives within a dialectical framework of structure and agency, in which each structure is understood as the path-dependent outcome of past agency. The logic of capital was not understood as a unitary, eternal law of motion anymore, but rather as multiple, competing *accumulation strategies*. The field of class struggle was re-specified in terms of competing *hegemonic projects* (Jessop 2007, 34).

The notion of structural selectivities is borrowed from Claus Offe (1974) who had argued that the state necessarily and structurally privileges the interests of the capitalist class, that the state is structurally selective towards these interests. Jessop modifies this understanding in his concept of strategic selectivity positing that the privileging of ruling class interests is less an automatic outcome of the structure of the state system itself than it is a contingent outcome of specific accumulation strategies and hegemonic projects (Jessop 1990, 260). Nevertheless, there is a structural bias towards capitalist interests, because one of the indispensable functions of the modern state is to maintain, reproduce or restore the conditions for capital accumulation. Maintaining these conditions may, however, involve catering to the interests of industrial workers if this is implicated in the given hegemonic project and/or accumulation strategy as was the case in the social democratic projects of the Fordist era in Northern and Western Europe.

Structural selectivities still feature within CPE, although only as one out of four modes of strategic selectivities: "*Structural selectivity* is a short-hand term for structurally inscribed strategic selectivity and denotes the asymmetrical configuration of constraints and opportunities on social forces as they pursue particular projects" (Sum and Jessop 2013, 214, emphasis in the original). This term thus refers to the structural mechanisms constraining or enabling social agents to pursue their interests through specific strategies and projects. But as CPE is concerned with both structuration and semiosis, it is also interested in the semiotic or discursive mechanisms involved in the evolutionary selection of economic and political imaginaries. Thus, the term "*discursive selectivity*" is introduced, referring to "the manner in which different discourses (whether everyday or specialized) enable some rather than other enunciations to be made within the limits of particular languages and the forms of discourse that exist within them" (Sum and Jessop 2013, 215). Structural and discursive selectivities are not thought of as entirely separate mechanisms, but—just as structuration and semiosis more generally—as two dialectically interrelated aspects of the moment of selection. For example, the ability of different branches of the labour movement to articulate their interests vis-à-vis the state or international institutions depends on their "structural power" that is determined by their position within the global economic system (Wright 2000, 962), however, it also depends on their ability to speak the appropriate language in a given political arena, to use the available hegemonic codes for their purposes or to extend their meanings, to depict their interests as in line with whatever "general interest" or to influence common sense and public opinion in their favour, in short, on their "discursive power".

The two other modes of strategic selectivities are agential and technological selectivities. In line with the SRA's and CPE's dialectic understanding of structure and agency, *agential selectivity* is the counterpart to structural and discursive selectivity and refers to "the differential capacity of agents to engage in structurally oriented strategic calculation—whether in regard to structurally or discursively inscribed strategic selectivities" (Sum and Jessop 2013, 217). There are strategic selectivities inscribed into the structures of global capitalism and there are selectivities inscribed into specific discourses and both require agents to be able to strategically orient their actions towards these structures and discourses, to analyse particular conjunctures and to effect change or continuity within them. Agential selectivity refers to the fact that "agents can make a difference" (ibid.) when they are able to read and exploit structural and discursive selectivities.

The notion of *technological selectivities* is an outcome of CPE's integration of Foucauldian concepts of technologies, thus, it refers to "disciplinary, normalizing and governmental technologies" (Sum and Jessop 2013, 205) rather than technology in the technical sense. The key for integrating Foucault into CPE is linking his concepts of discourse, dispositive and governmentality to Marxian and Gramscian concepts of capital accumulation, domination and hegemony in order to come up with a strategic-relational definition of dispositives already indicated above. Sum and Jessop explain:

"By combining Foucauldian interest in governmental technologies (with their implicit Marxian engagements) with a more explicit account of the contradictions and crisis tendencies of capital accumulation, we will obtain a more nuanced version of the semiotic-material moments of social development" (2013, 213–214).

In this perspective, Gramsci is the vehicle for synthesising Marx and Foucault, who are taken as complementing rather than contradicting each other. Citing Marsden (1999), Sum and Jessop argue that Marx's theory is better suited to answering "why" questions and Foucault's theory is more attuned to "how" questions (Sum and Jessop 2013, 207). Marx was interested in *why* the process of capital accumulation appears to be an alien power to people despite being produced and reproduced by them, why "to them, their own social action takes the form of the action of objects, which rule the producers instead of being ruled by them" (Marx 1890, 89), in short, why subjects and objects switch positions. Foucault was interested in *how* people are subjected to "technologies of power which determine the conduct of individuals and submit them to certain ends or domination, an objectivizing of the subject" (Foucault 1988, 18), how subjects are disciplined and normalised in such a way that the reproduction of social domination appears to be the effect of their own desire and choosing, in short, how "technologies of power" and "technologies of the self" (ibid.) interact in reproducing domination and hegemony: "This contact between the technologies of domination of others and those of the self I call governmentality" (Foucault 1988, 18–19).

This concept of *governmentality*, along with the dispositive concept discussed above, is included in CPE's notion of "technological selectivities" expressing "the asymmetries inscribed in particular disciplinary and governmental technologies as well as interwoven dispositives" (Sum and Jessop 2013, 211). These technologies shape individual choices and delimit their capacity to act, they contribute to the "conduct of conduct" (Foucault's definition of government)[3] and thus constitute a central aspect of the moment of selection in the evolution of economic imaginaries. Thus, the question of how governmental technologies contribute to the subjectivation of individuals and to the objectivation of social relations, limiting the scope of available identities and courses of action, selecting or normalising certain discourses and practices while excluding others, is a common concern of CPE and Foucauldian governmentality studies. CPE additionally is concerned with questions of when particular discourses or, rather, imaginaries become selected, what contradictions they are addressing, who the actors involved in their selection and retention are as well as why and how they are being reproduced, modified or resisted by subaltern groups (Sum and Jessop 2013, 226). These questions will also guide my analysis of decent work as an economic imaginary. Before, I introduce the methodological framework adopted for this study—Critical Grounded Theory.

---

3 In the English translation, the quote reads: "The exercise of power consists in guiding the possibility of conduct and putting in order the possible outcome. Basically power is less a confrontation between two adversaries or the linking of one to the other than a question of government" (Foucault 1983, 221).

3. Towards Critical Grounded Theory

In this chapter,[4] I present a distinctive methodology for my study—Critical Grounded Theory (CGT)—that was developed through collaborative work with Claes Belfrage (Belfrage and Hauf 2015). The chapter is divided into three parts. First, I return to the methodological aspects of critical discourse and dispositive analysis and reflect on their ability to shed light on the practical use of political and economic imaginaries. Second, the limitations of CDA provide an occasion for me to revisit the methodological literature on Grounded Theory to look for ethnographic tools and techniques that may be combined with CDA. The tensions between the critical-realist framework of CPE and the originally positivist method of Grounded Theory, third, necessitates an adaptation of Grounded Theory to the ontology and epistemology of critical realism to lay the groundwork for CGT. Fourth, CGT itself is introduced both conceptually and procedurally.

We have seen that, although semiosis is omnipresent and has to be given more weight within political economy research, it is not sufficient to study semiosis in and of itself by analysing discursive artefacts. If the production of meaning is to be accounted for in a meaningful way, it has to be embedded within an analysis of the actual practices of the actors engaging in meaning-making in terms of their political strategies and hegemonic projects, focussing on how specific economic imaginaries serve to underpin these projects and strategies and make them work for their interests. The CPE approach compels us to consistently differentiate the semiotic from the material dimension of economic arrangements in order to enable analysing their mutually constitutive interrelations. An analysis of the persistence of neoliberal imaginaries during the current economic and financial crisis, for example, would be incomplete without looking at who

---

4 Sections 3.1 to 3.4 partly correspond to Belfrage and Hauf (2015).

is continuing to circulate these imaginaries, to which projects and strategies they are connected and for what ends and with what effects they become enacted or challenged. In order to get access to this level of the "real", I want to argue, critical scholars will have to go beyond discourse analysis and do empirical, indeed ethnographic work. They have to go places and talk to people, i.e. conduct field trips and interviews to get information about how discourses or imaginaries become relevant in people's everyday lives and they need to know how to do it. This may seem self-evident and obviously critical scholars have begun to combine discourse analysis and ethnography in many cases, but only seldom in a systematic and reflexive manner.

The move from discourse to dispositive analysis indicates the need to combine discourse analysis with interviews and observations without providing clear guidance as to how this can be done in practical research. Therefore, Claes Belfrage and I (Belfrage and Hauf 2015) have proposed Critical Grounded Theory (CGT) as a method for Cultural Political Economy research. CGT as a distinct critical version of Grounded Theory is the result of decentring Critical Discourse Analysis and combining it with Grounded Theory tools of data generation and evaluation, which have to be adapted to critical realism, the ontological and epistemological foundation of CPE. Yet, CGT may be adapted to a range of other critical approaches in the social sciences as well.

3.1 Critical Discourse and Dispositive Analysis

The previous chapter already introduced some theoretical aspects of critical discourse and dispositive analysis as they become relevant for the theoretical elaboration of CPE. To recap, discourses are irreducible to language and speech and, therefore, cannot be adequately studied using *linguistic* discourse analysis alone. This is why CPE favours *critical* discourse analysis that pays due attention to their discursive and non-discursive context. CDA, however, is also limited, because it can only be productively employed if the research interest is primarily located on the semiotic level. However, "the 'imaginary' refers not only to semiosis but also to its material supports and this requires a broader toolkit" (Jessop and Sum 2012, 86). The move from CDA to dispositive analysis as proposed by the

Duisburg School is thus a welcome development that may help to clarify the methodological operationalisation of CPE.

Jäger (2001) argues that Foucault's concept of the dispositive ultimately laps into inconsistency, because he fails to see that dispositives are held together by human activity or labour mediating subject and object and that it is thus the subject that links discourse to reality. If, however, the subject and its labouring activity are (re-)introduced to move from discourse to dispositive analysis, the methodological framework has to be adapted accordingly. What is central methodologically, then, is less the discourse as such, its rules of formation and its inner regularities, than its practical use in social activities. To study how discourses "may be *enacted* as new ways of (inter)acting, [...] *inculcated* as new ways of being (identities), [or] physically *materialized*" (Fairclough 2009, 165, emphasis in the original) as new objectifications, we need a method that is capable of analysing discourses in terms of the social practices they are entangled with, the subjectivities and identities they bear upon and the materialisations or institutionalisations they may effect. Jäger and Maier (2009, 56–60), thus, propose a three-dimensional procedure for analysing dispositives in terms of their associated discursive practices, non-discursive practices and materialisations. In the first dimension, discursive practices and the forms of knowledge entailed therein can be reconstructed using the methods and techniques of (critical) discourse analysis. More often than not, this will involve media analysis, i.e. reconstructing a certain discourse by looking at how it is produced and circulated in different media such as newspapers, magazines, TV, or the internet. All the examples for discourse-analytical tools and possible steps of a discourse analysis Jäger and Maier (2009) provide are examples of media analysis. They are very careful to argue that discourse analysis of texts remains the central part of dispositive analysis, but has to be complemented by other tools and techniques such as participant observation or ethnographic interviews (Jäger and Maier 2009, 60).

In order to reconstruct non-discursive practices and their associated forms of knowledge, Jäger and Maier argue that "actions can be observed and described" (2009, 58) and actors can be questioned in ethnographic interviews, providing the second dimension of dispositive analysis. The third dimension is to reconstruct the materialisations of non-discursive practices, however, such materialisations (e.g. a building) cannot be interviewed and their meaning cannot be revealed by observation. The researcher, therefore, has to rely on her own background knowledge, but she "should aim to extend this knowledge by drawing on the pertinent literature and by questioning users, producers and other persons who are experts on the materialization in question" (Jäger and Maier 2009, 59). What Jäger and Maier explicitly do not provide is a recipe or a clear-cut method for how to do this in the concrete. They want to provide some suggestions for approximating the problem of discourses, actions and materialisations, rather than presenting a finished method ready for application. They conclude that, in addition to discourse analysis, "dispositive analysis comprises the analysis of non-discursive practices, for which methods developed in ethnography, such as ethnographic interviews and participant observation, provide important means" but "an explicit methodology for combining these approaches has yet to be developed" (Jäger and Maier 2009, 60). So, we are left with the suggestion to combine discourse analysis with participant observation and ethnographic interviews without indication as to how this could be achieved practically.

In acknowledging the limitations of CDA and the need to go beyond discourse, dispositive analysis points in the right direction methodologically. Nevertheless, it seems to reinforce the privileging of discourse, because it *a priori* places discourse analysis at its heart. Jäger (2001, 88) argues that discourse analysis can also be applied to non-discursive practices and materialisations, because ethnographic data can be turned into texts (protocols, transcripts, etc.). Although this is certainly true, it is not a satisfactory solution for CPE, because it would reduce ethnographic situations to their semiotic moment and erase their structural features by making everything a text. It would allow for interpreting meaning produced in these situations, but fall short of linking this to the level of social structures and causal mechanisms that CPE is interested in, too. For this, we need a methodology that is centred on the ethnographic immersion into the field prioritising the practical relevance of discourses for social actors in their everyday life. Ethnography should be made central to the retroductive research process in order to enable the investigation of discourses or imaginaries in terms of the lived experiences of the social actors producing, circulating, modifying or resisting them. Proper ethnographic tools and techniques need to be introduced, rather than analysing ethnographic data with discourse-analytical tools. Grounded Theory is one of the most popular ethnographic methodologies. Therefore next, although potentially counter-intuitive, Grounded Theory is explored as a rich source of ethnographic tools and techniques to be employed in the elaboration of CGT.

In the next section, I thus revisit the Grounded Theory literature to look for ethnographic tools and techniques that may be adapted to critical realism and combined with CDA to constitute a distinctive method we have labelled Critical Grounded Theory (Belfrage and Hauf 2015).

3.2 Grounded Theory Methods

At first sight, the very idea of a critical version of Grounded Theory seems to be an oxymoron. Grounded Theory, as developed by Barney Glaser and Anselm Strauss (1967), stands firmly in the tradition of positivist science, the very antithesis to critical science. It is therefore not surprising that the majority of critical scholars have disregarded Grounded Theory. Sum and Jessop reject it:

"Grounded theory is a theoretically agnostic, empiricist research method that [...] claims to avoid preconceived hypotheses that are imposed on the data and aims instead to ground its theory in a naïve observation of 'raw' data gathered without prior theoretical contamination" (2013, 123).

I want to argue, however, that this critique only holds for "objectivist grounded theory" (Charmaz 2006) most strongly associated with Barney Glaser (1992) who, indeed, was a *naïve* realist positing pure induction as the only scientific road to knowledge. However, Grounded Theory tools can be integrated into critical frameworks such as CPE by aligning them with the ontology and epistemology of *critical* realism.

In recent contributions, Grounded Theory has been developed further and the idea of pure induction is now hardly held up by any Grounded Theory scholar. It is increasingly recognised that observations are necessarily theory-laden and influenced by what is called "pre-concepts". Accessing reality in a pre-discursive or non-conceptual way is simply impossible. Most of these contributions (e.g. Charmaz 2006; Clarke 2011) push Grounded Theory away from positivism and towards social constructivism and postmodernism, arguing that the method has always been "paradigmatically neutral" (Glaser 2001). Charmaz (2006, 129), therefore, juxtaposes what she calls "objectivist grounded theory" and "constructivist grounded theory", the former wedded to the positivist tradition and the latter to the interpretive tradition of social science. Clarke and Friese take this argument one step further by pushing the "postmodernisation" of Grounded Theory forward, thereby actually replacing Grounded Theory with "situational analysis" and opening it up for postmodern feminism and discourse analysis (Clarke and Friese 2007). What is missing here is a third epistemological position between the naïve realism of Glaser (1992) and the radical constructivism of Clarke and others (e.g. Clarke and Friese 2007), occupying the ontological and epistemological space of critical realism.

Grounded Theory has become a highly popular method in the social sciences for its ability to construct, in a systematic manner, rich conceptual frameworks, or "grounded theories", out of, typically, ethnographically produced data. Grounded Theory as a method for qualitative social research goes back to the seminal work by Barney Glaser and Anselm Strauss (1967) *The Discovery of Grounded Theory*. The title is suggestive of the idea that the adequate "theory" is already there in the data, simply waiting to be "discovered", representing the naïve realism and positivism associated with the work of Glaser. Strauss has since moved in a different, more "post-positivist" direction that is less opposed to the use of existing theory in order to establish the context of a grounded theory (Strauss and Corbin 1990). As the questions of theory and context are central to the development of CGT, the disagreement between Glaser and Strauss deserves closer attention.

In *Basics of Qualitative Research*, Strauss and Corbin (1990) develop two different techniques to facilitate the "doing" of Grounded Theory. The first is the use of a "coding paradigm" (ibid., 99) as a tool for enhancing "theoretical sensitivity" in moving "upwards" from the data to "codes" to "categories". The second tool of note in this work is the "conditional matrix" (ibid., 158), which is closely related to the coding paradigm. It is a coding device to help the researcher locate the phenomenon under study within a broader structural context and analyse the interrelations between macro and micro conditions and consequences on a variety of scales from local action to the international level. Glaser, however, dismisses both techniques. He rejects the coding paradigm accusing it of being too prescriptive and, thus, "forcing theoretical coding concepts onto data to the max" instead of letting "whatever theoretical codes emerge where they may" (1992, 63). He also criticises the conditional matrix for the same reasons. Arguing that structural conditions at any of the matrix's levels are relevant to any Grounded Theory study, like Strauss and Corbin (1990, 161) do, for Glaser, again, means abandoning Grounded Theory in favour of what he calls "preconceived conceptual description" (1992, 98), or "pre-concepts". In other words, Glaser's ideal Grounded Theory is an arms-length, supposedly objective approach to ethnography and thus unsuited.

Strauss' move has opened Grounded Theory up to constructivism and notions of meaning-making (Charmaz 2006). Clarke (2011) has sought to capitalise on this by moving towards "situational analysis" and exposing Grounded Theory to postmodernism and discourse analysis. What can be learned from this intervention is the definitive rejection of positivist remnants of Grounded Theory and the reinforcement of the proposition that it is necessary to relate categories and properties not only to the emerging conceptualisation but critically to previously existing theories as well. What is disappointing for our purpose is Clarke's imitation of the postmodern gesture of rejecting comprehensive social theories in arguing that it makes no sense to formalise something that is constantly changing (ibid., 221). Favouring theorising over theory, she claims that it is unnecessary for Grounded Theory to aim for substantial and formal theories; instead, analysis should focus on the production of "sensitising concepts". In addition, this appears inconsistent with her call for "de-reification" (ibid., 220) and analysing relations of power and domination in order to unmask the "non-negotiable in social life" (ibid., 221). We maintain that the very notions of reification, power and domination presuppose a comprehensive critical theory of society. Obviously, for the present attempt to operationalise CPE, an approach that sustains the idea of comprehensive social theory, we would need another, more genuinely *critical* Grounded Theory.

There are several attempts at integrating critical theory into the Grounded Theory method. MacDonald (2001) seeks to find a critical perspective for grounded theories of nursing and health promotion. She recognises charges against symbolic interactionism and Grounded Theory for having an "astructural bias" (ibid., 118), i.e. being insensitive to social structure, thus neglecting the complex interdependencies between macro and micro and between structure and agency. She advocates that grounded theorists should not be afraid of the consideration of comprehensive social theory or what Glaser lambasts as "pre-concepts". She seems to imply, however, that on proper reading many of these charges are overstated or true only for a fraction of work based on symbolic interactionism and

Grounded Theory. Her argument takes up the disagreements between Glaser and Strauss, favouring Strauss' more context-sensitive approach. Nevertheless, she lapses into inconsistency. On the one hand, she contends that the conditional matrix can account for social structure. On the other hand, her feminist argument that "power is embedded in [...] structural phenomena that [...] exist separately from people's acknowledgement or understanding of them" (ibid., 121) suggests that she is in agreement with the contention that the historical specificity of the reifying effects of the economic structure of capitalism should be made more central to analysis.

Gibson rightly argues that any critical-theoretical Grounded Theory that endeavours to do so "without reflecting on society would lose its ability to be critical" (2007, 440). That is to say, from our perspective, to produce grounded theory, we need a theory of society for understanding its macro context. Unfortunately, he proceeds by challenging comprehensive social theory and, instead, proposes a more pragmatic accommodation involving the inclusion of participants as equal partners (ibid., 444). Moreover, Gibson fails to account for the dialectical relationship between structure and agency both theoretically and methodologically. Kushner and Morrow (2003, 34) introduce realist foundations in order to enable an emancipatory agenda for Grounded Theory and take further steps towards CGT. Oliver (2012) takes this effort one step further by specifically developing the critical realist foundations for Grounded Theory in order to enhance explanation and understanding as well as the normativity of praxis. She thus exposes Grounded Theory to the same philosophical balancing act as CPE, demonstrating the utility of the endeavour.

3.3 Critical Realism and Retroduction

As Oliver (2012) argues, critical realism can bridge the divide between the realist insistence that there is a reality existing independent from our knowledge of it and the constructivist idea that all meaning made of that reality, all knowledge of it is socially and discursively constructed. It avoids the pitfalls of both naïve realism and radical constructivism. I here briefly discuss critical realism and retroduction before outlining how a retroductive CGT research process may look like.

Critical realism has often been conceptualised as the philosophy of science actually underlying Marx's critique of political economy (cf. contributions to Brown et al. 2002). Jessop argues that the regulation approach, the direct predecessor of CPE, is implicitly critical realist (2002, 90) because of its links to Marx and Althusser. By the same token, CPE can be said to build on a critical realist foundation. Indeed, it is the foundation in critical realism that distinguishes CPE most notably from other, more radically constructivist "cultural" or "performative turns" in political economy. Critical realism, as elaborated by Roy Bhaskar (e.g. 1986) differentiates "real" structures or mechanisms, "actual" things or events and "empirical" observations or experiences. It seeks to uncover the generative mechanisms, often lying hidden behind what meets the eye, that cause observable phenomena. A mechanism is a relationship in the domain of the "real" that a scientific law refers to (Collier 1994, 43). If, for instance, Marx's "law of the tendency of the rate of profit to fall" is understood as a scientific law in the sense of critical realism, then there is a mechanism in the real world this law refers to—the fundamental crisis tendencies of capitalism are real regardless of when and where they become actualised and observable. This is also the reason why this notion of laws as tendencies does not allow for exact predictions. The generative mechanism is not deterministic in any sense similar to natural sciences. Rather, if an event occurs in the domain of the actual, the generative mechanism can only explain the cause of the event *ex post*. The social reality is an open system in which multiple mechanisms co-determine events, overlapping, reinforcing or counteracting one another. It is impossible to close the system experimentally in order to isolate a single mechanism like in natural sciences. The social reality is multi-causal, multi-layered, stratified and complex.

In order to identify generative mechanisms, the critical realist asks the following question: What must be true for this event to be possible? From an observable phenomenon, we go back to possible explanations for the phenomenon. This is the methodological principle of retroduction; retroductive arguments are arguments "from a description of some phenomenon to a description of something which produces it or is a condition for it" (Bhaskar 1986, 11). In order to arrive at possible explanations for the phenomenon, the critical realist relies on analogies with already known phenomena and on pre-existing theories as cognitive raw materials for the retroductive movement of thought. These pre-existing theories may be "proto-theories" (Collier 1994, 165), i.e. proto-scientific theories stemming from people's experiences in everyday life, as well as existing scientific theories about the phenomenon at hand we wish to deepen, challenge, refute or reconstruct. In discourse analytical terms, scientific theories serve as "special discourses", everyday forms of knowledge are "elementary discourses" while "interdiscourses" refer to those discourses in media, politics, popular culture and so forth that occupy an intermediate position between special and elementary discourses (Link 2011, 437–440). We have seen above that proto-theories are called "pre-concepts" in Grounded Theory, dismissed by objectivist Grounded Theory but embraced by constructivist as well as Critical Grounded Theory.

In CGT, these pre-existing theories and concepts are worked through during an initial phase of deskwork. During this initial phase, the researcher analyses the relevant scientific literature as well as media and policy documents before employing them in the construction of initial conceptualisations or "soft hypotheses". These will gently guide the researcher through the subsequent phases of ethnographic fieldwork. In these phases, ethnographic interviews, focus groups, participant observations or other ethnographic methods can be employed to produce rich qualitative data to be evaluated using the tools and techniques of Grounded Theory. Finally, the researcher revises, reconstructs or develops the initial proto-theories in the light of empirical findings. CGT is thus different from CDA and dispositive analysis, because the core of CGT is not textual analysis of fragments of discourses, from which other elements of the dispositive are related to better understand the discourse. Rather, the ethnographic immersion into the field is fundamental, in which the researcher employs pre-concepts to better understand how discourses and imaginaries become practically relevant in people's everyday lives.

Retroduction, thus, describes an on-going, spiral movement between the abstract and the concrete, between theoretical and empirical work, that involves both an interpretive and a causal dimension of explanation. It involves a moment of "dwelling in theory" (Burawoy 1998, 5), a deductive moment, in which existing theories and concepts are worked through and applied to the research object in a first instance to generate soft hypotheses sensitising the researcher's understanding of observations and guiding dialogue with participants. This moment is also the most discourse-analytical moment of CGT as scientific theories and media or policy discourses can be productively studied using the tools of CDA. These hypotheses are not "tested" for verification or falsification as in quantitative methods, neither are they "bracketed" or "suspended" as in constructivist Grounded Theory. In CGT, they are rather consciously put into dialogue with observations made in the field and with conceptualisations of participants. The perspectivity and subjectivity of the researcher, his interventions into the field "create perturbations that are not noise to be expurgated but music to be appreciated, transmitting the hidden secrets of the participant's world" (Burawoy 1998, 14). Retroduction then involves an inductive moment, in which the researcher is immersed into the field before working up empirical data into emerging conceptualisations, refining previous concepts, deepening understanding, altering explanations and reconstructing existing theory in order to appropriate the "real-concrete" as a "concrete in thought" (Jessop 2002, 98). The result is not an *objective* grounded theory discovered in the data, but a *critical* grounded theory reconstructed through a sophisticated retroductive research process. Let us now consider how such a process may look like in more detail.

3.4 A Retroductive Model of Critical Grounded Theory

We start the research process with critical observations or experiences of a social problem, of an issue or a process that we wish to explain, not as disinterested observers but as active members of a society ridden by social antagonisms and relations of exploitation, domination and exclusion, the explanation of which is a precondition for changing them. The aim of critical social science is to enable emancipatory practices by producing critical knowledge about society. Explanation in critical realism involves both causal and interpretive dimensions. In terms of interpretation, to get an initial understanding of how the problem is discursively construed and represented in both academic and everyday discourses, we analyse media discourses relevant to our problem, collecting, preparing and evaluating discursive materials such as newspaper articles, online forums, policy papers, transcripts of parliamentary debates and so on. We also retroduce by going back to possible explanations for the problem by exploring existing mid-range theories bearing on our topic as well as our preferred general approach, in my case CPE. Tentative explanations will serve as initial conceptualisations or soft hypotheses. Where positivist science will attempt to "test", i.e. verify or falsify hypotheses by isolating one possible mechanism after the other in a closed system, CGT employs initial conceptions in the dialogue with participants during repeated cycles of empirical fieldwork (e.g. ethnographic interviews, participant observation, focus groups, etc.) and theoretical deskwork in what is called "constant comparison" in Grounded Theory terminology. Emerging conceptualisations and interpretations are constantly compared to existing ones, thereby making the initial conceptualisations more and more refined and complex. Although "theoretical saturation" may never be achieved, at some point of the process, our conceptualisations are used to explain the social problem or process at a given point in time. Although each individual research project will have to end at some point, the retroductive process is indefinite as a matter of principle since theories are always provisional, incomplete and subject to revision as the most plausible explanations can only approximate the "real", which is never fully knowable.

Nevertheless, we end up with a number of potential outcomes: the reconstruction of mid-range theories, having deepened or broadened our knowledge, established new connections and challenged existing explanations. Depending on our specific project, this will hopefully result in societal impact serving emancipatory purposes. Moreover, the fieldwork itself and the feedback provided to participants may impact upon society. Perhaps less likely, the initial approach, in my case CPE, may be revised. Figure 4 illustrates the retroductive research process of CGT.

Figure 4: The Retroductive Research Process of Critical Grounded Theory

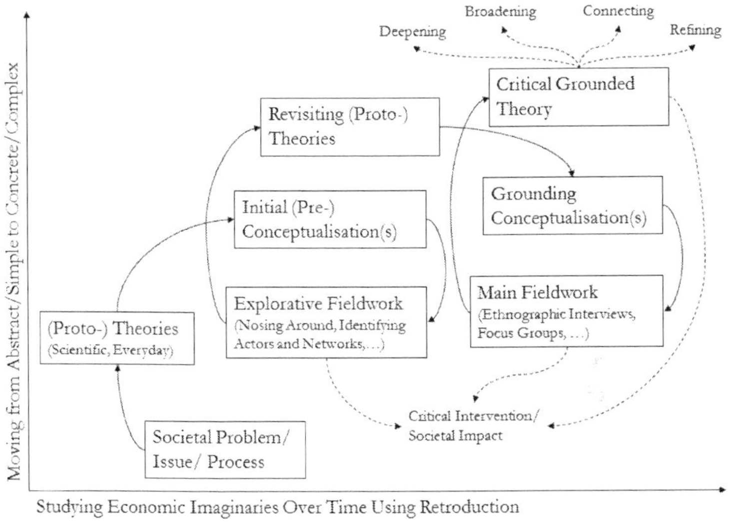

Source: Belfrage and Hauf 2015, 336

We have seen that, within a CPE framework, discourses, imaginaries and dispositives cannot be adequately studied deploying methods of discourse analysis alone. Analysing the interplay of the discursive and the non-discursive "requires a broader toolkit" (Sum and Jessop 2013, 165). In order to develop such a toolkit, we have adopted a distinctive way to integrate aspects of critical discourse analysis into a broader methodology that looks at imaginaries not *per se* but at how they become enacted in social practices, inculcated by social agents and materialised in institutions, strategies and projects—Critical Grounded Theory (Belfrage and Hauf 2015). I have presented an abstract model of how a retroductive CGT research process may look like. This model is necessarily ideal-typical and incomplete and will only become clearer and more specific when applied to concrete case studies. I do so in Chapters 6 and 7, analysing the practical relevance of the decent work discourse as an economic imaginary for strategies and practices of labour unions and social movements in Indonesia. Before, it is necessary to provide a clearer picture of how I have approached the case studies using CPE and operationalising it with CGT.

3.5 A CPE Approach to Decent Work

The aim of the present study is not to provide a (critical) discourse analysis of decent work *per se*. My main interest is not to analyse the rules of formation, the power effects and the politics of truth of the decent work discourse on a global scale. Although decent work is a global discourse, my interest neither is to reconstruct decent work from a global perspective, focussing on how the discourse has been produced and organised within the ILO. Rather, I want to investigate the ways in which the global decent work discourse becomes locally and practically relevant to the strategies and practices of Indonesian labour unions and social movements and how it relates to other, alternative discourses, strategies and practices deployed by them.

Studying decent work in the concrete, rather than in the abstract, means to look at concrete practices in local contexts and at how they become enabled or constrained by the discourse. A critical analysis of decent work as a global discourse will thus form part of this study (see Chapter 4), albeit a decentred and shortened one that mainly serves the purpose of providing the larger historical and discursive context of the local practices that are of primary interest here. This is a necessary step to get to the core of the present study—a *critical grounded theory of decent work as an economic imaginary*, grounded in ethnographic research on the local relevance of decent work and other discourses for Indonesian labour unions and social movements (mostly but not exclusively within the garment, textiles and shoes industry). In order to arrive at the concrete/complex level of everyday strategies and practices, I look at how decent work policies have been implemented in Indonesia, not *in toto*, but by analysing specific approaches towards decent work in one particular sector. I have chosen the garment, textile and shoes industry as an entry point, because it is both one of the most globalised industries worldwide and one of the most important sectors of industrial development in Indonesia. Poor working conditions and low wages in the global garment industry are well documented (e.g. Wick 2005) and regularly make it to the headlines of Western newspapers. At the same time, the garment sector has continued to be said to be the key industry in the transition from a primarily agricultural to an industrial regime of accumulation: "apparel is typically the entering industry for countries embarking on a program of industrialization, particularly export-led industrialization" (Bonacich et al. 1994, 13).

A CPE/CGT approach to decent work has to start with the historical context of its research object. Without reflecting on the historical development of decent work, it cannot be adequately understood or explained. For better or worse, this requires a historical macro level reconstruction of the specific conjuncture out of which the decent work discourse emerged, i.e. an engagement with the history of neoliberal globalisation regarding the "big picture" of how neoliberalism emerged from the crisis of Fordism and effected profound changes in the world of work such as the feminisation of labour and the restructuring of capital accumulation along global commodity or transnational supply chains (see Chapter 4.1). It also requires a more meso level reconstruction of how global labour regulation has changed over the last decades in response to global restructuring, contrasting how labour regimes were organised in the Fordist era with new forms of labour regulation emerging in the era of globalisation. Especially the questions of how and why private forms of labour regulation such as Corporate Social Responsibility (CSR) have emerged and how they connect to the official structure of the ILO and its policies have to be addressed (see Chapter 4.2). Here, the debate about a social clause within the WTO system, its failure and subsequent relegation to the ILO will also be briefly discussed. Finally, the historical context of Indonesia as a case study has to be illuminated in terms of the history of the Indonesian labour movement from independence, to the Suharto era, to *Reformasi* and the present day (see Chapter 5). These historical excursuses are brief and only include those aspects that are important for the empirical analysis in Chapters 6 and 7.

Applying the concepts and categories of CPE, decent work is here conceptualised as an economic imaginary, in other words, as the semiotic moment of a wide network of diverse social practices connected to the regulation and organising of labour—whether local collective bargaining processes, national decent work country programmes, or global mobilisations around decent work. Given the vagueness and the potential infinity of decent work related issues, the decent work discourse has to be operationalised and its different discourse strands disassembled. When entering the field of decent work in Indonesia through the ILO, one gets the impression that every ILO project—from HIV/AIDS education to the training of police forces to deal with mass demonstrations more effectively—is related to decent work. This comes as no surprise since decent work has become the overarching discourse for all of the ILO's activities in the era of globalisation. When entering the field through the garment, textiles and shoes industry, it is easier to narrow the focus down to a realistic research plan. The most important ILO project in that sector is Better Work Indonesia (BWI), a joint project of the ILO and the International Finance Corporation (IFC) that I want to analyse as an example of how the ILO's global decent work agenda is implemented in particular, local settings, taking Indonesia's garment industry as a case study (see Chapter 6.1). The difference in wording between *decent* and *better* work does not preclude this kind of operationalisation. To the contrary, Better Work is one of the concrete programmes of the ILO forming part of the larger decent work agenda.

The decent work agenda of the ILO, however, is only one of the discourse strands that are central to the discourse as a whole. Since 2008, the International Trade Union Confederation (ITUC) has been organising the World Day for Decent Work on 7 October. Decent work, thus, has become a rallying cry of the international trade union movement, too. The domestic workers" movement, for instance, has also upheld the right to decent work in its mobilisations (Schwenken 2012). NGOs working in the field such as the Clean Clothes Campaign (CCC) often endorse the concept, too. This strand is certainly different from the ILO strand and needs to be analysed in its own right. During my research stays in 2011 and 2012, I was able to gather information about a particular multi-stakeholder initiative that was negotiating a voluntary protocol on freedom of association in Indonesia's sportswear industry at the time—the Play Fair Alliance (PFA, see Chapter 6.2). In my view, this form of private regulation is part of the decent work discourse, although it represents another discourse strand. Hypothetically speaking in CPE terminology, the ILO can be seen as a *hegemonic* actor in this field and BWI subsequently as a hegemonic approach towards decent work in Indonesia's garment industry. Similarly, traditional trade unions and NGOs are *sub-hegemonic* actors and the multi-stakeholder initiative that negotiated the protocol on freedom of association could be a sub-hegemonic approach. As we have seen above, CPE here envisages a third dimension—counter-hegemony and resistance. In Chapter 7, I look at possible actors and approaches that may fall into this category, again entering the field through the garment sector, but also looking beyond it to open up the horizon for a broader discussion of recovered *counter-hegemonic* imaginaries, strategies and practices of labour unions and social movements in Indonesia, taking the Indonesian People's Movement Confederation (KPRI) as a case study.

The CPE perspective and the concept of economic imaginaries reduce the complexity of decent work and its context while still enabling a rich and differentiated account that does justice to the topic. It helps to differentiate the semiotic from the material dimensions of decent work, seeing it both as a discursive formation and as a set of practices that has already been (partially) institutionalised in different contexts. It helps, for example, to differentiate the hegemonic ILO discourse on decent work and the ways it has already been selected and retained within the ILO, from alternative (sub-hegemonic) versions of the decent work discourse appropriated by trade unions and human rights, development or labour NGOs that may compete with the hegemonic version in ongoing cycles of variation, selection and retention. It also draws attention to potential resistance to decent work and counter-hegemonic discourses, i.e. economic imaginaries contesting both hegemonic and sub-hegemonic decent work discourses. The CPE perspective serves to understand the vagueness of the decent work agenda, which symbolically proclaims the right to decent work for all without providing substantial language on what decent work means in the concrete. It is exactly this vagueness, the big gap between the global discourse and the wide range of (trans-)local practices it may be used to justify, that makes decent work an economic imaginary *par excellence*. Initially, its discursive or semiotic dimension was more important in order to gather support from different actors. The symbolic right to decent work for all workers made it an attractive concept for trade unions and NGOs, while the emphasis on employment creation and competitiveness allowed employers and states to endorse the concept.

When thinking about it from a CPE perspective, decent work promises to be a contested discourse, both within the ILO and outside. Different versions of the decent work imaginary may circulate in different settings and on different scales (variation), diffused and appropriated by particular actors that have particular interests and strategies (selection) and enacted or institutionalised in specific projects, programmes and campaigns (retention). There may also be counter-hegemonic imaginaries, i.e. radical alternatives challenging the decent work discourse fundamentally (resistance). The question arising is: In what way has the global discourse on decent work informed (trans-)local strategies? Who is taking up the decent work discourse, in which context and why? How does the meaning of decent work change as the discourse moves between different sites and scales? Which strategies, projects and practices are appropriating decent work and for what ends? And, of great significance here, which are contesting or resisting it? Remember that in CPE social imaginaries are understood as addressing or processing contradictions based in social forms, so looking at decent work as an economic imaginary also means asking about the contradictions it addresses and the ways in which these are contained within the imaginary, albeit necessarily partially and temporarily. Therefore, it also means being attentive to how these contradictions may escape containment and thus resurface as conflicts and crises. Obviously, this will entail reflecting on the basic contradiction between capital and labour, how it is being regulated in the wage relation, how decent work imaginaries are addressing it and how recurring labour conflicts continually demonstrate that this fundamental contradiction of capitalism cannot easily be contained.

3.6 A CGT Study of Decent Work

Thus theoretically and methodologically equipped and with these questions in mind, I set out on a research journey that is described in this section. I describe the individual steps I took in undertaking a CGT study of decent work, taking Indonesian labour unions and social movements as a case study. This will recount the research process in chronological order, so readers may retrace how I initially approached the research problem by analysing the pertinent literature, how I operationalised it into a set of research questions and initial conceptualisations, how I deployed these during my first fieldtrip to Indonesia, rethought them back home revisiting special and inter-discourses before conducting my second fieldtrip and finally how I constructed a theoretically informed and empirically grounded argument about decent work.

The theoretical approach and the methodological operationalisation have already been discussed in the abstract above. This section reflects on these elements of the book in the concrete from the position of the researcher in the research process. Reflexivity and self-reflexivity are cornerstones of Grounded Theory (Breuer 2010). The researcher is an active part in the process and therefore she needs to reflect on her activity.

The process presented here will thus include self-reflexion, taking the subjectivity of the researcher and his relationship to the sites and actors under investigation into account. It will necessarily be "messy", because CGT is inherently "messy", iteratively shifting between discourse-analytical and theoretical deskwork and ethnographic fieldwork, between data collection, interpretation and analysis, constantly comparing tentative initial conceptualisations with ongoing observations made in the field, with emerging new conceptualisations and with those of participants. I do not hide this "messiness" behind a sterilised and artificial account of a linear research process that could be neatly presented as a positivist sequence of elaborating theory, collecting and analysing data, testing hypotheses and presenting results (cf. Suddaby 2006). Adhering to the conventions of positivist science is impossible for CGT studies, even if this requires more patience from the reader.

Approaching the problem of decent work

The retroductive research process of CGT starts, as we have seen above, with recognising a research problem that relates to a societal problem, process or conflict. In Marxian terms, what are the societal contradictions that decent work aims to address? In more Foucauldian terms, what is the "dominant strategic function" of decent work, what is the "urgent need" that decent work responds to? In order to get an initial understanding of what decent work is, I reviewed historical and theoretical literature relevant for this topic as well as analysed scientific discourse on decent work. The results of this initial step are presented in Chapters 4.1 and 4.2 in some detail. Here, let me just briefly summarise that stage in order to clarify how I proceeded next.

CPE, as inspired by Foucault, looks at the historical moment in which a new discourse, such as decent work, emerges and traces its development back to what came before. This "genealogical" method does not aim to determine the "origin" of the decent work discourse, but rather to investigate what enabled its "emergence" (McNay 1994, 89). Embedding this genealogy into the CPE framework, with its foundation in regulation theory, means to look at the conditions of emergence in terms of the different periods of capitalist development, different regimes of accumulation and different modes of regulation.

In short, decent work emerged in the context of neoliberal globalisation, which itself marks the transition from Fordism to neoliberalism. The societal problem arising in this context that decent work responds to is twofold. On the one hand, decent work responds to the problem of indecent working conditions, poverty wages and social insecurity. Globalisation has led to increasingly informal and precarious employment and decent work is ostensibly designed to rectify this problem by introducing new labour policies. This discourse strand can be found in hegemonic sites (mainly the ILO and associated governments and business associations) as well as some sub-hegemonic sites (e.g. service-oriented NGOs and "business unions"). On the other hand, decent work responds to a problem of legitimation in the current conjuncture of global capitalism. Social movements have contributed to a crisis of legitimacy by challenging the hegemony of neoliberal globalisation, criticising multinational corporations for sweatshop conditions in their supplier factories and raising public awareness about labour and human rights violations. Decent work responds to this legitimation problem by symbolically proclaiming the right to decent work for all without challenging the structural mechanisms causing indecent working conditions in the first place. This discourse strand is mainly to be found in counter-hegemonic sites (e.g. movement-oriented NGOs and social movement unions). Some sub-hegemonic sites may also occupy a third space in between the two general lines and navigate between acknowledging the legitimatising function of decent work and seizing the opportunities for incremental change arising therefrom (e.g. development NGOs and social democratic unions).

These two perspectives express the basic tension within the decent work discourse. Both perspectives are also mirrored in the academic literature. An example of the first perspective, although only in part, is Leah Vosko's feminist analysis of decent work. Although acknowledging the "hegemony-reinforcing" (Vosko 2002, 40) role of the ILO during the Cold War, she argues that the emergence of the decent work discourse in the era of globalisation reveals a growing presence of counter-hegemonic forces inside the ILO and at its margins. For her, decent work represents a counter-hegemonic potential if the discourse is appropriated by progressive trade unions, women's groups and other NGOs to struggle for better working conditions and labour rights of vulnerable groups of workers outside or at the margins of formal employment systems. Guy Standing (2008) represents the second, less optimistic view of decent work. He laments that decent work has marginalised the traditional ILO regime of industrial relations and adversarial bargaining and interprets its emergence as a sign of defeat of organised labour against neoliberal hegemony. Both perspectives are discussed in more detail in Chapter 4.2.3. The point here is to make clear how I initially approached the research problem by identifying this basic tension within the decent work literature. It drew my attention to the question of whether the decent work imaginary should be seen as reinforcing or countering neoliberal hegemony. I turn this question into an initial (pre-)conceptualisation of decent work to guide my empirical research: Decent work can function both as a pro-hegemonic and a counter-hegemonic imaginary vis-à-vis neoliberalism, depending on which actors appropriate it, in which context, for which projects and strategies and with which objectives and interests they do so.

The second step of the CGT research process is the exploration of the field.

Exploring the field and selecting the cases

The first research trip to Indonesia was undertaken in March 2011. Its main purpose was to explore the field, getting to know the most important actors and organisations and their networks. This exploration was done very much in the spirit of Grounded Theory, "nosing around" (Breuer 2010, 62) the field without tightly defined goals other than getting a feeling for what is currently relevant in the field, discovering new and theoretically interesting aspects of the research problem, talking to the different actors in the field about their ways of thinking and acting and reflecting on how this relates to my initial conceptualisation. This fed into the final case selection. In order to ensure reflexivity, I started to keep a field diary about my experiences, conversations, observations, explanations and interpretations as they developed over time. According to Grounded Theory, "all is data" (Glaser 1998, 8), so I documented all the thoughts, ideas, associations, questions and problems I had that were potentially relevant for my research interest. The diary enabled me to keep track of how my initial conceptualisations changed over time through dialogue with participants. It enabled constant comparison of emerging conceptualisations with existing ones as well as "theoretical sampling" (Breuer 2010, 57) regarding the next site to be explored, the next participant to be interviewed, or the next case to be analysed. Theoretical sampling describes the Grounded Theory mode of putting together a research sample, which does not define the sample *a priori* according to a fixed research design. Instead, the sample evolves over time as the research process unfolds. The researcher decides on additional cases or phenomena to be analysed according to conceptual relevance. Theoretical knowledge derived from analysing exploratory data, for example, forms the basis of deciding on which data should be collected next and where it could be found. During the exploration, however, theoretical sampling was combined with "snowball sampling" (Przyborski and Wohlrab-Sahr 2008, 180–181), that is, conceptually relevant cases were identified drawing on emergent conceptualisations, but interviewees were contacted via previous interviewees, so that not all theoretically interesting phenomena were analysed empirically to the same extent. Here, difficulties in field access necessitated a certain degree of pragmatism.

Access to the field was gained through the labour rights NGO *Trade Union Rights Centre* (TURC). TURC is a think tank and advocacy NGO supporting the Indonesian labour movement by providing legal advice, trainings, information and research on the legal, political and economic situation of Indonesian workers to trade unions and NGOs. Their knowledge of the most important actors in the field and their networks provided the ideal starting point for "snowballing" through the field, that is, key informants introducing additional key informants to be interviewed. I chose to access the field through TURC, rather than the ILO, because my main interest is the local relevance of the global decent work discourse for trade union strategies, rather than the implementation of the decent work agenda through the ILO itself. Nevertheless, it was important for me to understand which unions were cooperating directly with the ILO, participating in decent work related ILO projects and thus most likely to actively make use of the decent work discourse. As already mentioned, my non-exclusive focus is on the garment, textile and shoes industry. Therefore, part of the task was to identify which union confederations have federations within that sector. This was quite difficult since not all confederations are organised sectorally. KASBI (*Kongres Aliansi Serikat Buruh Indonesia*, Congress of Indonesian Labour Unions' Alliance), for example, has federations that are organised by city, province and district rather than industrial sector. Nevertheless, 65 per cent of KASBI members reportedly are garment workers (Union Interview, January 2012) and should therefore be included in my study.

Interviews with trade union and NGO representatives as well as academics were conducted as semi-structured, guideline-based "expert interviews" (Meuser and Nagel 2005). During the explorative stage, gaining "context knowledge" about the field was more important than "operative knowledge" (ibid., 75) from within the field. Thus, I mainly talked to informants from NGOs and academia in order to reconstruct their context knowledge and saved conducting interviews with representatives from trade unions and the ILO for the second stage, that is, the main fieldwork (see below). Additionally, two group discussions were conducted with members of labour NGOs (TURC, KPKB). After having talked to representatives from additional Indonesian NGOs (Sedane Labor Resource Centre (LIPS), Women's Group for Workers' Justice (KPKB)) as well as donor NGOs (Friedrich-Ebert-Stiftung (FES), American Center for International Labor Solidarity (ACILS)), I was able to map the landscape of Indonesian trade unions and labour NGOs, their networks and their relationships to the ILO (see Figure 5). This in itself is a relevant outcome of the exploratory research given the extreme fragmentation, complexity and diversity of the Indonesian labour movement.

Figure 5: Mapping the Field of Indonesian Trade Unions and Labour NGOs (March 2011)

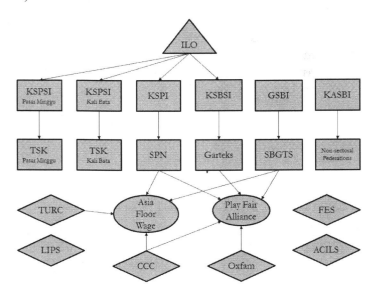

Source: author's compilation

As can be seen, the ILO only has direct relationships with four out of six confederations on the national level. This is due to the fact that the ILO as an international organisation can only collaborate with employer's organisations and trade unions that are officially recognised by the Indonesian government. As of March 2011, these were the two branches of KSPSI (*Konfederasi Serikat Pekerja Seluruh Indonesia*, Confederation of All Indonesian Trade Unions), KSPI (*Konfederasi Serikat Pekerja Indonesia*, Confederation of Indonesian Trade Unions) and KSBSI (*Konfederasi Serikat Buruh Sejahtera Indonesia*, Confederation of Indonesian Prosperity Labour Unions). GSBI (*Gabungan Serikat Buruh Independen*, Federation of Independent Labour Unions) and KASBI were excluded from ILO projects and programmes and thus could not benefit from any capacity-building or training efforts organised by the ILO on the national level.

The second row of Figure 5 shows national union confederations, while the third row shows their respective sectoral garment, textile and shoes federations. Rows four and five show national and international labour NGOs as well as two initiatives or campaigns and their members or affiliates. The history of Indonesia's trade union movement from independence, to the Suharto regime, to *Reformasi* is discussed in some detail in Chapter 5. Figure 5 will gain further meaning when the historical background of how this complex landscape evolved can be taken into account. Here, the point is to clarify how this kind of mapping helped me with operationalising my research interest and sampling the interviewees.

I tried to identify relevant projects or campaigns addressing at least one of the major components of the decent work agenda from the local level. I was looking for a "critical" or "most likely case" (Flyvbjerg 2006, 231) of a local appropriation of the global decent work discourse. TURC serves as the national focal point for a regional trade union-NGO alliance campaigning for an *Asia Floor Wage* (AFW) in the garment industry. Although a living wage standard is missing from the ILO's core labour standards, wages undoubtedly are a major determinant of decent work. During the exploration, I envisaged the AFW alliance to be a promising candidate to investigate the local appropriation of decent work vis-à-vis other discourses and strategies. The idea of an AFW is discussed in the academic literature. It has its place in special discourses on labour struggles in Asia (Merk 2008, 2009, 2011a) and it is being pushed by international NGOs such as the Clean Clothes Campaign (CCC). From a discourse-analytical perspective, the AFW appears to be a major strategic effort of Indonesian trade unions and labour NGOs. The local relevance of the AFW campaign, however, has to be put into perspective by contrasting expectations raised by academic and media discourses with actual ethnographic data obtained from the field. Although two garment federations (SPN, GSBI-SBGTS) are members of the alliance, they reported that the campaign was not taken up very well by Indonesian trade unions. Some unions such as KASBI resigned after an initial phase of discussions. One of the reported reasons is that the AFW alliance is seen as dominated by national NGOs (TURC) and international NGOs (CCC) rather than by Indonesian labour unions themselves. The initiative for an AFW came from India and it seems to be alive and well in South-Asian countries such as Bangladesh and Sri Lanka. In Indonesia, however, it does not seem to resonate with the local priorities of garment unions.

Most members of the AFW alliance are also members of the *Play Fair Alliance* (PFA), which is campaigning for freedom of association in Indonesian factories producing sportswear for transnational corporations such as Nike or Adidas. Freedom of association and the right to collective bargaining belongs to the four core labour standards. The PFA was much more successful in moderating a process of negotiations among trade union confederations, supplier factories and buyers/ brands. Therefore, I decided to drop the AFW and replace it with the PFA as a critical case for analysing decent work from the "local appropriation perspective".

Although this perspective is my main interest, I aim to contrast it with official decent work policies in more narrowly defined terms, that is, with the ILO's approach towards realising decent work in Indonesia's garment, textile and shoes industry. *Better Work Indonesia* (BWI) is the first monitoring project of the ILO in Indonesia. It is a partnership of the ILO and the International Finance Corporation (IFC) starting operations in 2010. It offers technical services to both global buyers and local suppliers of garments and textiles produced in Indonesia with the aim of improving global competitiveness and compliance with core labour standards. It builds on ten years of experience drawn from the pioneering Better Factories project in Cambodia and it targets garment factories in the Greater Jakarta Area. Both its institutional setup and its sectoral and regional focus make it a "critical case" (Flyvbjerg 2006) for analysing decent work from the "global regulation perspective".

Given that KASBI was excluded from BWI and, at the time, not part of the PFA, I was determined to analyse their strategies towards improving working and living conditions for garment workers as a third contrasting case, whether they could be framed as belonging to the decent work imaginary or to another, possibly competing discourse. During the exploration, I came across the case of PT Istana, a garment factory in Northern Jakarta that declared bankruptcy and announced the closure of the factory in 2007. When negotiations about severance pay for the 1,000 workers (most of them women) ended in dispute, members of the workplace union SBKU-Istana—member union of FSBKU (*Federasi Serikat Buruh Karya Utama*), then affiliated with KASBI—decided spontaneously to occupy the factory in order to force the employer to pay severance pay according to the law. Although the factory occupation at PT Istana can hardly be called a success story of industrial production under workers' control, it clearly shows that there are more radical and militant union strategies within Indonesia's garment sector I had to include in my analysis if I wanted to avoid reproducing their marginalisation by official discourses of decent work.

The case of PT Istana, however, is only an example of one particular factory on the local level. If I was to analyse it properly in terms of economic imaginaries and political strategies, I would have to find a way to link it to a larger campaign, project or initiative on the national level comparable to BWI or the PFA. By speaking to activists with intimate knowledge of the case of PT Istana and related cases, I learned about the Indonesian People's Movement Confederation (KPRI, *Konfederasi Pergerakan Rakyat Indonesia*), a newly established multi-sector alliance of Indonesian social movements aiming to link urban struggles (such as the factory occupation at PT Istana) and rural struggles (land reclaiming and agricultural cooperatives) by joining labour unions, peasants' and fishermen's organisations as well as women's and indigenous people's movements under the umbrella of KPRI. Although or maybe because KPRI does not fit neatly into the conventional perception of what decent work is about, it is a critical case for analysing the edge of the decent work discourse or, as the case may be, alternative competing imaginaries beyond decent work. The fact that radical union strategies like factory occupations did not surface in the academic literature on Indonesian labour struggles and were only discovered during exploratory fieldwork underpins the methodological argument about CGT as the necessary combination of theoretical work, discourse analysis and ethnographic immersion into the field.

Revisiting theories and grounding conceptualisations

The following table shows the exploratory interviews and group discussions conducted in March 2011.

	Expert Interviews	Group Discussions	Organisations
Trade Unions	1		GSBI
Labour NGOs	4	2	TURC, LIPS, FES, ACILS TURC, KPKB
Academics	3		Universitas Indonesia
Sum	8	2	

Table 1: Expert Interviews and Group Discussions Conducted During Exploration

Between April and October 2011, these interviews and group discussions were transcribed and evaluated according to rules and techniques of CGT. Transcription forms an active part of the research process and the interpretation of data. It should thus be done by the researcher herself, rather than be delegated to student assistants or automated systems (Breuer 2010, 68). Transcripts were then segmented thematically and partially paraphrased, before codes and categories were developed to enable thematic comparison between interviews. These emergent codes and categories were then put into dialogue with revisited existing theory and employed to ground my initial (pre-)conceptualisations and revise them in light of exploratory empirical findings and additional theoretical perspectives. Emerging ideas and associations were documented as memos in my diary to ensure reflexivity and retraceability. The steps of data evaluation Meuser and Nagel (2005) propose for analysing expert interviews are taken from classic Grounded Theory methodology (Strauss and Corbin 1990). This means that they understand codes to emerge from working inductively with data without the use of existing theory. They distinguish this Grounded Theory mode of coding from Mayring's (2008) qualitative content analysis, which allows for codes and categories to be derived deductively from the theoretical framework of the study.

The spiral movement between theoretical and empirical work, combining deductive and inductive moments typical for the retroductive method of CGT, necessitates another third way between these two poles. On the one hand, reflexive openness has to be maintained to minimise the risk of merely reproducing preconceived suspicions and maximise the likelihood of discovering new aspects and perspectives. Therefore, the initial step of "open coding" (Breuer 2010, 80) primarily produced "*in-vivo* codes" (ibid., 78, emphasis added), that is, codes developed from within transcripts, close to the original language of the interviewee in order to let participants speak for themselves, at least in the first instance. The point here is that it is necessary to reconstruct the knowledge of experts according to their own system of relevance and priority. On the other hand, linking emerging conceptualisations to existing ones and putting data into dialogue with theory is crucial for CGT as we have seen above. Thus, subsequent steps of translating *in-vivo* codes into "theoretical codes" (ibid.) and further into categories were more theoretically informed by the general approach of CPE (especially the notions of variation, selection and retention as well as hegemony, sub- and counter-hegemony) and by mid-range theories about labour regulation.

What I had learned from the exploration was that my initial (pre-) conception was probably too optimistic. Actors and strategies that could be categorised as "counter-hegemonic" did not seem to make any use of the narrowly defined ILO discourse of decent work. The ILO itself was perceived very critically by many respondents, because it is associated with labour market flexibilisation, which was identified as one of the major obstacles to decent work in the emphatic sense. Scepticism towards the ILO was closely related to scepticism towards the four official national trade union confederations (see above) and their capacity to effectively improve the working and living conditions of Indonesian workers. The official decent work discourse did not seem to resonate with the local priorities of the other, more radical and militant labour unions; they appeared to have their own strategies and imaginaries of how the situation of Indonesian workers shall be improved. These strategies and imaginaries potentially transcend the decent work discourse in narrowly defined terms. The resulting grounded conceptualisation, revised from the initial one (see above), gently guided me through the subsequent stage of the main fieldwork. It can be summarised as follows: Decent work can function both as a hegemonic and a sub-hegemonic imaginary vis-à-vis neoliberalism, depending on which actors appropriate it in which context, for which projects and strategies, with which objectives and interests. Whether counter-hegemonic imaginaries can be found within, at the edge or beyond the official decent work discourse remains to be seen.

Conducting the main fieldwork and constructing a critical grounded theory

Between November 2011 and February 2012, the main fieldwork was conducted. Having identified the three cases of BWI, PFA and KPRI and having revised my initial conceptualisation, I was now ready to investigate the cases in greater detail. The following table shows the expert interviews and group discussions and relates them to the cases. Where context knowledge about the field was more important than operational knowledge about the individual cases, the "cases" column shows "context".

	Expert Interviews	Group Discussions	Organisations	Cases
Trade Unions	2		GARTEKS, SPN	PFA, BWI
	3		KASBI (2x), GSBI	PFA
	2		KSN (2x)	KPRI
	1		FSBKU	KPRI
		4	SBGTS (2x), GARTEKS (2x)	PFA, BWI
		1	FSBKU	KPRI
Labour NGOs	4		Akatiga, KPKB, LIPS, FES	Context
	4		LBH, TURC, Oxfam (2x)	PFA
	1		PRP	KPRI
		1	Akatiga	Context
International Organisations	3		ILO (3x)	BWI
Transnational Corporations	1		Adidas	PFA
Academics	2		Universitas Indonesia (2x)	Context
Total	21	6		

Table 2: Expert Interviews and Group Discussions Conducted During Main Fieldwork

Access to participants, again, was gained by a modified "snowball sampling" technique that incorporated the purpose of "theoretical sampling" (Przyborski and Wohlrab-Sahr 2008, 177–181). In some cases, however, access to participants that were theoretically interesting (e.g. workplace unions participating in BWI) was impossible for me. I tried to compensate this lack of ethnographic data from the local level (especially in the case of BWI) by collecting data from other levels (national, regional, global) and other sources (media and academic discourses). Nevertheless, the diversity of primary and secondary data collected for this study constitutes a methodological challenge for the application of CGT. At least, problems with field access restraining theoretical sampling have to be made transparent and reflected upon. CGT does not uphold the Grounded Theory ideal of "theoretical saturation" (Breuer 2010, 110; Przyborski and Wohlrab-Sahr 2008, 182), because it sees the "real" as never fully representable in theory. Every form of knowledge production is preliminary and incomplete. This makes a pragmatic, at times "messy" approach to sampling less problematic than in positivist research. As long as it is made clear that a CGT does not provide an objective theory about an abstract object regardless of time and space, but a critical theory about a particular object in a particular conjuncture that incorporates the subjectivity and perspectivity of the researcher at a given point in time, she can construct the CGT using the data available to her at that time while being open and reflexive about the limitations of the scope of the argument.

For example, the CSR officer of Adidas agreed to give me an interview after I was introduced to her by a previous informant. Interviewing representatives from international buyers participating in the PFA promised to be conceptually relevant for analysing the multi-stakeholder initiative. Other buyers such as Nike, Puma or Pentland, however, were not available for interviews. The Adidas interview does not provide a sufficient sample to substantially include the buyers' perspective, but it could be used to complement the unions' perspective. The scope of the argument is limited to the trade unions participating in the PFA, but the analysis of their strategies can benefit from contrasting their view with that of the employers or the brands.

Data analysis was done similar to the way discussed above and electronically assisted by the qualitative data analysis software MAXQDA. First, transcripts were segmented thematically and paraphrased. Second, open *in-vivo* codes emerged before theoretical codes and categories were developed. Third, categorisation and (re-)conceptualisation fed into the construction of a critical grounded theory.

Table 2 implies that KASBI members were interviewed as part of the case study on the PFA. This is due to the fact that KASBI had joined the PFA in the meantime between exploratory and main fieldwork. Also, another national trade union confederation entered the stage of the Indonesian labour movement while I was there—the National Union Confederation (KSN, *Konfederasi Serikat Nasional*). It is affiliated with KPRI and was formed by a number of federations that had split off from KASBI for reasons that are discussed in Chapter 7, drawing on two additional follow-up interviews conducted in March 2013. Before, let me introduce the historical context of this study in greater detail.

4. Neoliberal Globalisation and Labour Regulation

In this chapter,[5] I outline the historical context of the present study. First, a brief history of neoliberal globalisation is sketched in order to clarify the broader macro context, out of which the global discourse on decent work emerged. The roots of globalisation in the crisis of Fordism, the neoliberalisation and feminisation of labour and the emergence of global commodity or transnational supply chains is introduced in general terms before, second, relating these historical processes of global restructuring to the history of global labour regulation more specifically, looking at the ILO's traditional role, the social clause debate within the WTO, the emergence of private labour regulation and the decent work agenda.

4.1 A Brief History of Neoliberalism

In this section, I discuss the roots of globalisation in the crisis of Fordism, the neoliberalisation and feminisation of labour and the emergence of global commodity or transnational supply chains. Beginning with Fordism and its crisis, driving the emergence of neoliberal globalisation, I also reflect on how regulationist concepts such as Fordism, although primarily developed for Western Europe and North America, can be applied to countries of the Global South, such as Indonesia. The analytical relevance of the gender dimension becomes clear when processes of global restructuring are related to new international and social divisions of labour.

---

5 This chapter partly flowed into Hauf (2015).

4.1.1 The Crisis of Fordism and the Forces of Globalisation

Fordism and its crisis

According to the familiar account from regulation theory, Fordism was a relatively stable mode of capitalist development that rested on the successful articulation of mass production and mass consumption. The Fordist regime of accumulation was one of "intensive accumulation with growing mass consumption" (Lipietz 1988, 23), i.e. accumulation rested on growth in productivity and corresponding growth in effective demand. The central institutional form of Fordism, most regulationists agree, was thus the wage relation, which was regulated in such a way that the basic contradiction between wages as costs of production and wages as sources of demand was temporarily resolved or processed by tying wage increases to growth in productivity. The ideal-typical form of regulating the wage relation in Fordism is said to represent an institutionalised compromise between capital and labour within national economies, forged by strong organisations representing their respective interests (labour unions and business associations) and mediated by the Keynesian welfare state, stabilising mass consumption and thus capital accumulation (Hirsch 1995, 78).

In CPE terms, one of the economic imaginaries associated with Fordism was thus the social democratic idea that workers and employers are best seen as "social partners" within national economies whose interests can be aligned to forge national compromises linking rising capital profitability with gains in social prosperity. This imaginary conceives of capitalism neither in Marxist terms as a structurally contradictory and crisis-prone mode of production, nor in neoclassical terms as a self-regulating free market economy but, rather, as a social market economy that produces the desired outcomes only if it is properly regulated and embedded within a broader setting of social institutions, including corporatist structures of collective bargaining and welfare state policies. The ideological function of the social democratic imaginary of Fordism can be attributed to the competition of systems between the Western and the Eastern power blocs. In the face of an actually existing alternative, it was necessary for capitalism to prove that it was capable to deliver wealth and social security for the majority of people while maintaining the economic superiority vis-à-vis the Soviet bloc. The competing imaginary associated with Marxism, contending that capitalism is inherently contradictory and will sooner or later enter into crisis no matter how Keynesian policies aim to avoid this, had to be displaced by an imaginary that depicts capitalism as contradiction-free and crisis-free.

This imaginary had a strong material base in the varying corporatist structures of the industrial nations of Western Europe and North America that, to varying degrees, succeeded in securing relatively high wages and social standards for the "standard employee" of Fordism (white, middle-class, male breadwinner) and sustaining high profits primarily for industrial and merchant capital. In fact, the post-World War II boom was a relatively long phase of continual economic growth without major crises that "for the first time in the history of capitalism, made continuous raises of wage incomes and a certain degree of mass prosperity not only compatible with the profitability of capital, but even made them its foundation" (Hirsch 1995, 76, my translation). The material base of the Fordist imaginary, however, was contingent on continuous gains in productivity, a condition that eventually eroded during the 1970s when the crisis of Fordism broke out.

The crisis of Fordism cannot be discussed here in sufficient length and detail to capture all of its complexity. The point here is merely to provide some conceptual and historical background for understanding the forces of globalisation from a regulationist vantage point. The "oil shock" of 1973 and the breakdown of the Bretton Woods system of fixed exchange rates following the "Nixon shock" of 1971 that made the US (United States) Dollar inconvertible to gold were crucial manifestations of the crisis of Fordism (Parnreiter et al. 1999, 16). Although regulationists argue that its major cause was a structural decline in the profitability of capital in the metropolitan countries (Hirsch 1995, 84), they also stress that it cannot be reduced to an economic crisis but, rather, has to be interpreted in terms of an economic, political and social crisis of the whole social formation. The decisive economic nuclei of the Fordist crisis were depleting reserves of productivity, falling rates of profit, declining tax revenues and subsequent pressures on the Keynesian welfare state. The Fordist mode of regulation began to transform itself from a foundation to a constriction of capital accumulation: "The compatibility of capital profit and mass prosperity came to an end" (Hirsch 1998, 22). On the international scale, the crisis of Fordism is closely connected to the crisis of US hegemony, which was not the least triggered by the lost war in Vietnam and the immense costs of maintaining the huge military apparatus. Additionally, Europe and Japan were economically successful and became a serious competition for the US on the world market. Whereas the Fordist period was marked by a strong US hegemony within the Western bloc, post-Fordist restructuring processes led to a world order dominated by the "capitalist triad" comprised of the US, Europe and Japan (Hirsch 1995, 91).

In search for strategies for recovering from the crisis, economic and political elites began to espouse trade liberalisation and internationalisation of production. Commodity, capital and financial markets were liberalised from regulatory restraints in order to boost cross-border investment and trade. The breakdown of Bretton Woods meant that international financial markets became deregulated, exchange rates became more volatile and speculative and the domestic market orientation of Fordism made way for a more global orientation of capital accumulation. The US Dollar became threatened by devaluation and the consequential "Volcker shock" pushing US interest rates up to 20 per cent in 1981 had immediate and catastrophic effects on peripheral countries. The US Dollar exchange rate rose sharply, meaning for indebted countries[6] that their debts and interests (to be paid in US Dollars) skyrocketed overnight (Novy et al. 1999, 17). The profitability crisis of central Fordism gave birth to the debt crisis of the Global South, which in turn provided the background for neoliberal "structural adjustment programmes" and their devastating effects on social security and social reproduction in the periphery (Federici 2014, 102).

These are the forces behind global restructuring in the form of neoliberal globalisation. Before looking at post-Fordist restructuring and the emergence of transnational supply chains more closely, the Global South's world market integration during Fordism is briefly discussed.

Fordism and the periphery

The familiar account of Fordism as mass production plus mass consumption mediated by the welfare state carries a strong bias towards Western Europe and North America. Within countries of the Global South, Fordism showed a different face—and there were controversial debates about the question of whether the accumulation regimes of these countries

---

6 Most peripheral economies got into international debt in the 1970s, when cheap credits were available due to deregulated financial markets and decreased investment in the metropolises, because their trade balance deficits rose when demand for raw materials and simple manufactured goods from the centre declined (Hirsch 1995, 87).

should be labelled in relation to central Fordism at all or whether their distinctiveness demands a term of its own.

This relates to the international regime as an institutional form and its Fordist shape. According to regulation theory, it is misleading to think of economies as national in the first instance that become interconnected via foreign trade in the second instance. Rather, every national economy is from the outset embedded within an "international regime" (Boyer 1990, 40), which comprises the international division of labour, the world market and the international state system. The strength of this account is that it allows for both thinking about the world market in terms of a single international regime and about the different ways of how national economies become integrated into the world market. For example, the metropolitan economies of Western Europe and North America organised accumulation primarily within the borders of nation states while growth in developing economies was mostly export-oriented. During Fordism, the rich countries of the North primarily imported raw materials from poor countries of the South to be used in industrial production for the domestic market. They were dependent on international exchange, but the dynamic of accumulation primarily rested on domestic demand, which was bolstered by the welfare state. A smaller portion of finished goods was exported back to developing countries, which tried to emulate the Northern model by launching programmes of "import substitution industrialisation" (ISI). Both accumulation strategies were complementary within the "old [international] division of labour" (Lipietz 1987, 47), with the Global North producing finished industrial goods and the Global South producing cheap raw materials and agricultural goods that were exchanged via foreign trade. This form of the international division of labour is closely linked to the history of colonialism and imperialism, that is, the violent expansion of capital accumulation originating in Europe and subjugating the rest of the globe as sources of raw materials and market outlets for excess production.

During Fordism, however, many countries of the Global South sought to free themselves from being confined to the role of raw material suppliers and started to look for opportunities to add more value to their products so as to generate more wealth within their borders. The strategy by which developing countries aimed to emulate the Fordist regime of auto-centred accumulation became to be known as "import substitution industrialisation" (Parnreiter et al. 1999, 13). Instead of exporting raw materials and re-importing finished goods, leaving the bulk of value-added in the Global North, countries of the Global South tried to embark on an auto-centred path to industrialisation, underpinned by protectionist policies and informed by *Dependencia* theories of unequal exchange and over-exploitation (cf. Ebenau et al. 2013, 226). The ISI strategy emerged in Latin America after the world economic crisis of the 1930s and started to spread to Asia in the 1950s. In the 1960s, problems with the ISI strategy became apparent. Lipietz (1987, 61) identifies three main reasons for the "failure" of early import substitution: the Fordist labour process cannot be emulated simply by importing machinery without constructing the corresponding social relations, domestic purchasing power amongst workers and peasants was not enough to foster mass consumption and the strategy necessarily led to trade deficits and debts since imports of capital goods were increased and had to be paid off with increased exports of primary goods—the controversial "terms of trade" problem. He terms these early experiments with ISI "sub-Fordism" and describes them as "a *caricature* of Fordism, or as an attempt to industrialize by using Fordist technology and its model of consumption, but without either its social labour process or its mass consumption norms" (Lipietz 1987, 62, emphasis in the original).

The emerging crisis of central Fordism, however, shifted the international division of labour as capital started to search for cheap labour in developing countries in the 1970s. The three levels of the Fordist labour process (conception and organisation, skilled manufacturing and unskilled assembling) were reorganised into a "*new, vertical division of labour* between levels of skill inside branches of industry" (Lipietz 1987, 71, emphasis in the original). Labour-intensive tasks defined as "unskilled" were relocated to low wage countries in the periphery as a major strategy to overcome the profitability crisis of Fordism. These countries, however, had to meet a number of political conditions that cannot be derived from the economic "needs" of the centre: their government must be autonomous from direct foreign domination, it must be autonomous from the old ruling classes and it must be autonomous from the popular masses: "In short, it usually requires a *dictatorship* to break the old balance and to use the state to create managerial personnel who can play the part of the ruling classes within a new regime of accumulation" (Lipietz 1987, 73, emphasis in the original). Lipietz is here referring to countries such as Portugal (dictatorship until 1974), Spain and Greece (dictatorships until 1975) and South Korea (dictatorship until 1987), all of which were targeted by the extension of Fordist accumulation as peripheral regions for relocating labour-intensive production at different points in time. We could here add Indonesia, ruled by military dictator Suharto until 1998 (see below for specificities pertaining to Indonesia).

As ISI became more and more to be seen as a failure, it was increasingly replaced by or, rather, rearticulated with the strategy of "export-oriented industrialisation" (EOI) or "export-substitution" as Lipietz (1975, 73) calls it. He differentiates two different logics within the EOI strategy: "primitive Taylorization" and "peripheral Fordism" (Lipietz 1987, 74). The first logic refers to relocation of labour-intensive industries such as textiles and electronics to countries or regions with very low wages, long working hours and bad conditions such as the "export processing zones" of South Korea and Taiwan in the early 1970s. It is in these industries that young women were especially targeted to recruit a cheap, seemingly docile and acquiescent labour force (see below for more on the feminisation of labour). Given the inhumane and exploitative working conditions in these early export-oriented industries, Lipietz also speaks of the first logic as "bloody Taylorization" (1987, 76). The second logic refers to the way that peripheral countries such as South Korea in the later 1970s, Mexico or Brazil have sought to move beyond the stage of primitive Taylorisation by establishing a growing home market for manufactured goods that becomes the second pillar of growth next to the export-oriented sector. Peripheral Fordism thus combines ISI and EOI in specific ways (Lipietz 1987, 79).

Lipietz is careful to argue that "Fordism is not taking over the whole periphery" (Lipietz 1987, 81) and that the logic of peripheral Fordism is not the only logic operating in the periphery. Given the differences between countries grouped under the concept of "peripheral Fordism", it should be handled with care so as to avoid universalising Fordism globally to an extent that does not correspond to real interdependencies anymore. Nevertheless, Lipietz (1987, 109) wants to show that "primitive Taylorization" and "peripheral Fordism" are useful concepts to grasp the interrelations of central and peripheral regimes of accumulation within the new international division of labour. These concepts, however, have been criticised as US- and Euro-centric, because they conceptualise peripheral regimes of accumulation in terms of the dynamics of central Fordism, which is set as the norm, instead of allowing for alternative, including non-capitalist, development strategies (Alnasseri 2004, 144). Sum (1997) criticises the concept of "peripheral Fordism" for not being specific enough to capture the various development paths of different countries across the continents of Latin America, Africa and Asia. She, therefore, suggests speaking of "exportism" (Sum 1997, 174) in the cases of the extroverted economies of East Asia rather than "peripheral Fordism" to capture the differences and specificities of these countries. Nevertheless, she also differentiates between "simple" and "complex exportism" (Sum 1997, 178), the former defined as mainly or exclusively connected to EOI, the latter as a specific articulation of EOI and ISI, not dissimilar to Lipietz's concepts of "bloody Taylorism" and "peripheral Fordism". She does, however, stress the dependency of exportist economies more than Lipietz given their extraversion, their most important feature. Sum (1997, 182) contends that it is exaggerated to call the form of Taylorist production emerging through EOI strategies "bloody" and suggests speaking of "flexible Taylorism" to emphasize the fragmentation of the labour process across different production sites by way of subcontracting and outsourcing.

I do not intend to intervene in this theoretical debate at this point. What is important for me is that both authors aim to locate the local specificities of national regimes of accumulation and modes of regulation within a larger international regime or mode of international integration. There is always a dialectic of the general and the particular at work in trying to pin down what is distinctive and what is generic about a certain growth model. Whether to call it "peripheral Fordism" or "complex exportism" is less important than the analytical content: Fordism was a phase in the history of capitalist development that, in very different ways, affected all countries over the globe. The history of Fordism, however, cannot be written in the abstract, but has to be reconstructed by looking at the specificities of concrete cases. Below, I therefore include a discussion of Indonesia's economic development under Fordism as part of the contextual chapter on Indonesia. Before, let me briefly discuss the neoliberalisation and feminisation of labour that has driven the emergence of transnational supply chains, as a highly gendered strategy for recovering from the Fordist crisis.

4.1.2 Neoliberalisation and Feminisation of Labour

Capitalism has always been global. It has evolved as a "world system" (Wallerstein 2004) in conjuncture with imperialism and colonialism. Foreign trade ratios grew until World War I in what is sometimes called the "first globalisation" (Faubert 2011) to relatively high levels that were surpassed quantitatively only by the "second globalisation" starting in the 1970s. What is really new about neoliberal globalisation qualitatively is the emergence of transnational supply chains.

The emerging crisis of central Fordism, as noted above, shifted the international division of labour as capital started to search for cheap labour in developing countries in the 1970s. Within the "new, vertical division of labour" (Lipietz 1987, 71), labour-intensive tasks were relocated to low wage countries in the periphery as a major strategy to overcome the profitability crisis of Fordism, resulting in the emergence of "global commodity chains" (Gereffi and Korzeniewicz 1994) and the replacement of import substitution with export orientation. Emerging global commodity or transnational supply chains[7] came to be dominated by transnational corporations (TNCs). Export countries are competing over the most favourable conditions for foreign direct investment by TNCs. Since low wages and weak social (as well as environmental) standards are the only "comparative advantage" of most countries of the Global South, downward competition between them resulted in the "race to the bottom" (Ehmke et al. 2009, 26). In trying to attract foreign capital, labour markets were increasingly restructured according to the neoliberal dogma of "flexibility", thereby eroding labour standards and working conditions.

---

7 The "global commodity chain" (GCC) approach was initially developed by Gereffi and Korzeniewicz (1994), differentiating producer-driven from buyer-driven supply chains (e.g. automobile vs. clothing industry). It was then iteratively reformulated as the "global value chain" (GVC) and the "global production network" (GPN) approach. The GVC approach goes beyond the producer- vs. buyer-driven typology of the GCC approach and develops a five-dimensional typology instead (Gereffi et al. 2005). The GPN approach goes beyond both by stressing that supply chains are networks rather than linear structures and that they are embedded in wider social, political and economic relations (Coe et al. 2008). These frameworks have informed a huge and diverse body of literature. While I do not aim to intervene in the debate about which framework is more adequate, I hereinafter use the term "transnational supply chain" (Hurley and Miller 2005) that builds on the GCC approach but explicitly incorporates the informalised and feminised segment of home work at the bottom end of the apparel supply chain.

Transnational supply chains are highly complex. Hurley and Miller (2005) use the metaphor of an iceberg to depict the intricate web of contracting, subcontracting and sub-subcontracting in the global garment industry. The tip of the iceberg is the respective lead firm, in most cases a global retailer such as Walmart or merchandiser of branded goods such as Nike and Adidas. They place orders with multinational manufacturers (Tier 1), themselves often large TNCs, which in turn subcontract parts of the production process to medium (Tier 2) and small manufacturers (Tier 3) to meet short turnaround times or low prices dictated by the lead firm. Sub-subcontracting goes down to the level of home workers, the most precarious, informal and feminised segment of the supply chain. Above the waterline and thus visible is only the relationship between buyer and Tier 1 manufacturer (Hurley and Miller 2005, 23). The subcontracting networks below the waterline are more invisible, making it hard for anyone to trace the production process and to monitor working conditions but making it easy for TNCs to shift the responsibility for bad working conditions and labour right abuses on to their subcontractors. Downward pressure on turnaround times and prices increases further down the supply chain, "bringing associated problems of excessive overtime and sub-minimum wages" (Hurley and Miller 2005, 26). Stephanie Barrientos' "gendered employment pyramid" (2007, 244) further explains that beneath the level of paid home work there is an even larger background of unpaid domestic and care ("reproductive") work largely performed by women, upon which global production systems are built up.

Globalisation has also restructured the "care economy" (Chorus 2013) in profound ways. Rising labour market participation of women in Northern countries has not led to a more equal redistribution of care work between women and men as many hoped for. Rather, "social reproduction" continues to be seen as a women's task, despite their full integration into the "productive" economy of capitalist wage labour. On the discursive level, gender regimes have been modernised to depict men and women as equals, one of the successes of the feminist movement. On the material level, however, gendered divisions of labour persist and continue to reproduce gender hierarchies. This contradictory process has been called the "rhetorical modernisation" (Wetterer 2003) of gender regimes. The practical solution to the reproduction problem in many cases has been the commodification of care work and its delegation to ethnically *other* women—migrant women workers without or with limited citizenship rights acting as "new maids" (Lutz 2001) in middle-class households of rich countries. As a result, globalisation leads to the emergence of global "care chains" (Lutz 2005) as the hidden counterpart of transnational supply chains.

The new international division of labour, thus, has also contributed to shifting gendered divisions of labour. This process is often referred to as the feminisation of labour. Globalisation is often understood as a process fuelled by technological and financial innovations. True in some sense, Sylvia Federici points out that from a labour perspective another aspect is more important:

"In my view, the technological and financial revolution that has accompanied the globalisation process and enabled it in some respect is less significant than the ability of capital to cut the cost of labour by massively expanding the world labour market" (Federici 2012, 52–53, my translation).

The crucial factors, according to her, are "the increase in numbers of workers available for exploitation, the disciplining of these workers and the cut in labour costs" (Federici 2012, 53, my translation). She identifies two major mechanisms by which the world population available for wage labour has been increased: continuous "primitive accumulation" through a new round of global enclosures driving people off their customary lands and forests, depriving them of their means of subsistence and forcing them to look for wage labour on plantations or in the cities and increased employment of women who have previously been excluded from the realm of wage labour (Federici 2014, 94).[8]

The "feminisation of labour" is thus an integral part of globalisation, seen as the major strategy of capital to resolve the profitability crisis of Fordism. Post-Fordist restructuring processes have to be read through a gender lens. Usually, feminisation of labour is understood to grasp two different, though interrelated processes: the increase in female labour market participation and the proliferation of precarious, "flexible" labour relations and insecure working conditions, previously seen as typically female, for both men and women (Standing 1989, 1999). As ISI was increasingly replaced by EOI, bringing "bloody Taylorization" (Lipietz

---

8 An example from Indonesia of the first mechanism is the palm oil industry. Primary forests are slashed and burned to make way for palm oil plantations; indigenous people are driven off their land and turned into day labourers working on the plantations or forced to migrate to the cities to look for informal employment (Humanity United n.d.). The land reclaimings discussed in Chapter 7.2 offer an alternative to these people.

1987, 74) to the periphery, labour-intensive industries such as garments, textiles and consumer electronics were relocated to countries or regions with very low wages, long working hours and bad conditions, especially in "export processing zones" in countries of the Global South designed to attract foreign capital through legal incentives (tax breaks, exemptions from customs, restrictions of labour rights and so on). In these export-oriented industries, young women were especially targeted to recruit a cheap, seemingly docile and acquiescent labour force—an expectation these women were soon to prove wrong when they started to collectively organise for their interests (Salzinger 2004).

It was mentioned above that during Fordism, the basic contradiction between wages as costs of production and wages as sources of demand was temporarily resolved or processed by tying wage increases to growth in productivity in order to enable workers to buy and consume the very products they have produced. In contrast, neoliberalism processes this contradiction in a very different way. In the new international division of labour, workers and consumers are geographically separated. It is not the same (national) group of workers anymore who sells their labour power and uses the wage to purchase commodities. Now, workers in the Global South are the producers while consumers are mostly located in the Global North or are members of the global wealthy elites. Sparke terms this shift as one from "national mass consumption" to "uneven global consumption" (2013, 115). This means that wages in the South are not expected to form the basis of effective demand and, thus, should be as low as possible from capital's point of view to maximise profits. Against Marx's intuition, neoliberal accumulation regimes in the South may even capitalise on wages below subsistence level, because they can secretly rely on a large reservoir of unpaid subsistence work, mostly performed by women to ensure the social reproduction of people and communities. As feminist scholars of the Bielefeld "subsistence approach" have argued, this is not a pre-modern anomaly within capitalism but the silent *modus operandi* of capitalism itself:

"Since a part of the population performs the necessary subsistence work without causing costs for capital, the opportunities for capital to appropriate surplus labour are massively expanded. The marginal mass is not located outside or at the margin, it is rather an integral part of the capitalist system" (Bennholdt-Thomsen cited in Feministische Autorinnengruppe 2013, 107–108, my translation).

4.2 History of Global Labour Regulation

As mentioned before, these processes of global restructuring have altered the terrain of global labour regulation in every respect. The Fordist development paradigm based on Keynesianism and national welfare states has been replaced by the neoliberal development paradigm based on supply-side economics and "international competition states" (Hirsch 2005, 145). It is in this context that the discourse on decent work has emerged. Therefore, building on the previous narrative of Fordism and neoliberal globalisation, this sub-chapter reconstructs the history of global labour regulation to provide an account of the historical context of the decent work agenda. I start with the historic role of the ILO during Fordism in the context of the Cold War. I then discuss the "social clause" debate of the 1990s as well as the emergence of private self-regulation of business. I end with the decent work agenda itself.

4.2.1 The ILO in Historical Context

> "Universal and lasting peace can be established only if it is based upon social justice." (ILO 1919, Preamble)
> "Labour is not a commodity." (ILO 1944, I a)

The ILO was founded in 1919 as part of the treaty of Versailles that ended World War I. The preamble of the ILO constitution states the overarching objective of the ILO in its founding years: securing peace through policies promoting social justice. Unjust working conditions and social hardships are seen "to produce unrest so great that the peace and harmony of the world are imperilled" (ILO 1919, Preamble). It also defines a set of more specific objectives that need to be addressed to improve such conditions in order to prevent unrest and disharmony: working hours, unemployment, living wages, health care, social security, migrant work, equal remuneration, freedom of association and vocational education (ibid.). The 1944 Declaration of Philadelphia was amended to the original constitution and further specified principles and objectives reflecting the experiences of World War II.

Standing (2008, 357) notes the connection of the proposition that labour is not a commodity to Karl Polanyi's (1944) *The Great Transformation*, in which he argued that land, labour and money are fictitious commodities, because they are not produced for the market. A critic of both economic liberalism and Marxism, Polanyi envisioned a "double movement" between the forces of marketisation/commodification dis-embedding the market from society and spontaneous counterforces of social protection re-embedding the market societally. The ILO's self-proclaimed goal was the "de-commodification of labour", i.e. the removal of labour from capitalist competition in order to prevent deteriorating working conditions causing social unrest. Standing argues that when "the ILO was set up, the motives of its founders were to arrest the march of socialism and to regulate the excesses of industrial labour markets" (2008, 357). As such, the ILO at that time can be seen as representing what has been called "the social democratic imaginary of Fordism" above. It aimed to socially regulate markets for them to produce more socially favourable outcomes. Only if international competition among capitalist states was not carried out on the backs of labour could a repetition of the social upheavals of the inter-war period and a spread of socialism be prevented.

In order to create a "level playing field" of working conditions (Maupain 2013, 23), the ILO was a core mechanism (or a central "node") of the international regime of Fordism, based on the regulation of national labour markets. Through the principal instrument of ILO conventions, the ILO obliged member countries to implement ratified conventions into national law, but it lacked a binding mechanism of enforcement in cases of non-compliance. Nevertheless, the Fordist period saw a remarkable output of ILO conventions setting the standards for Keynesian welfare states with regard to how they were to regulate their labour markets. By 1969, when the ILO won the Nobel peace prize, it had adopted 130 conventions covering such diverse topics as child labour, minimum wages, employment benefits, discrimination and social security. These conventions were constructed around Keynesian welfare states and national market economies with limited international competition. This model is closely linked to the Fordist regime of accumulation and mode of regulation. It is thus not surprising that the crisis of Fordism coincided with a crisis of the ILO's original model. According to Standing, "the zenith of the ILO coincided with the zenith of labour decommodification around the world" (2008, 359). The unfolding crisis of Fordism, the rise of neoliberalism as a policy paradigm replacing Keynesianism and the beginning globalisation process put immense pressure on the ILO to restructure itself in order to retain its regulative function.

Neoliberal globalisation and the above mentioned "race to the bottom" lead to an increasing re-commodification of labour. National states are now competing over the most favourable conditions for global capital's search for profitable investments; and the cost of labour is the main mechanism through which many countries of the Global South aim to achieve competitiveness. After the end of the Cold War and the downfall of the Soviet bloc, accelerating the process of neoliberal globalisation, it was not the ILO that hosted discussions about how to address the race to the bottom but the World Trade Organisation (WTO), established in 1995. Rorden Wilkinson argues that this was due to a "peripheralization of the ILO" (2002, 206) within the remodelled institutional framework of global governance after 1995. The ILO is the only international organisation with a tripartite structure, comprising representatives from labour unions, employer associations and member states. It is thus the only international organisation in which "organized labour have had a role in the decision-making procedures" (Wilkinson 2002, 205). As such, it was not included in the legal framework of the new WTO, which established "primary linkages" (ibid., 212) only to the International Monetary Fund (IMF) and the World Bank and "secondary linkages" (ibid., 213) to organisations such as the World Intellectual Property Organisation. The ILO was not incorporated legally into the new system of global economic governance, but the WTO established "rhetorical linkages" (ibid., 216) to the ILO to displace the resurging debate about formally linking trade agreements and labour standards.

In the period immediately preceding the emergence of decent work, discussions about how to best prevent downward harmonisation of labour rights and social standards within transnational supply chains centred around the idea of a "social clause" within the regime of the WTO, linking labour standards to trade agreements and allowing for trade sanctions against states who would fail to comply with minimum standards.

4.2.2 The Social Clause Debate and the Emergence of Private Regulation

Whereas scholars, activists and unionists from the Global North have tended to stress the progressive potential of a multilateral "social clause" (e.g. Scherrer and Greven 2001, 128), postcolonial and feminist scholars have argued that social clauses may actually be counterproductive with regard to protecting the most vulnerable workers at the bottom of transnational supply chains. Naila Kabeer (2004), for instance, argues that the enforcement of labour rights through trade sanctions may not only lead to declining employment in export industries but, more importantly, to the transfer of jobs from the formal to the informal economy, where women are concentrated and working conditions are far worse. The Western gaze tends to victimise "Third World women" (Kabeer 2004, 10) working in "sweatshop" export factories and neglect the positive aspects of formal factory work in comparison with available alternatives in the informal economy. Kabeer (2004, 4) maintains that women workers, trade unions and NGOs in the Global South have resisted the idea that social clauses will serve their interests, but other stakeholders have resisted the social clause proposal as well.

First of all, neoliberal economists and TNCs from around the globe have rejected it because it contradicts the ideology of free markets and free trade. Second, governments of developing countries have criticised it for basically serving protectionist interests of the North vis-à-vis their low-cost competitors from the South (Kabeer 2004, 8; Vosko 2002, 22). This became clear when the issue of free trade and labour standards was discussed at the first and second WTO Ministerial Meetings in 1996 in Singapore and in 1998 in Geneva respectively without conclusion. Wilkinson explains that the failure "to comprehensively resolve the trade-labour standards issue ensured that it was to resurface as one of the many concerns of the protesters at the organization's third Ministerial Meeting" (2002, 218) in 1999 in Seattle. Labour standards and working conditions were thus one of the factors fuelling what became to be known as the "Battle in Seattle" (Summers 2001)—the first major mobilisation of the anti-neoliberal globalisation movement.

On the other hand, the International Confederation of Free Trade Unions (ICFTU), at the time the largest international trade union organisation, supported the proposal for a social clause and launched a campaign for labour standards to be incorporated into the WTO regime. Mark Anner (2006) argues that the ICFTU launched this campaign despite internal differences among its affiliates from North and South. He explains that the ICFTU carries a "European bias" due to power imbalances between Northern and Southern unions in terms of membership, leadership and financial resources (Anner 2006, 71–72). Although

Southern unionists were aware of these power imbalances and raised concern that a social clause may prioritise Northern interests—labour rights for formal-sector workers—at the expense of Southern demands related to development, they supported the campaign because at the same time they recognised the need for transnational labour solidarity in the context of neoliberal globalisation and the race to the bottom. Anner calls this "the paradox of labour transnationalism" (2006, 65) and further argues that while Northern unionists were successful in convincing their governments to support the social clause campaign, their Southern counterparts "never managed to assuage the fears of developing countries that a labour standards clause would not be used for protectionist purposes" (2006, 77). These countries' governments continued to resist the social clause proposal fiercely.

After the collapse of the WTO negotiations in Seattle, given the widespread opposition against the social clause from a coalition of diverse actors, the attempt to implement a social clause within the WTO regime ultimately failed. As a result, the matter of global labour regulation was referred back to the ILO at a time when the organisation struggled to retain relevance in the age of globalisation, as Standing (2008) argues. The impasse at the WTO "fuelled the adoption of the ILO's [1998] Social Declaration, whose form resembles a social clause yet it is *not* attached to trade" (Vosko 2002, 22, emphasis in the original). Instead of championing a binding regime of "hard law" labour regulation linked to trade sanctions, the ILO moved away from the Fordist "ratification model" (Elias 2007, 51) and resorted to a neoliberal model of "soft law" labour regulation based on voluntariness and promotional measures. In line with the United Nations' Global Compact, the ILO began to embrace voluntary codes of conduct (CoCs) and Corporate Social Responsibility (CSR) policies.

CoCs and CSR have emerged in the 1990s in response to criticisms of inhumane working conditions in world market factories raised by anti-sweatshop campaigns forming part of the just mentioned anti-neoliberal globalisation movement:

"The big wave in adopting codes of conduct […] emerged as a response to consumer campaigns. Fearing that consumers might reject products made under poor conditions, major corporations, such as Levi Strauss, Reebok, Liz Claiborne and later Nike, decided to address the labor standards problem" (Hassel 2008, 239).

One of these campaigns was the international anti-sweatshop campaign targeting Nike's subcontracting practices in Asian countries such as Indonesia. Topics such as child labour, misery wages, abuse of workers, union busting and safety and health were subject to public criticism. Such criticism pressured Nike to re-legitimise their production practices by adopting a CoC. Christian Ulbricht (2012) explains that Nike's reaction to this criticism went through four phases. Phase 1 (1990–1992) was marked by repudiation of criticism. Subcontractors were argued to be independent companies. Nike denied responsibility for working conditions and wage levels in their factories. After continued "naming and shaming" campaigns, phase 2 (1992–1996) saw the adoption of Nike's first CoC in 1992, a unilateral code with weak monitoring provisions. During phase 3 (1996–1997), Nike sought to consolidate its image as a socially responsible corporation by allowing independent monitoring. However, public pressure continued after new scandals surfaced; and Nike reacted by improving its CoC and by setting up a Corporate Responsibility Department in 1998 (Ulbricht 2012, 456–457), the same year that the ILO adopted the "core labour standards" framework (see below). Today, Nike has turned CSR from necessary evil to one of the fundamentals of its marketing and advertising strategy. Put differently, Nike moved from rejecting criticism to capitalising on criticism. Nike's *Better World Manifesto* captures the public image the company seeks to establish by co-opting criticism nicely:

"Don't tell us what we can't do. Don't tell us not to dream. Big fat hairy audacious dreams. Like making the world better through sport. Sport is our passion. Sport inspires hope, instills discipline, reduces depression and disease. It raises self-confidence, raises awareness, rallies communities, defines nations, defies gravity and denies prejudice. Sport laughs in the face of racism. It flicks a towel on sexism's ass and kicks sand in the face of discrimination. It makes neck hairs stand to attention. Hell it's even been known to stop wars. That's a pretty impressive resume. Sport, you're hired. We won't rest until every living, breathing person on this planet has access to it and we won't stop making the best gear to propel humanity forward. Without wrecking our global playground in the process. We will do good with a vengeance. And to all cynics and naysayers, we're going to make the world better for you anyway. Because like sport, we don't discriminate. We've made the world better but we still want a better world. Nike Better World" (Nike n.d.).

Buying Nike sports shoes is a good example of what Žižek means by "'cultural capitalism': we primarily buy commodities neither on account of their utility nor as status-symbols; we buy them to get the experience provided by them, we consume them in order to make our life pleasurable and meaningful" (Žižek 2009, 52). Shoes are not only bought to satisfy a material need. Partly, they are bought as status-symbols to show that the buyer can afford these pricey shoes. Since the anti-sweatshop campaign against Nike in the 1990s, however, it has become more important for the corporation to craft an image of social and environmental responsibility in order to secure demand. Attaching an ethical aura to its products has become central to Nike's business model. Nike's *Better World Manifesto* indicates the advertising strategy of alluding to consumers' global awareness. When you buy a Nike shoe, you are not guilty of supporting a system of slave-like sweatshop conditions anymore. You are, on the contrary, helping to build a better world. It projects an ethical imaginary onto Nike's business model. Other, more material aspects of the business model, such as sourcing at the lowest possible price putting downward pressure on wages and working conditions, remain largely untouched, however. The "cynics and naysayers"—presumably those who continue to criticise Nike—are silenced within that imaginary.

Ulbricht concludes that the "valorisation ['*Inwertsetzung*'] of criticism in terms of advertising and marketing of socially fair working conditions has surely contributed to the survival of the company" (2012, 465, my translation). He conceptualises CSR as a myth that was produced by co-optation of criticism, but a myth that other corporations subsequently had to orient themselves towards as well. Today, CSR has become a mainstream strategy of virtually all major TNCs. As consciousness about the limited effects of codes of conducts and CSR policies grows, calls for more encompassing and more binding systems of labour monitoring and auditing are getting louder. CSR policies have been widely criticised for failing to deliver on the promise of improving working conditions (see e.g. contributions to Burckhardt 2011). The ILO tried to improve their effectiveness by promoting its "core labour standards" (ILO 1998) as the general frame of reference for minimum standards to be implemented in company codes. These core labour standards have been laid out in the ILO's 1998 *Declaration on Fundamental Principles and Rights at Work*: freedom of association, prohibition of child labour, prohibition of forced labour and prohibition of discrimination. These have become one of the pillars of the ensuing decent work agenda, to which I turn next.

4.2.3 The Decent Work Agenda

Scientific discourses on decent work can be clustered around a basic tension between optimistic and pessimistic views regarding its progressive potential. The following juxtaposition does not represent a full review of the available literature, nor does it represent a full CDA of the decent work discourse. Rather, two prominent discursive positions are examined in order to tease out the paradoxes of decent work as a sensitising concept for the subsequent empirical analysis grounded in ethnographic fieldwork.

An example of the optimistic view is Leah Vosko's (2002) feminist perspective on decent work. Revisiting Robert Cox's essay *Labor and Hegemony* (1977), she agrees with him that the ILO was implicated in maintaining hegemonic power relations until the end of the Cold War. Cox had argued that a certain form of corporatism had been institutionalised in the ILO's tripartite structure, locking in "a form of productive relations, one based on an ideology of non-antagonistic relations and on bureaucratized structures of representation and control" (1977, 389). This form of corporatism, however, was typical for the Fordist mode of regulation, which was based on national class compromises between capital and labour mediated by national welfare states. Corporatist trade unions privileged the Fordist "standard employment relationship" (formal, full-time, permanent employment with relatively high wages often reserved for white middle-class "male breadwinners" (Pfau-Effinger 2004)) and abandoned both informal, marginalised workers (often female and migrant) within the centre and workers in the periphery.

In contrast to the hegemonic function the ILO fulfilled during the Cold War, Vosko argues that the emergence of the decent work discourse in the era of globalisation reveals "a growing counter-hegemonic presence inside the ILO and especially at its margins, where transnational coalitions between organized labour, emerging labour organizations in the informal sector and NGOs are growing" (2002, 20). For her, decent work is underpinned by two rather different, if not contradictory pillars. The first is the ILO's focus on core labour standards, a minimum set of conventions codifying universal labour rights every member state must ratify as specified in the *Declaration on Fundamental Principles and Rights at Work* (ILO 1998). The four core labour standards are freedom of association, prohibition of child labour, prohibition of forced labour and prohibition of discrimination. These are codified in eight core conventions:

- Freedom of Association and Protection of the Right to Organise Convention, 1948 (No. 87)
- Right to Organise and Collective Bargaining Convention, 1949 (No. 98)
- Forced Labour Convention, 1930 (No. 29)
- Abolition of Forced Labour Convention, 1957 (No. 105)
- Minimum Age Convention, 1973 (No. 138)
- Worst Forms of Child Labour Convention, 1999 (No. 182)
- Equal Remuneration Convention, 1951 (No. 100)
- Discrimination (Employment and Occupation) Convention, 1958 (No. 111)

The core labour standards have been criticised from a feminist vantage point for encouraging a "basically voluntarist approach to labour regulation, severing ILO conventions from their principle mechanism of implementation (ratification into domestic law) and endorsing business 'self-regulation' through things like voluntary codes of conduct" (Elias 2007, 47). These "soft law" tendencies reveal that the core labour standards approach works within and to the benefit of what Elias calls the "neoliberal development paradigm" (2007, 51).

The core labour standards, however, are only one of the pillars of the decent work agenda. The second pillar, according to Vosko (2002, 20), is the ILO's new commitment to extend existing labour rights and social standards to marginalised groups of workers who have previously been excluded from these rights as exemplified by the *Convention Concerning Home Work* (ILO 1996). Taking the latter as an example, Vosko concludes that instruments aimed to improve working conditions and labour rights of marginalised workers represent a victory for counter-hegemonic forces within the ILO, but they lack force. Although she acknowledges that this victory may be largely symbolic in nature (Vosko 2002, 33), she agrees with Prugl (1999) that it is pivotal for the global feminist movement, because the ILO for the first time has moved beyond the male standard employee of Fordism and addressed the needs of mostly female informal and marginalised workers, especially in and from the Global South. Therefore, while the first pillar of decent work potentially has the negative effect of reinforcing hegemonic power relations within the ILO, the second pillar, according to Vosko (2002), reveals the counter-hegemonic potential of the decent work discourse if appropriated by progressive trade unions, women's groups and other NGOs.

The CPE view adopted here, however, directs attention to the question of whether—and if so, how—the symbolic victory of the feminist movement *on paper*, on the level of what can be called a "discursive economy of representation" (Chowdhry 2004, 233), translates into actual improvements of working conditions of women workers *on the ground*, in the material economy of exploitation, or whether it runs the risk of getting tangled up in what Elias calls a "hegemonic politics of co-option" (2007, 50). In other words, does the decent work agenda's new concern with the informal sector provide the material basis for moving beyond the neoliberal development paradigm? Or does it merely accommodate feminist claims discursively without providing the material means to challenge the structures of neoliberal capitalism, thereby actually serving to reinforce neoliberal hegemony?

Guy Standing (2008) certainly believes in the latter. He represents the second, pessimistic view of decent work. He laments that decent work has marginalised the traditional ILO regime of industrial relations and adversarial bargaining and interprets its emergence as a sign of organised labour's defeat by neoliberal hegemony. The *Convention Concerning Home Work* is a good example for contrasting the optimistic with the pessimistic view of decent work. Standing, although agreeing that the convention represents an attempt to extend labour rights to marginalised workers and that the ILO's new concern with labour relations beyond the male standard employment relationship of Fordism is to be welcomed, calls it "a dead letter" (2008, 366), looking at the lack of ratifications rather than the standard-setting process. Standing, a former ILO official with an insider's view, discusses the role of the ILO in the era of globalisation in historical context. He argues that, while the ILO had an important role in the Keynesian regulation of national labour markets during Fordism, it has recently struggled to retain this role, because neoliberal globalisation has undermined its foundations. The ILO failed to adequately respond to the neoliberal imaginary of "supply-side economics", which originated from the economics departments of Universities of Chicago and Columbia and was quickly taken up by powerful international organisation such as the IMF and the World Bank. Instead of confronting the structural adjustment programmes of these organisations, shock therapy policies in the former Soviet Union and their disastrous effects on labour and social policies worldwide, "the ILO did not respond" (Standing 2008, 363), resulting in a loss of credibility and voice. The subsequent proliferation of neoliberal policies geared towards the flexibilisation of labour markets further gave rise to the phenomena typical of the neoliberal world of work (feminisation, casualisation, informalisation, outsourcing, subcontracting, etc.), further undermining the regulating function of the ILO. After a failed attempt to counter this development with a *Convention on Contract Labour*, the ILO resorted to restructure itself under the Christian-democrat Director-General Michel Hansenne, resulting in the 1998 Declaration limiting the body of the international labour code to the above-mentioned core labour standards. For Standing, this represents a major setback:

"The four core standards enshrined in the Declaration are 'negative rights' that lie outside the sphere of social or work rights. Banning 'the worst forms of child labour', banning 'forced labour', campaigning against gender discrimination and defending freedom of association are matters of common and civil law. They do not constitute a strategy or a progressive agenda" (Standing 2008, 367).

The 1998 Declaration further weakened the ILO, because it envisages only promotional measures to improve implementation of core standards, rather than the possibility for sanctions: "Soft law was replacing binding law" (Standing 2008, 367). Standing links this development to the ILO's endorsement of emerging forms of private self-regulation such as voluntary CoCs and CSR policies, representing "a further way by which the traditional ILO regime has been marginalized" (2008, 368). The more recent emergence of decent work as the overarching theme of the ILO under Director-General Juan Somavia is seen in a similar vein. Standing (2008, 370) criticises decent work as a "slogan" and a "mantra" leaving "too much room for flabby platitudes" due to its inherent vagueness. The language of "social dialogue", central to the decent work discourse, replaced traditional understandings of industrial relations and collective bargaining, resulting in a "non-confrontational mode that sidelines equality while espousing the vagueness of 'decency', 'fairness' and 'dialogue'" (Standing 2008, 371). In this perspective, decent work is largely an ethical rhetoric that masks the fact that the ILO lacks the power to substantially challenge hegemonic power relations in the era of neoliberal globalisation.

To sum up, the 1998 Declaration laid the groundwork for the decent work agenda by codifying the core labour standards that have been criticised for being compatible with the neoliberal development paradigm (Elias 2007; Standing 2008) and for reinforcing hegemonic power relations within the ILO (Vosko 2002). The 2008 *Declaration on Social Justice for a Fair Globalization* (ILO 2008a) further specified the decent work agenda. It was now defined as consisting of four pillars: employment creation, social protection, social dialogue and fundamental principles and rights at work (i.e. core labour standards). The ILO is a tripartite organisation and, as such, represents a specific configuration of relations of forces that become inscribed into its agenda. If decent work is seen as a compromise or a "skilful effort at mediating escalating tensions inside the ILO between global capital, backed by a majority of industrialized states and an increasingly vocal group of member states, trade unions, women's organizations and other NGOs concerned with improving the lives of marginalized workers" (Vosko 2002, 20), it is thus not surprising that decent work is a discourse that is attractive to both workers and employers, because each have injected their own imaginary of what decent work should mean into the agenda. For employers and most states, the objective of employment creation allows for continuing with neoliberal supply-side economics and policies of competitiveness. The notion of social dialogue replaces adversarial bargaining, as Standing (2008) notes and thus works in the interest of global capital to minimise industrial action and labour unrest. Fundamental labour rights—as universal human rights rather than appendices of international trade agreements—and social protection, on the other hand, can be seen as concessions to trade unions and developing countries. The question is whether or not the decent work agenda has the potential to move beyond the neoliberal development paradigm or whether it serves to reinforce neoliberal hegemony by accommodating criticisms of neoliberalism discursively without providing the material means to actually change neoliberal production processes.

The potentials and limitations of decent work

Kabeer (2004) is careful to argue that her scepticism of global labour standards in trade agreements—informed by postcolonial and feminist theory—is different from the neoliberals' stance against regulation in that it is not founded on the belief in the self-regulating capacities of free markets. On the contrary, she argues that the "struggle for labor standards needs to be broadened and made more inclusive by transforming itself into a struggle for a universal 'social floor'" (Kabeer 2004, 28) in order for all workers to be able to struggle for better working conditions without being afraid of losing their jobs or having to enter into the informal labour market for new or alternative employment. Similarly, Barrientos views decent work in general and social protection in particular as providing "the basis for a more holistic approach to enhancing workers' rights in global production" (2007, 251) vis-à-vis the narrow focus on social clauses and codes of conduct. The progressive potential of decent work is largely seen in the rhetorical inclusion of informal workers, especially women workers and in the social protection pillar that—if put into material practice— would better cater to the needs of women who are forced to flexibly switch between paid home work for the global market and unpaid housework for their families (Barrientos 2007, 243). The ILO had long ignored the feminist discourse on social reproduction, but the decent work agenda seems to change this by addressing all forms of work, whether paid or unpaid, whether male or female, whether permanent or temporary, at least rhetorically.

Female migrant domestic workers, for example, are among the most marginalised, informal and precarious workers in the global economy. In many countries, they are not only explicitly excluded from national labour law; they also suffer from low wages and long working hours and do not enjoy any form of social protection (Schwenken 2012). Although horror stories about slave-like conditions in countries such as Saudi Arabia abound, their struggle for decent work shows that these women are not faceless victims of globalisation, but workers who organise collectively to fight for their rights. Three years of intense campaigning by organised domestic workers have resulted in the adoption of the ILO's (2011a) *Convention Concerning Decent Work for Domestic Workers* in 2011, entering force in 2013.

Helen Schwenken (2012) argues that the Domestic Workers Convention is a major step forward in terms of recognising the rights of domestic workers *as workers* and making visible their hidden labour. The intense campaign preceding the adoption of the convention was unique in that it was carried out by domestic workers' organisations themselves in coalition with trade union federations. Successful cooperation of formal trade unions and more informal organisations and networks in this case is a practical example of the progressive potential of decent work as suggested by Vosko (2002). The decent work agenda clearly enabled domestic workers to fight for the recognition of their rights as workers and the convention extends existing labour rights to this previously excluded group of informal workers. The demand for decent work for domestic workers passed the moment of *variation* and became *selected* within the standard-setting procedure of the ILO. Within the discursive economy of representation, domestic workers now enjoy the same rights as other workers. However, the question remains whether this feminist victory on legal territory translates into new forms of material practices on the ground. In other words, does the imaginary have enough powerful backing to become further materialised or institutionalised in the "actually existing economy" (Sum and Jessop 2013, 166) of global care chains?

Schwenken (2012) is cautiously optimistic about the convention and sees its progressive potential largely in the ways it has enabled discussions about the informal economy, labour migration and gender relations within the ILO—topics that have long been ignored but become more and more important under globalisation. She is, however, less optimistic about the convention's power to substantially challenge the structural conditions governing the field of transnational domestic work, i.e. neoliberal gender, migration and labour regimes. The instrument of an ILO convention is largely semiotic in nature and does not in and of itself have the power to challenge the neoliberal development paradigm. The conditions for domestic workers to organise and fight for concrete improvements on the ground are nevertheless improved. If and how domestic workers will be able to make use of these new opportunities is an empirical question that depends on local balances of power and conjunctures of social struggles in particular contexts.

The question, again, is whether the symbolic success of feminism in the discursive economy of representation translates into material improvements of actual working and living conditions. In the CPE terms of this study, the different views of decent work discussed above can be conceptualised as competing imaginaries of decent work—a *feminist imaginary of decent work* stressing its progressive potential for regulating the informal economy and a *"business case" imaginary of decent work* foregrounding CSR and business self-regulation. To reiterate, the CPE perspective helps to understand the vagueness of the decent work agenda, which symbolically proclaims the right to decent work for all without providing substantial language as to what decent work means in the concrete and how it may be achieved practically. It is exactly this vagueness, the big gap between the global discourse and the wide range of (trans-)local practices it may be used to justify, that makes decent work an "economic imaginary" (Sum and Jessop 2013, 182) *par excellence*. Initially, its discursive or semiotic dimension was more important in order to gather support from different actors. The symbolic right to decent work for all workers made it an attractive concept for trade unions, women's organisations and other NGOs, while the emphasis on employment creation and competitiveness allowed for employers and states to endorse the concept. The vagueness of the discourse allows for all stakeholders to subscribe to their own decent work imaginary, while leaving open the question of which practical routes are to be taken towards the realisation of decent work.

In CPE terms, does the feminist imaginary of decent work have the potential to become counter-hegemonic vis-à-vis neoliberalism or does it remain sub-hegemonic in that it "can be subsumed and contained within the hegemonic codes" (Sum 2005) of neoliberalism? Answering this question requires careful empirical analyses of concrete cases in terms of how decent work imaginaries materialise to constitute new forms of labour praxis in particular contexts. This is the objective of the empirical analysis in Chapters 6 and 7, taking Indonesia as a case study. Before, I want to further outline the historically specific context for my case study of labour struggles in Indonesia.

5. Trade Unions and Labour Politics in Indonesia

In this chapter, a historical outline of labour politics in Indonesia from independence, to the Suharto-era, until *Reformasi* and the present day is provided to prepare the empirical analysis in the next chapters. First, existing literature on the history of Indonesian labour politics is reviewed. This is necessary in order to set the stage for the empirical analysis in Chapters 6 and 7. Some of the claims about the role of NGOs and newly emerging trade unions from the literature are contrasted with empirical insights gained from ethnographic fieldwork below. Second, the current situation of organised labour in Indonesia is described, drawing on ethnographic fieldwork as well as media and document analysis. Three points are of particular importance in this context.

First, Indonesia has a history of radical labour traditions. Until Suharto took power in a military coup in 1965, the biggest trade union confederation SOBSI (All-Indonesia Central Workers' Organisation) was closely aligned with the Communist Party of Indonesia (PKI) and claimed some 2.7 million members in 1960. The tradition of radical, mass-based labour organising was broken when the PKI and SOBSI were crushed by violent repression after the 1965 coup d'état, killing up to a million alleged communists in one of the biggest democides after World War II. The history of these crimes against humanity is only now starting to be discussed in Indonesia.

Second, under the 30 years of Suharto's authoritarian rule over Indonesia, autonomous labour organising was suppressed. The only legal labour organisation (SPSI, All-Indonesia Trade Union) was dominated by the state, permeated by the military and aligned with the employers. This form of "authoritarian state unionism" (Lambert 1997) is part of a political legacy that extends into the landscape of today's labour politics and trade unions and poses significant challenges to independent labour organising.

Third, after a popular mass movement ousted Suharto, in which workers and intellectuals played a significant role (Ford 2009), a democratisation process—called *Reformasi*—commenced in 1998. Since then, independent trade unions have begun to re-emerge, laying the foundation of what today is a vibrant though fragmented labour movement. The reformed Indonesian labour law made it easy to establish new independent workplace unions that have since formed new federations and confederations (La Botz 2001). The old authoritarian state unions, however, have not been replaced by these newly emerging, genuinely democratic unions. Rather, they are now competing with one another over members and political influence.

5.1 From Independence to the New Order

Indonesia declared independence after World War II in 1945, when Japanese occupation troops had to leave the country following their defeat. The most important figure of the nationalist movement, Sukarno, became the first president of the newly independent nation, with Mohammad Hatta as vice-president. Before the war, Indonesia had been a Dutch colony since 1816 (the Dutch East Indies colony), when the Dutch state took over possessions from the Dutch East India Company (La Botz 2001, 62). The Dutch East India Company had been active in the region since early in the 17th century, competing with other colonial powers, primarily Portugal. The Netherlands recognised Indonesian independence only after a bitter war of liberation and international diplomatic pressure forced them to do so in 1949. In this liberation war, trade unions and peasant organisations existing at the time were heavily involved. According to Rita Tambunan (2010), communist or socialist trade unions on the one hand and Islamic-oriented trade unions on the other deferred their political differences in favour of the common struggle against the colonial master.

The time between 1949 and 1965 is referred to as *Old Order* or *Guided Democracy* and was marked by the government of Sukarno. Sukarno had founded the Indonesian National Party (*Partai Nasional Indonesia*) in 1927/1928 and since then had been the leader of the nationalist movement. Besides this party, the two most important parties were the Muslim Masyumi Party (*Partai Majelis Syuro Muslimin Indonesia*) and the Communist

Party of Indonesia (*Partai Komunis Indonesia*, PKI) (La Botz 2001, 91). In the 1950s, the PKI supported the nationalist politics of Sukarno. In all of these parties, there were different trade unions represented to varying degrees. In 1950, the PKI had only a couple of thousand members; in 1959, the number rose to 1.5 million and up to 3 million by 1965, with an estimated total of 20 million followers (according to a publication by the RAND corporation, Pauker 1969, v) making it the biggest communist mass movement at that time outside the Soviet power bloc. In the trade unions of that time, communists were the most influential force. Even Sukarno himself advocated a specifically Indonesian combination of nationalism, religion and communism ("*Nasakom*") to appease the three main political forces—the army, Islamic groups and the communists (La Botz 2001, 105). In 1962, he appointed two communist leaders, Aidit and Njoto, as ministers into his government. In August 1965, Sukarno declared Indonesia's withdrawal from the IMF and the World Bank. He envisioned an axis from Jakarta to Phnom Penh and Hanoi to Peking and Pyongyang and he proclaimed the arming of the popular masses in the context of *Konfrontasi* with neighbouring Malaysia (Parente 2009, 13). The balancing act between the nationalist military and the communist PKI, which had been one of the central foundations of Sukarno's rule, was shifting towards the communists. This development came to a violent halt in 1965 after the coup d'état that brought General Suharto to power.

What exactly happened on 1 October 1965 remains subject to debate until the present day. A group of military personnel and lieutenants calling themselves the September 30th Movement kidnapped and killed six top army generals. They accused these generals of plotting a coup d'état against Sukarno (Roosa 2006, 3). They occupied the national radio station and mobilised hundreds of troops to the inner city of Jakarta. The September 30th Movement, however, "collapsed just as suddenly as it had erupted" (ibid.). The only surviving general, Suharto, took command of the army and orchestrated a counter-attack the same day. He officially declared that the killings were an attempted coup masterminded by the PKI and launched a counter-coup gradually seizing power, *de facto* making him the president by 1966. Information linking the attempted coup to the PKI, however, was inconclusive and there never was an official investigation besides the "show trials" (Roosa 2006, 6) at that time. Alternative interpretations are suppressed to this day. The only survivor of the September 30th Movement reported in 1978 that he had informed Suharto of the planned action beforehand (ibid.). John Roosa, in the most recent analysis of the incident beyond speculation and conspiracy theory, therefore concludes that the army circles around Suharto were at least informed, if not implicated in the September 30th Movement, using it as a simulacrum "to set in motion their long-standing plan for displacing Sukarno and attacking the Communist Party" (2006, 194) with Western backing. He thus gave his book the comprehensive title *Pretext for Mass Murder: The September 30th Movement and Suharto's Coup d'État in Indonesia* (Roosa 2006), arguing that the incident did not represent a coup or a movement in any real sense, but a pretext for the counter-coup and for the anti-communist violence that would ensue (cf. La Botz 2001, 114).

After Suharto's counter-coup, the military committed mass murder against alleged communists and potential opponents with the help of anti-communist segments of the population, especially Islamic militias. In a series of massacres, between 500 thousand and 1 million people were killed (Ford 2009, 30). This democide is registered as one of the biggest politically motivated mass murders in post-World War II history. According to La Botz, the US government tacitly approved of the massacres. He cites US Ambassador Green writing to Secretary of State John Foster that he had "made it clear that Embassy and USG [U.S. government] [were] generally sympathetic with and admiring what [the] army [was] doing" (Green cited in La Botz 2001, 144). The communist movement was crushed and the PKI was banned. The ban of the PKI remains in place until today.

In fact, all trade unions were banned as well or, rather, forced to disband and integrate into a state-controlled monopoly trade union, first called FBSI (*Federasi Buruh Seluruh Indonesia*, All-Indonesia Labour Federation) and later restructured and renamed to SPSI (*Serikat Pekerja Seluruh Indonesia*, All-Indonesia Trade Union) (Ford 2009, 33–35). Communist organisations such as the trade union federation SOBSI (*Sentral Organisasi Buruh Seluruh Indonesia*, All-Indonesia Central Labour Organisation) and the peasant organisation BTI (*Barisan Tani Indonesia*, Peasants' Front of Indonesia) as well as Islamic unions such as GASBINDO (*Gabungan Serikat Buruh Islam Indonesia*, Amalgamated Indonesian Islamic Labour Union) and SARBUMUSI (*Serikat Buruh Muslimin Indonesia*, Indonesian Muslim Labour Union) were banned. FBSI/SPSI thus became the only legal labour organisation in Suharto's *New Order* regime. Dan La Botz (2001) explains that SPSI was not an instrument for organising workers but for controlling and suppressing them:

"Controlled by Golkar [Suharto's party], permeated by the military and allied with the employers, SPSI could no longer be called a labor union. Workers no longer had any organizations to fight for even their most minimal needs for better conditions or higher wages. SPSI was a fascist labor front constructed to control workers, not represent them" (La Botz 2001, 123).

5.2 Industrial Relations under Suharto

Industrial relations under the New Order were founded on the national ideology of *Pancasila* and geared towards economic development, political stability and societal modernisation. Pancasila refers to a specifically Indonesian version of authoritarian corporatism that was already used by Sukarno, but Suharto extended it to restructure the whole of Indonesia according to an organic vision of society (Ford 2009, 31) leaving no room for conflict. This organic vision of society constructs Indonesia as a national "family", dictates harmony onto its family members and displaces conflict among them. Applied to the field of labour as a doctrine known as Pancasila Industrial Relations, this ideology outlawed strikes and industrial disputes, deeming them unnecessary within the harmonious family of Indonesian society. La Botz, again, labels the Pancasila Industrial Relations discourse "a fascist theory of industrial relations" (2001, 123).

Building on this ideological foundation, New Order industrial relations were organised from above according to the needs of national development. As Ford argues: "From its inception, the New Order had sought legitimacy through promises of economic prosperity and political stability, explicitly positioning its development programs as the means by which a Pancasila state was to be achieved" (2009, 33). Economic development became a major priority of Suharto's regime. The New Order state could thus be called a "developmental state" (Parente 2009), although it represented an authoritarian developmentalism from the outset, not dissimilar to other authoritarian developmental states in the region such as South Korea. Although downplaying the authoritarian aspect of Suharto's developmental state, Robert Parente (2009) rightly argues that its approach to economic policy constituted the Indonesian version of Keynesianism, including some "limited welfare programs" (La Botz 2001, 124).

In CPE terms, Pancasila was the crucial economic imaginary glossing over the antagonism between capital and labour and processing the contradictions based in the social forms of capitalism. Pancasila Industrial Relations were one of the cornerstones of Indonesia's mode of regulation in the era of Fordism. With regard to its regime of accumulation, Indonesia like many other developing countries shifted from import substitution to export orientation between the 1970s and the 1980s. The state-led industrialisation strategy initially employed ISI as a means to "strengthen domestic capital through protective policies that aimed at securing an integrated national industrial base" (Lambert 1997, 58). Suharto established a host of state-owned enterprises in capital-intensive industries such as steel, oil, petrochemicals and metal processing. This form of state-led industrialisation, however, was contingent on access to oil revenues that were huge during the oil boom of the 1970s (Parente 2009, 16). When international oil prices collapsed in the mid-1980s, the ISI strategy had to be replaced or at least complemented by export manufacturing to compensate for lost income from oil (La Botz 2001, 119). Thus, the advent of EOI "meant that the labour-intensive light manufacturing sector began to grow very rapidly" (Ford 2009, 35), especially the textiles, garments and footwear industry.

This shift from ISI to EOI also meant a shift in economic policy priorities from protectionism to free trade since Indonesia was now competing over foreign investment (Lambert 1997, 59). Lambert argues that this shift made changes in the structure of authoritarian state unionism necessary. Export industries were built up in large factories concentrated in large bonded zones (i.e. export processing zones). Lambert explains: "In this context, the primary purpose of state unionism was to ensure, as far as possible, the ideal conditions for effective mass assembly production, that would be attractive to foreign investors" (1997, 60). Passivity of workers and their control by state unions was therefore crucial for maintaining labour discipline. The increasing level of strike action in the early 1980s made clear that the old structure of FBSI was failing to fulfil this purpose. FBSI was therefore renamed and restructured to SPSI in 1985 (ibid., 61) with even more military control over labour.

In response to growing international pressure to comply with ILO standards, SPSI was restructured again in the early 1990s. In an attempt to demonstrate a "liberal democratic image" (ibid., 63) to the international community without changing the fundamentals of Pancasila Industrial Relations, some changes were made to the organisational structure of SPSI to accommodate claims to freedom of association and the right to collective bargaining. Indeed, the Suharto regime began to promote local SPSI unions, "arguing that their absence is problematic for stable industrial relations" (ibid., 69). For Lambert, this late restructuring of SPSI does not represent a step towards democratic reform of authoritarian state unionism, but little more than "pretend democracy" (ibid., 71). SPSI remained an instrument of control, not representation. It remained a "state apparatus" (ibid., 77) deeply integrated with the military, rather than a genuine trade union. Labour activists trying to organise workers therefore had to seek out NGOs for assistance in setting up independent worker groups outside of SPSI. The early 1990s labour reform, however, legalised independent enterprise unions where no SPSI unit existed. This provided some limited space for autonomous labour organising in the factories that would become essential for the resurgence of Indonesia's labour movement.

5.3 Resurgence of the Labour Movement and *Reformasi*

Lacking trade unions that actually represented the interests of wage earners in conflict with the state and the employers, parts of the workforce began to organise outside of SPSI. Forms of alternative organising ranged from semi-illegal autonomous trade unions, some of which successfully launched wildcat strike actions in the early 1990s, to legal NGOs concerned with labour law and labour politics and other labour NGOs (Ford 2006). Many of these NGOs, emerging in the late 1980s, saw grassroots organising and policy advocacy as their main task (Ford 2000, 71). Many emanated from the students movement and were founded by students aiming to join forces with independent labour organisations in the struggle against Suharto. According to Vedi Hadiz, there were three crucial factors in the defeat of the Suharto regime: the Asian financial crisis of 1997,[9] the decline

---

9 The Asian financial crisis of 1997 marked the spectacular end of the so-called "Asian miracle" of the Southeast-Asian "tiger" states (Parente 2009, 25). It originated in Thailand as a currency crisis of the Baht, but quickly spread to other countries, including

in support for Suharto from important parts of his own power base and increasingly militant mass protests staged by an alliance of students and workers and supported by fractions of the urban middle classes (2000, 18). La Botz explains the role of NGOs within the liberation struggle:

"NGOs played a key role in helping workers organize. NGOs helped workers create organizations, aided them in strikes and advised them when they engaged in informal bargaining. NGOs also helped to link the alternative labor movement to the wider effort to build a democratic movement for civil rights and political reform" (La Botz 2001, 129).

In the European context, the emergence of NGOs has been interpreted as the privatisation of formerly public functions and as the institutionalisation and, thus, de-radicalisation of the "new social movements" (Hirsch 2003). In Indonesia, on the other hand, some NGOs played a part in radicalising civil society against Suharto. However, La Botz argues that "Indonesia had its share of both imperial and government-financed NGOs" (2001, 130), which were funded by the regime and its Western allies and targeted against the burgeoning opposition. Most NGOs, however, were founded by oppositional groups or former student activists, serving as space for the articulation of critique and dissent that was otherwise not available in the authoritarian New Order. Alongside alternative trade unions and grassroots workers' groups, these NGOs constituted the embryonic forms of organised opposition against the Suharto regime (Ford 2000, 70).

Although politically and ideologically these NGOs ranged from religious to secular and from socialist to conservative, they were united by the common demand for democratisation. Human rights and democracy were the primary goals of these organisations, most of which were convinced that these could not be achieved within the Suharto regime, but only in direct confrontation with it. Labour NGOs provided a legal framework for labour activism, acted as legal advisors to the independent labour movement, conducted research and trained activists in strategies of organising. They were a central prerequisite for the emergence of independent trade unions in the late 1990s: "In fact, [...] the NGOs acted

---

Indonesia. The Rupiah was allowed to float, the currency depreciated quickly, external debt skyrocketed, banks were closed, unemployment increased, inflation soared, and food riots ensued. Parente argues that the subsequent intervention of the IMF, dictating a neoliberal "structural adjustment program", contributed to Suharto's downfall, because it aggravated the social situation through measures like the removal of fuel and food subsidies (2009, 41).

as surrogate labor organizations", as La Botz (2001, 135) explains. After the fall of Suharto, many of these labour NGOs continued to exist. Some were providing legal advice for activists and unionists or lobbying for workers' issues. Others aimed for an official status as legally registered trade unions and struggled for better working and living conditions through collective bargaining and industrial action (Ford 2000, 74–75).

When Suharto was ousted by a popular mass movement, initiated by student and worker activists, in May 1998 following the Asian financial crisis, a process of democratisation called *Reformasi* ensued that promptly opened up new spaces for political articulation and organisation, which remained closed for almost 35 years of military dictatorship. Indonesia ratified the *Freedom of Association and Protection of the Right to Organise Convention* (ILO 1948), enabling new trade unions to be founded on the local, provincial and national levels virtually overnight.

La Botz (2001) describes various forms of labour organisations that have emerged or re-emerged after the end of the New Order regime. For example, SARBUMUSI has been re-established, the Muslim trade union that was one of to the most powerful unions in the Sukarno period. La Botz argues that SARBUMUSI has little chances of attaining its old significance (2001, 172) despite being supported by external donors such as the American Center for International Solidarity (ACILS) of the American Federation of Labor and Congress of Industrial Organizations (AFL-CIO). However, as I argue in the next chapter, external support and foreign funding by Western NGOs can be a problem for trade unions as well. ACILS also funded the reformed wing of SPSI that had split off from the rest of SPSI after May 1998 and was called *SPSI-Reformasi* at the time of La Botz's research (2001, 174). Both the non-reformed wing of SPSI and SPSI-Reformasi continued to be seen as "yellow unions"[10] by many independent activists, heavily bureaucratised and top-down in their approach with many old leaders and officers still in power. SPSI, still funded by Golkar, was seen as representing the interests of the old oligarchy, while SPSI-Reformasi was accused of being masterminded by ACILS' external US influence (ibid., 175). Nevertheless, La Botz argues that SPSI-Reformasi remained an important part of the new labour

---

10 "Yellow union" is a term for employer-sponsored or state-led pseudo-unions that goes back to the early 20th century, when such pseudo-unions, labelled as "yellow", were established in Europe to undermine the "red" syndicalist or socialist unions. The term is also used in Indonesia; it emerged from the interview material.

movement given that they claimed more members than any other union and had a wide infrastructure at their disposal allowing for large-scale networking and organising. For him, the question is whether or not a new generation of young unionists and activists will manage to further democratise the organisation from within and thereby accomplish a more democratic and militant kind of unionism (ibid., 180).

La Botz also discusses more genuinely independent trade unions emerging in the struggle against Suharto. First, the Indonesian Prosperity Labour Union (*Serikat Buruh Sejahtera Indonesia*, SBSI) was founded in 1992 as a quasi-illegal labour organisation with the assistance of labour NGOs and labour lawyers and Muchtar Pakpahan as the leading figure (Ford 2009, 66). Under Suharto, SBSI grew rapidly although being forced to work underground. The organisation became a threat to the regime and Muchtar was incarcerated for several years as a political prisoner (La Botz 2001, 199). He became a kind of martyr of the new labour movement and was released from prison only after Suharto was replaced by his protégé Habibie. During *Reformasi*, SBSI became the largest and most important union organisation of Indonesia with hundreds of thousands of claimed members in all provinces and all sectors, according to La Botz (2001, 217). The challenge was to transform a militant activist underground organisation into a professional trade union. This challenge was met on the one hand but, on the other, this also meant for SBSI to run the risk of de-radicalisation and bureaucratisation, which is well-known from the history of European trade unions. La Botz (2001, 224) argues that this risk can only be avoided if labour unions maintain the relationships to those social movements from which they emerged and continue to fight not only for collective bargaining agreements and legal rights, but also for social justice and societal change more broadly. La Botz (2001, 225) is sceptical as to SBSI's prospects of retaining its social movement roots given the type of social democratic unionism of Western Europe around which it is modelled. He therefore turns to another, more radical independent trade union organisation.

Second, the National Front of Indonesian Labour Struggle (*Front Nasional Perjuangan Buruh Indonesia*, FNPBI) was founded by Dita Sari, a student activist who began to organise workers and establish local plant-level unions in the 1990s. Like Muchtar, Dita was imprisoned for several years before being released in 1999 but, in contrast to Muchtar, she remained in prison during Habibie's interregnum, because she was seen as radical or even communist due to her affiliation with the socialist Democratic People's Party (*Partai Rakyat Demokratik*, PRD). During *Reformasi*, the army's influence in politics and the hegemony of anti-communist propaganda was, if at all, only slowly diminishing. It is thus remarkable that the FNPBI was relatively successful in mobilising workers for economic struggles while the PRD remained marginal in the political arena. According to Dita, the FNPBI strategy rests on the combination of economic and political struggles. Organising independent labour unions and winning collective bargaining agreements remain important tasks for Dita, but her ideas go beyond that and include the vision of a future radical workers' party (La Botz 2001, 243–244). While La Botz seems to advocate the PRD as a viable socialist alternative for Indonesia, their election results in 1999 (less than 0.1 per cent) create doubt. In 2004 and 2009, the PRD did not run for parliamentary elections anymore.

What became of Dita Sari and the FNPBI is touched upon, when the preceding discussion—based on an analysis of existing scientific discourses on the new labour movement of Indonesia—is contrasted with everyday discourses of Indonesian labour activists recorded through ethnographic fieldwork more than ten years after La Botz's research in the remainder of this chapter.

We have already seen that the Indonesian labour movement has been reignited after the ousting of Suharto in 1998 by a popular mass movement in the aftermath of the Asian financial crisis. After the ratification of the ILO's 1948 *Convention Concerning Freedom of Association and Protection of the Right to Organise*, new trade unions from the enterprise to the national level were mushrooming virtually overnight. Newly emerging, genuinely independent and democratic trade unions are now competing with the old authoritarian state unions over members and influence. In CPE terms, a huge amount of *variation* in the trade union landscape was produced through the democratic opening, challenging the sedimented meanings of Pancasila Industrial Relations and re-politicising organised labour's discourses and practices. The *selection* and *retention* of certain forms of trade unionism at the expense of others will partly depend on unions' material resources (e.g. funding by their members, the state, the employers and/or external donors) and their discursive resources such as their respective imaginaries of decent work (or beyond).

National trade union confederations

SPSI still exists today, although there were many splits and divisions in the organisation. As mentioned in the previous section, the first split within SPSI had already started in the last months of the New Order, producing SPSI and SPSI-Reformasi. Those unions and federations that remained in SPSI formed a national trade union confederation called KSPSI (*Konfederasi Serikat Pekerja Seluruh Indonesia*, Confederation of All-Indonesian Trade Unions) as the direct successor of SPSI. KSPSI later split up again to form two competing KSPSI confederations, the one known as KSPSI-Kalibata and the other as KSPSI-Pasar Minggu, named after the location of their headquarters in Jakarta. Unions and federations affiliated with SPSI-Reformasi restructured themselves to form the national trade union confederation KSPI (*Kongres Serikat Pekerja Indonesia*, Congress of Indonesian Trade Unions). The formation of KSPI was supported by the International Confederation of Free Trade Unions (ICFTU) and it officially affiliated itself with the ICFTU. In sum, there are now three national trade union confederations that are either direct successors of SPSI or have split off from it. As of now, at least on the national level, KSPSI unions continue to be seen as "yellow unions" by many workers, although there is debate whether it may be transformed into a genuinely democratic and independent trade union as a new generation of workers and union leaders rises.

The before-mentioned SBSI of the late Suharto era laid the foundation for another, more genuinely independent national trade union confederation—KSBSI (*Konfederasi Serikat Buruh Sejahtera Indonesia*, Confederation of Indonesian Prosperity Labour Unions). In 2003, there has however been a split in KSBSI over accusations against Muchtar Pakpahan who was criticised for his authoritarian style of leadership. The high international profile he gained as a labour activist against Suharto and political prisoner increasingly contrasted with the perception of him within his own organisation as potentially misusing financial resources and clinging onto power for too long. The unions that split off from KSBSI restructured and renamed themselves to SBSI-1992 so as to indicate that they wanted to take up the more militant tradition of the early SBSI. KSBSI, on the other hand, further became institutionalised into the industrial relations system of Indonesia and gained international recognition by the Christian World Confederation of Labour (WCL). When the ICFTU and the WCL merged in 2006 to form the International Trade Union Confederation (ITUC), the new ITUC therefore had two affiliates in Indonesia, KSPI and KSBSI.

The process of institutionalisation and recognition, however, came at a price. Muchtar's successor, Rekson Silaban, secured for himself a seat on the Governing Body of the ILO from 2005 as well as on the Executive Board of the WCL and later on the General Council of the ITUC. The high international profile of the KSBSI leadership reflected the declining priority for local organising efforts. According to an informant from Universitas Indonesia, KSBSI now represents something of a "labour aristocracy" with "union elites struggling to gain access to the centre of power" (Scholar Interview, December 2011). The ILO reportedly addresses Rekson as speaking for and representing the interests of Indonesian workers, which is problematic because KSBSI, while enjoying greater political influence, has fewer members than other confederations, especially on the shop-floor level. Rekson has close ties with Jusuf Kalla from the old Golkar party who acted as vice-president under Susilo Bambang Yudhoyono from 2004 to 2009 and again under Joko Widodo from 2014. He supports the idea of labour market flexibilisation and tries to find a middle ground between workers' and employers' interests. As the informant put it, "he is more the ILO's voice than the workers' voice" (Scholar Interview, December 2011), which is why many of the other trade unions often exclude him from strategic discussions. Whereas KSPSI certainly remains a "yellow union" on the national level, KSBSI has moved from semi-illegal and therefore sometimes militant unionism to a degree of institutionalisation that has rendered at least the leadership "yellow" in the eyes of many workers.

There are, however, other national trade union confederations that have emerged after the fall of Suharto. Dita Sari's FNPBI has been mentioned before. Similar to Muchtar, Dita gained a high international profile due to her prominent role as a labour activist and political prisoner in the late New Order. According to La Botz (2001, 167) and Ford (2009, 168), FNPBI belonged to the most important new trade unions in the first years of the post-Suharto period, but when research was conducted for the present study in 2011 and 2012, FNPBI was hardly mentioned in the interviews at all. What had happened? Ford argues that the declining relevance of FNPBI is partly due to its failure to secure ongoing international support because of its leftist political agenda (2009, 171). She argues: "Its openly leftist stance and choice of a political approach to trade unionism forced FNPBI to the periphery of the labour movement" (Ford 2009, 168). This could be interpreted as arguing that it was FNPBI's political unionism—the idea that organised labour has to play a political role in the democratisation process rather than a mere economic role on the shop floor—that frustrated workers and contributed to its decline.

Evidence from my own research, however, suggests that it was not the political approach to unionism itself, but the way it was put into practice by Dita as the leading figure of FNPBI. After years of leading sometimes militant labour struggles and mass demonstrations, she decided to accept an offer to join the Ministry of Manpower and Transmigration in 2010 alongside other former labour activists. Although hopes were high among the labour movement that having activists from their midst working from within the system would help to further their demands, disappointment soon took over. As a spokesperson of the Manpower Ministry, Dita was responsible for migrant worker issues. Indonesian migrant workers are mostly female migrant domestic workers and often suffer horrible human and labour rights abuses in destination countries such as Malaysia or Saudi Arabia. One labour NGO observer summarises the experience:

"Dita Indah Sari has lost the trust of workers. That's what I heard. Especially in the case of Indonesian migrant workers. Recently, one of them, Ruyati or Rumiyati, was beheaded in Saudi Arabia. Many workers have asked themselves, why the Manpower Minister has so many advisors from the field of labour activists if this kind of thing is still happening. They owe an explanation. How come that they could not alarm the minister earlier? But instead what they did is remain silent. Well, the workers don't need silent advisors. They need someone who has power, who speaks out about where the problem is and isn't afraid of losing their position" (NGO Interview, November 2011).

The case of Dita Sari, therefore, can be interpreted as another case exemplifying the price of institutionalisation and official recognition turning into co-optation. Frustrated with the limited results of Dita's switching sides from the labour movement to the government, some union federations until then affiliated with FNPBI broke away and joined yet another national trade union confederation—KASBI (*Kongres Aliansi Serikat Buruh Indonesia*, Congress of the Indonesian Labour Union Alliance). Since then, FNPBI has faded from the visible landscape of Indonesian trade union confederations.

KASBI was founded in 2003 as the Action Committee of Independent Labour Unions (*Komite Aksi Serikat Buruh Independen*, KASBI). Local enterprise-level unions, province and city-level union federations as well as leftist students' and workers' groups were part of this action committee. When it restructured itself to form a national union confederation rather than an action committee in 2004, it renamed itself but retained the well-known abbreviation. KASBI explicitly positioned itself as anti-capitalist and anti-imperialist, arguably making it the most radical of the Indonesian union confederations at that time. This radical stance is also reflected in KASBI's connection to students' and workers' groups such as the Working People's Alliance (*Perhimpunan Rakyat Pekerja*, PRP), a leftist labour NGO composed of members of the independent union movement and the leftist student movement. The issue of NGO influence in trade unions is a very sensitive one that repeatedly became politicised and caused fragmentations and splits within the labour movement.

For example, one of the union federations that participated in the action committee was the Federation of Independent Labour Unions (*Gabungan Serikat Buruh Independen*, GSBI). Like other independent unions, GSBI emerged during the last years of the New Order as a clandestine alternative to SPSI. Assisted by the labour NGO SISBIKUM (*Saluran Informasi Sosial dan Bimbingan Hukum*, Channel for Social Information and Legal Guidance), two plant-level unions were founded in 1996 and 1997— PERBUPAS (*Perkumpulan Buruh Pabrik Sepatu*, Association of Footwear Factory Workers) and ABGTeks (*Asosiasi Buruh Garmen dan Tekstil*, Association of Garment and Textile Workers)—that would later merge into GSBI's garment federation SBGTS (*Serikat Buruh Garmen Tekstil dan Sepatu*, Garment Textile and Footwear Labour Union). Still linked to and funded by SISBIKUM, GSBI officially registered as a trade union federation in 1999. Elena Williams (2007, 45) and Michelle Ford (2009, 174) report that GSBI severed its ties to SISBIKUM in 2001 after quarrelling over transparency, authority and union independence. The NGO interfered with GSBI's working relationships to a degree that became unacceptable to the union. Similarly, when KASBI decided to declare itself a national union confederation in 2004, GSBI moved out of the network because of differences with KASBI's leadership and the political influence of NGOs like PRP. Instead of joining KASBI, GSBI decided to move towards becoming a national union confederation of its own (Union Interview, January 2012).

External NGO influence ultimately also contributed to the split of KASBI. Once the most radical and militant of the newly emerging independent trade union confederations, KASBI has recently gained more official recognition and is set on a path of institutionalisation into Indonesia's industrial relations system. One example of this is KASBI's participation in the multi-stakeholder negotiations of a private protocol on freedom of association, mediated by the Play Fair Alliance, which is analysed in more detail below. The strong presence of international NGOs such as Oxfam Australia was one of the reasons for some member unions of KASBI to disagree with this path and eventually to split off from KASBI to form the new trade union confederation KSN (*Konfederasi Serikat Nasional*, National Union Confederation) taking KASBI's place at the most leftist end of the union spectrum.

The following figure summarises the development of Indonesian national trade union confederations.

Figure 6: Indonesian National Trade Union Confederations

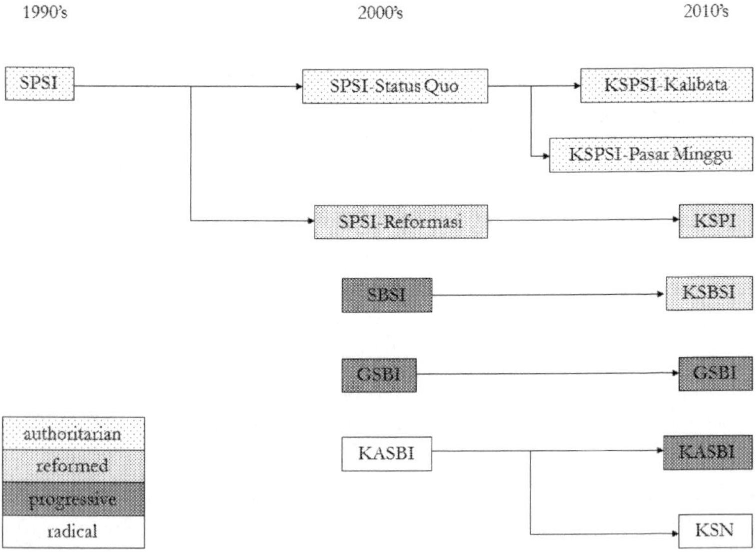

Source: author's compilation

There are at least seven union confederations today (on the right side of the figure). Only the top four of these are officially recognised by the Indonesian government and, by the same token, by the ILO. Out of these four, two are direct successors of SPSI and continue to be seen as "yellow unions" by labour activists. KSPI has emerged as the reformed wing of SPSI. SBSI has emerged as a progressive, social democratic trade union but, as indicated above, has moved away from its original activist stance in the process of institutionalisation and consolidation. That is why its present form is colour-coded orange rather than pink to capture the shift from progressive to reformed unionism. The progressive union GSBI continues to seek official recognition as a national trade union confederation, just like KASBI. For the latter, however, the process of gaining more recognition and becoming more integrated into the industrial relations system has also shifted the organisation away from radical and militant union strategies towards more moderate forms of progressive unionism. This shift is also indicated by colour coding. Member union federations alienated by this shift have since formed KSN as a new confederation staunchly defending the radical approach of "social movement unionism" (Scipes 1992).[11]

Garment, textile and footwear union federations

Most of the national trade union confederations are organised by industrial sector. The two branches of KSPSI both have their own federation in the garment and textile sector, both named FSP-TSK (*Federasi Serikat Pekerja - Tekstil Sandang dan Kulit*, Federation of Textile Garment and Leather Trade Unions) or TSK in short, only to be differentiated by the suffix Kalibata or Pasar Minggu. Despite its name, KSPI's affiliate in the textile and garment sector is the large SPN (*Serikat Pekerja Nasional*, National Trade Union). KSBSI's garment and textile federation is called FSB-GARTEKS (*Federasi Serikat Buruh - Garmen dan Tekstil*, Federation of Garment and Textile Labour Unions) or GARTEKS in short, headed by Elly Rosita Silaban, Rekson's wife. GSBI's garment federation SBGTS (*Serikat Buruh Garmen*

---

11 Kim Scipes (1992) has used the term "social movement unionism" to denote a new type of unionism in the Global South that goes beyond both bourgeois and Leninist conceptions of unionism. Social movement unions are not only concerned with workplace issues, but "are major actors in the struggle for democracy, human rights, and social justice in their countries" (Scipes 1992, 81). Initially suggested by Peter Waterman, it was first applied by Rob Lambert and Eddie Webster to South Africa (Waterman 2004, 217). Kim Moody and Peter Waterman have since reformulated the concept as "international social movement unionism" (Moody 1997) and "new international social unionism" (Waterman 2004) respectively.

Tekstil dan Sepatu, Garment Textile and Footwear Labour Union) has already been mentioned (see also Figure 5). KASBI and KSN, on the other hand, have not organised their member federations based on industry but rather based on local proximity in the cities, provinces and districts where they organise their members. Nevertheless, many workers organised in KASBI and KSN are garment, textile or footwear workers. The majority of the members of most of the federations that have split off from KASBI to form KSN are working in the garment industry (NGO Interview, January 2012).

Interestingly, yet unsurprisingly, the leadership of the old authoritarian trade unions is predominantly composed of elderly men who were already active in SPSI's leadership under Suharto. The independent trade unions emerging in the struggle against Suharto, on the other hand, have recruited their leaders from their membership. The independent garment union federations, representing a vast majority of women workers, thus elected female leaders. GSBI-SBGTS is headed by woman leader Emelia Yanti, GARTEKS by Elly Silaban and KASBI even has a female president on the confederation level, Nining Elitos. Women's representation and active participation within the union apparatuses seems to correlate with the degree of independence and intra-union democracy enabling or restricting workers' self-representation and self-organisation.

Each of these union confederations and federations is included to differing degrees in the different projects and initiatives that I analyse next. Each has its own imaginary of what decent work is and its own strategy of how it may be achieved. In CPE terms, the dynamic post-Suharto period produced a huge *variation* of different, competing trade union strategies and contested decent work imaginaries. The empirical analysis of the three cases in the next chapters is conducted in this context as a comparative study of contrasting cases. They are here seen as actively contributing to the *selection* and *retention* of some of these strategies and imaginaries as well as the filtering out or marginalisation of others. The question is what kinds of imaginaries the different projects and initiatives produce and circulate, what kinds of strategies and practices they enable or restrict and how these can be employed by counter-hegemonic forces to challenge the hegemony of neoliberalism.

Before, a general discussion of the situation of organised labour in Indonesia at the time of research, based on interviews as well as media and document analysis, is provided to give an impression of the field that the three cases subsequently discussed form part of or intervene in.

5.4 The Current Situation of Organised Labour

On 3 October 2012, over two million workers joined the first nation-wide general strike in Indonesia since 50 years. They demanded substantial wage hikes and an end to the outsourcing and contract worker system. All across the country, mass actions and demonstrations occurred; hundreds of thousands took to the streets, with militant actions like the blocking of toll roads and violent clashes with the police. There has not been as much and intense labour unrest since before the Suharto era. Since the 1980s, Indonesia has been a fast growing export economy and after the shock of the Asian crisis of 1997, recovered quickly. The export growth rate was as high as 26.5 per cent in 2000, while it was still 15.3 per cent in 2010 (World Databank), despite the global financial and economic crisis of 2008. These impressive figures contrast starkly with a massive lack of "decent work"— low wages, long working hours, unpaid overtime, precarious employment, union busting, physical and psychological abuse, lack of occupational health and safety measures and other violations of labour and human rights of those who are producing economic wealth—the workers.

Labour unions' priorities: wages, contracts, freedom of association

The labour movement has been reignited since a popular mass movement ousted Suharto in 1998 in the aftermath of the Asian crisis. After years of stagnant real wages despite strong economic growth, workers are now starting to demand a greater share of Indonesia's new wealth. 2011 has been the first year of what some observers call a "wage war" (NGO Interview, December 2011) gaining momentum. At the end of each year, the minimum wages for the next year are being negotiated on provincial and district/city levels. Due to decentralisation after *Reformasi*, each province has its own minimum wage—the *Upah Minimum Provinsi* (UMP, Provincial Minimum Wage). Within provinces, each district or city in turn has their own minimum wage—the *Upah Minimum Kabupaten/Kota* (UMK, District/City-Level Minimum Wage). In addition, there are sector-specific minimum wages on the provincial and the district/city levels (UMSP, UMSK). Minimum wages are negotiated in tripartite wage councils between local governments, employers and unions, but final decisions are made by provincial governors. The question of which unions are represented in these wage councils, however, is contentious and in most cases, these are the unions that have the best relationship to the state, i.e. KSPSI and its various split-offs and incarnations.

Transparency and accountability of the union representatives in these councils is a problem in terms of representation and democracy. Different episodes illuminating this problem have been reported during interviews. When the 2012 minimum wage for Batam province was negotiated, KSBSI was leading the negotiations for the unions in the wage council. They accepted a minimum wage that was below the level the other unions were ready to accept. The other unions, therefore, mobilised their members and pressured the provincial government and the KSBSI officials to re-open negotiations, much to the employers' association disapproval (NGO Interview, December 2011). In Tangerang, representatives from KSPSI, SPN and TSK first agreed to raise the minimum wage for 2012 from 1,290,000 to 1,381,000 Rupiah. Other unions such as GSBI and KASBI, however, continued to pressure members of the wage council through mass demonstrations and highway blockages and finally an agreement was reached to raise the UMK to 1,529,000 Rupiah, the same level as Jakarta (Union Interview, January 2012).

The minimum wage is supposed to be based on government calculations of the price of a commodity basket covering the decent living needs (KHL, *Kebutuhan Hidup Layak*). This basket is calculated for a single worker without family. Labour unions criticise the calculation as too restrictive in terms of what counts as a living need. There is continuous debate about the items to be included in the basket and unions have proposed different alternative concepts for minimum wage calculation (see Chapter 7.1). Even if measured against the government-issued KHL, more than 80 per cent of provinces have failed to fix their minimum wage at a level higher than or equal to the KHL (Scholar Interview, December 2011). This means that most provinces officially provide minimum wages that are below subsistence level. What is more, even this low-level minimum wage is often not paid by companies, because they can avoid it by claiming that their economic performance precludes them from doing so. The ILO's Global Jobs Pact Country Scan for Indonesia states that non-compliance with minimum wage regulations has gone up from 38.2 per cent to 43.7 per cent between 2008 and 2009 (ILO 2010, 30), when Indonesia and the rest of the world was hit by the global financial and economic crisis.

According to virtually all unionists interviewed, wages are one of the most pressing issues of organised labour in Indonesia. One respondent argued that "wages will always be the most important issue to organise workers" (Union Interview, January 2012). The other priorities articulated by the unions interviewed include labour market flexibility and the proliferation of precarious employment (in particular outsourced and temporary contract work) as well as freedom of association and union busting.

One of the paradoxes of organised labour in Indonesia relates to labour market flexibility and precarious employment, i.e. outsourced and short-term, temporary contract work. The same laws that were drafted with the assistance of the ILO to align Indonesian labour laws with international labour standards are also the laws that implemented a "flexibility regime" (Tjandraningsih and Nugroho 2008) in the Indonesian labour market. On the one hand, Labour Law No. 13/2003 (the Manpower Act) regulated issues such as the right to strike, dismissals and severance pay in a way that was "surprisingly favorable to workers" (Caraway 2004, 42). On the other hand, however, it also legalised the spread of outsourcing and contract work. Although the bill restricts the employment of outsourced workers to "non-core business", this remained a grey area and allowed for the massive expansion of outsourcing. Similarly, the use of short-term contracts is legalised by the Manpower Act, which further undermines job security of Indonesian workers. For these reasons, there was fierce resistance from progressive trade unions before the bill was passed (Uwiyono 2007, 196). Also, the ILO was subsequently seen by them as promoting labour market flexibility and therefore as siding with the employers and the pro-business government: "Actually, the trade unions blame the ILO for the bad working conditions in Indonesia, because they support the Labour Law No. 13/2003. Before we had better regulation, a better labour law than today" (NGO Group Discussion, March 2011). At the time of research, approximately 40 per cent of the formal labour force was employed as outsourced workers. On 17 January 2012, Indonesia's Constitutional Court ruled that outsourcing in this form violates the constitution and the workers' "right to a decent job and a decent life" (Jakarta Globe, 20 Jan 2012). The Manpower Act shall be amended accordingly. The issue of outsourced and temporary contract work remains highly contested until today.

The rise of outsourced and contract work also undermines freedom of association, because employers can simply refuse to renew contracts of union activists instead of openly sacking them for union activities, which is illegal. It also serves to discipline workers and discourage them from collectively exercising their labour rights, because the "only way that they can maintain employment is to work hard and keep their heads down in the hope that their contracts are extended" (Tjandraningsih and Nugroho 2008, 7). Outsourced and temporary workers are much harder to unionise than permanent workers. Tjandraningsih and Nugroho conclude:

"In Indonesia, trade unions have encountered the flexibility regime within a climate of free association brought about by the era of *Reformasi*. Unions' ability to take advantage of the opportunities presented by *Reformasi* has been undermined by a combination of poor economic conditions and the implementation of flexibility. In the current labour climate, joining a union is considered to be a threat to ongoing job security, rather than a viable way of defending one's rights" (2008, 9, emphasis in the original).

Freedom of association and defending against union busting is the third priority articulated by the union activists interviewed. In addition to the problem of "outsourcing as union busting by stealth", as Michelle Ford (2013, 236) calls it, leaders and members of independent trade unions continue to face more open union busting activities, violating an essential core labour standard. This includes forced relocation, denied promotion, interference with union activities, discrimination against unionists and intimidation through psychological or physical violence. Often, local thugs are hired to intimidate independent union organisers (Union Interview, January 2012).

In addition to these forms of "employer anti-unionism" (Ford 2013), freedom of association and the right to collective bargaining are further undermined by inter-union conflict and competition between the old "yellow" unions and the new independent unions that employers can exploit to their advantage. Wherever there is more than one union in a workplace, employers can support the old bureaucratic union structures and discriminate against new, more genuinely democratic unions. Ford's interviews have confirmed that "management has continued to favour the workplace units of the direct successor to the Suharto-era union or set up 'yellow' enterprise unions in attempt to silence genuine unionists" (2013,

228). One of the cases that both has been discussed in the literature and emerged as a case of continued relevance in my interview material is PT Panarub. I include a discussion of this case as part of the analysis of the protocol on freedom of association below.

The end of the era of cheap labour?

Between late 2011 and early 2012 when the main fieldwork for the present study was conducted, the situation of organised labour was marked by intense and sometimes violent labour struggles. For example, there was a bitter three-month strike for higher wages at the Freeport gold and copper mine in West-Papua, where police and security forces shot dead at least nine protesting workers (New Matilda, 16 December 2011). There were stronger and more militant protests in Western and Central Java, Batam and other provinces around the issue of fixing the minimum wage for 2012:

"In the latest of a series of rallies to demand better pay, tens of thousands of workers in Bekasi and Tangerang, in West Java and Banten respectively, blocked roads connecting neighboring regencies to the capital on Thursday, causing severe traffic congestion. Police officers failed to prevent the workers from occupying the roads, causing hours of excruciating traffic snarls. In Bekasi, workers closed seven toll gates in the industrial area, causing traffic jams on the inner-city toll road. Traffic congestion occurred on Jl. Industri, heading to the Lippo Cikarang Industrial area and Jababeka I and II. In Tangerang, some 10,000 people protested in front of Apindo's Tangerang office on Jl. Gatot Subroto, carrying banners, posters and flags, forming a long train of marchers and motorcycle convoys, leaving kilometer-long traffic queues in their wake" (Jakarta Post, 21 January 2012).

All of this gave signs of a new, reawakened labour movement willing to fight for workers' rights and making use of new democratic spaces opening up through democratisation with growing success. From 2011 to 2012, the legal minimum wage—in Indonesia this most often means effective wage (see ILO 2006, 14)—for Jakarta increased by 20 per cent to 1.52 million Rupiah (ca. 157 US Dollar). From 2012 to 2013, following the unprecedented general strike, it rose again by 44 per cent to 2.2 million Rupiah (ca. 228 US Dollar). For the first time, Jakarta's minimum wage was raised to the KHL level. Nevertheless, wage levels still are among the lowest in the region. Political decision makers, however, have realised that providing decent wages and labour conditions for Indonesia's workers is crucial for the future of the largest economy within the Association of Southeast

Asian Nations (ASEAN). President Yudhoyono said: "The era of cheap labour and injustice is now over" (Jakarta Post, 1 December 2012), following the general strike and subsequent mass actions that often ended in violent clashes with the police or private security forces. "We have to overcome and manage justice appropriately to prevent it from becoming a time bomb" (Jakarta Globe, 1 December 2012), he added.

These developments may give a glimpse of what the situation of organised labour in Indonesia looked like at the time of research. It was spanned by the contradictions of the strengthened labour movement with rising workers' aspirations for social welfare on the one hand, Indonesian employers and foreign investors fearing that higher wages may hamper business climate on the other and the Indonesian state trying to forge compromises that neither endanger growth prospects of the economy nor social peace. Workers have succeeded to push for substantial wage hikes through "traditional" working class strategies such as mass demonstrations and large-scale strikes, including militant direct actions. In Indonesia, where minimum wages are negotiated in tripartite forums but the final decision is made by the provincial governor, these more radical strategies were successful in pushing local governments to accommodate workers' demands. Moderate "social dialogue" strategies, on the other hand, have often failed to fulfil workers' demands due to the local balances of power, in some cases of minimum wage negotiations behind closed doors causing militant mass protests of discontent workers.

Whereas "social dialogue" may have been a viable strategy for labour in a central Fordist context of national class compromise that makes rising wages compatible with business interests, in a peripheral neoliberal context of transnational supply chains it is the least favourable starting point for labour. This is because workers at the bottom of "buyer-driven commodity chains" (Gereffi and Korzeniewicz 1994) in labour-intensive industries lack bargaining power in isolated negotiations with employers since they can easily be replaced and their wages are not expected to provide effective demand for the goods they have produced. On the individual company level, the balance of forces is to the disadvantage of workers, questioning the efficacy of "social dialogue" strategies. Indonesian unions must therefore compensate for the lack of economic power by developing "political power" (Behrens et al. 2006, 21), i.e. the capacity to influence policy- and decision-making processes through collective action. Political power can be employed to pressure local governments when workers shift from the economic to the political sphere, where the balance of forces is more advantageous to them. Mass mobilisations, large-scale strikes and other confrontational labour strategies are sources for such power. This is the larger context, in which the following analysis of the three cases is situated.

6. Contested Imaginaries of Decent Work

To recapitulate, the aim of the present study is to analyse the paradoxes of decent work in terms of whether and how this discourse works to reinforce *or* challenge the hegemony of neoliberalism. This is to be undertaken by finding answers to a number of questions. Does it help counter-hegemonic forces such as progressive trade unions, social movements and activist NGOs in their strategies and practices to struggle for better living and working conditions? How do they make use of or appropriate the discourse? How does decent work relate to potential alternative discourses, strategies and practices of unions, movements and NGOs?

In this and the next chapter, the results of ethnographic fieldwork in Indonesia are presented. First, the ILO's approach towards decent work in Indonesia is examined by looking at the Better Work Indonesia project. Then, the work of the Play Fair Alliance in Indonesia is discussed as an example of multi-stakeholder initiatives towards decent work. These two approaches are juxtaposed as contested and competing economic imaginaries of decent work. In the next chapter, this is complemented by an outlook on labour unions and social movements in Indonesia envisioning recovered imaginaries beyond decent work.

6.1 The Better Work Programme

The global Better Work Programme is a typical example of the kinds of initiatives the ILO is carrying out in the area of Corporate Social Responsibility (CSR) under the umbrella of decent work. It was initiated in 2001 as the Better Factories Cambodia project as an attempt to help the Cambodian garment industry to secure orders following the phase-out of the Multi-Fibre Agreement in 2005. After the Cambodian experience had been reported as a success story benefitting both employers and workers (Ferenschild 2011), Better Work was exported to other countries such as Indonesia, Vietnam, Lesotho, Jordan, Haiti and Nicaragua since 2008. Better Work is a partnership of the ILO and the International Finance Corporation (IFC) and, as such, an example of the new approach of the ILO to seek "soft money from international agencies" (Standing 2008, 381) to make up for decreased regular budget funding. The problem with this soft money is that the ILO becomes dependent on external donors and its programmes become donor-driven. The IFC is part of the World Bank Group and has the mandate to promote private sector development in developing countries. It is not known for its stance against the neoliberal development paradigm or its concern for marginalised workers. The joint venture of the ILO and the IFC, therefore, further exacerbates the contradictions within the decent work discourse. Better Work makes the "business case" for decent work while maintaining that workers will benefit simultaneously.

Better Work Indonesia (BWI) is the first monitoring project of the ILO in Indonesia starting operations in 2010. It aims to improve both company compliance with core labour standards and industry competitiveness in global supply chains, focussing the global garment and textile industry. It offers technical services to both global buyers and local suppliers of garments and textiles in terms of quality assurance, monitoring and evaluation and impact assessment. It builds on ten years of experience drawn from the pioneering Better Factories Cambodia project. The idea is a classic win-win-situation: Participation in Better Work would give the garment companies a competitive advantage on the global market, because CSR management, auditing and certification are now integral parts of transnational supply chains. The workers, of course, would benefit from better working conditions through improved company compliance. Before going into details of the empirical analysis of BWI, some remarks on the Cambodian experience drawn from the available literature are necessary since it is the purported "success story" of Better Factories Cambodia (BFC) that has enabled the emergence of BWI.

6.1.1 Better Factories Cambodia

BFC started operations in 2001. At that time, the phase-out of the Multi-Fibre Agreement (MFA) by 2005 was a done deal. After that, Cambodia would no longer be able to benefit from fixed export quotas for garments and textiles. During the last years of the MFA's existence, however, the United States and Cambodia entered into a bilateral Trade Agreement on Textile and Apparel (TATA) signed in 1999, which "set export quotas for garments from Cambodia to the United States, which Cambodia was entitled to no matter what, but also offered a possible 18 per cent annual increase in these export entitlements, provided that the government of Cambodia supported the implementation of a program to improve working conditions" (Sibbel and Borrmann 2007, 237).

The TATA was thus one of several bilateral free trade agreements initiated by the Clinton administration that linked free trade with labour standards following the breakdown of the social clause debate within the WTO. The governments of the United States and Cambodia approached the ILO, requesting a project that would help implementing the labour clause of the TATA. This gave birth to BFC.

While the "initial purpose was to inform ongoing US quota allocation decisions" (Arnold and Shih 2010, 407), it aimed to improve company compliance with core labour standards and Cambodian labour law. The main activity of BFC was monitoring working conditions in export garment factories, reporting the findings to supplier factories and making suggestions for improvements. It also engaged in capacity-building of employers' and workers' organisations, technical training and government consulting. Participation in BFC was voluntary but conditional for making use of export quotas, which is why "virtually the entire sector" (Sibbel and Borrmann 2007, 238) of export garment production registered with BFC. After the phase-out of the MFA and the end of TATA in 2005, BFC continued operations although the formal quota incentives for monitoring and improving working conditions made way for more informal incentives to convey an image of Cambodia as an "ethical producer" of garments and textiles for the global market (Arnold and Shih 2010, 402).

Achievements of Better Factories Cambodia

Within mainstream discussions of global labour standards and Corporate Social Responsibility, BFC is generally reported as a success story. Based on an analysis of the synthesis reports, which BFC publishes half-annually, Sibbel and Borrmann, for example, conclude that "overall progress in improving working conditions is substantial and has been so right from the beginning" (2007, 242). Their quantitative indicator is the rising average rate of implementation of suggestions for improvements made by BFC to supplier factories, without specifying in which areas the suggested improvements have or have not been implemented. Other benefits for workers, for them, include training activities such as "a soap opera airing on national television aimed at educating workers on ways of solving disputes and their rights and responsibilities in conducting legal strikes" (Sibbel and Borrmann 2007, 243). This could, of course, also be inter-preted as a benefit for the employers, since it aims to reduce the number of wildcat strikes and other militant working class actions.

Other benefits for Cambodian employers include more orders and more buyers due to the ethical image of Cambodia's export garment industry created with the help of BFC. Furthermore, both local suppliers and international buyers can save money by reducing auditing and monitoring costs. Supplier factories do not have to deal with the monitoring requirements of multiple buyers anymore, but can rely exclusively on BFC's monitoring mechanism. International brands and retailers too can cut monitoring costs by signing up to BFC to replace their own auditing and monitoring programmes (Sibbel and Borrmann 2007, 244). Jeroen Merk of the Clean Clothes Campaign (CCC) agrees that saving monitoring costs is one of the benefits of BFC for employers (2012, 8). He also agrees that BFC has benefitted workers through improved working conditions, although his examples are meagre: "Some [workers] noted evidence of improvements after (BFC) monitors visited their factory: a first aid kit was installed, doors were opened and the toilets were cleaned" (Merk 2012, 11). In his report for the CCC and the Community Legal Education Centre, Merk also discusses the limitations of BFC.

Limitations of Better Factories Cambodia

Whereas some improvements of working conditions have been recorded, especially in the area of occupational safety and health, Merk notes that BFC's impact on less visible issues such as freedom of association and the right to collective bargaining has been limited (2012, 12). He explains that "even if labour rights organisations generally consider the BFC as a positive development, it is a sad fact that working conditions in Cambodia remain highly inadequate" (Merk 2012, 15).

The first area of concern is the lack of enforcement powers on the side of BFC. Whereas "enforcing the labour law is not the mandate of BFC" (ibid.), trade unions and labour NGOs do inform BFC about labour right violations such as unfair dismissals of unionists and activists hoping for their assistance in addressing them. One labour organisation has explained that they would "no longer inform the BFC because it can't do anything" (ibid.). This connects to the second area of concern, namely freedom of association. Even Sibbel and Borrmann, otherwise rather silent on the downsides of BFC, admit that freedom of association "remains a serious issue" (2007, 242). Union leaders and members continue to be harassed or unfairly dismissed. The establishment and the activities of independent workplace unions continue to be obstructed by management. Merk notes an interesting analogy to the Indonesian problem of "yellow unions":

"There are a number of pro-business or corrupt unions that compete with the independent unions for representation in the factories. One union leader argues that wherever 'GMAC [Garment Manufacturers' Association in Cambodia] factories have poor conditions, this is because the union in that factory is organised by the employer so the ILO is unable to get a sense of the realistic conditions in the factory'" (2012, 16).

Union busting against independent trade unions remains a major problem. After a massive three-day strike for higher minimum wages in September 2010, hundreds of union activists have been unfairly dismissed. Even worse, "retaliation has become a hallmark of labour-management relations in Cambodia and includes the assassination of union leaders" (Merk 2012, 18). These murders, far beyond the realm of mere labour right violations, go unnoticed in BFC's synthesis reports (Hughes 2007, 846).

Other limitations of BFC include the limited scope of its monitoring activities. BFC, much like the CoCs of TNCs themselves, only addresses Tier 1 factories with direct contract relationships to transnational buyers; i.e. it replicates the limitations of other instruments of global labour regulation in that it does not have the capacity to effect change in actual labour practices further down the supply chain (Ferenschild 2011). Home workers remain below the waterline and thus invisible to BFC. Sub-contracted factories and factories that do not produce for export are not covered (Merk 2012, 19).

Whereas BFC claims that workers and their unions are included in all aspects of its operations, it gives access to its factory reports only to management. Unions are thus unable to keep track of their grievances and how they are addressed, if at all. Merk suggests that "workers should be at the centre of the process, which requires full access to auditing results [increasing] worker control over the very programs that focus on improving working conditions" (2012, 20). The question remains, however, whether putting workers at the centre and in control of BFC is compatible with its organisational structure and purpose, which is more geared towards the interests of Cambodia's export garment industry than to those of the workers toiling within it.

BFC is also not dissimilar to other, more private forms of labour regulation in that it places the brunt of the responsibility for respecting labour rights on the supplier factories. Buyer brands and retailers are shifting their responsibility onto suppliers without substantially changing sourcing practices or paying higher prices that would in turn allow better conditions or higher wages. Falling prices and shorter lead times continue to apply downward pressure on conditions and wages (Merk 2012, 23). Arnold and Shih, who have interviewed the GMAC representative Ken Loo, put it this way:

"At the end of the day, Loo concludes, buyers do not pay more for high labour compliance; it is a pass/fail system and a cost that suppliers must bear. In other words, buyers may require labour compliance but the cost of implementation is generally passed on to suppliers" (2010, 420).

Another important weakness of BFC is its failure to address the issues of excessive overtime and living wages. Cambodian garment workers continue to work for 70 hours a week or more (Merk 2012, 25). The BFC synthesis reports claim that overtime is mostly voluntary, but in a context, where the minimum wage is far below subsistence level, accepting overtime voluntarily to make ends meet comes close to forced overtime. BFC only measures whether a factory complies with Cambodia's minimum wage regulations, not whether the minimum wage is sufficient to support a decent living standard of workers and their families. What is more, real wages have actually declined 14 per cent between 2000 and 2012: "In other words, garment workers have become poorer since the BFC was launched" (ibid.). In contrast, between 1996 and 2001, which was a period of labour militancy, spontaneous mass demonstrations and wildcat strikes, large wage increases were won through hard struggle (Hughes 2007, 844).

These more confrontational union strategies were thus more successful from a labour perspective than the "social dialogue" strategies promoted by BFC.

Given these serious limitations of BFC, Arnold and Shih conclude that "categorisations of Cambodia as a 'success story' for a fair or more equitable globalisation are premature" (2010, 419). Caroline Hughes goes further in arguing that in a context of surging mass demonstrations and militant strikes, it was the strategy of the ILO "to replace public collective action with demobilizing and regimenting forms of participation by isolated representatives of the movement in negotiations with powerful political actors behind closed doors" (2007, 843). She explains that BFC has had a threefold effect. It served to delegitimise spontaneous mass mobilisations and defuse militancy, weaken independent unions vis-à-vis their government- or employer-sponsored competitors and pre-empt more autonomous forms of local organising and transnational networking for support and solidarity (Hughes 2007, 844–845). Setting up an extensive system of monitoring and reporting has failed to raise wages or substantially improve working conditions, but it has succeeded in deflecting, displacing or pre-empting militant labour activism and autonomous labour organising. BFC is thus a very different "success story" than the one that is officially circulated.

The BFC case has clearly shown that there is a contradiction or at least tension spanning the relationship between international competitiveness and working conditions. The goal of improving competitiveness of an export industry capitalising on low wages as the main "competitive advantage" effectively rules out raising wages substantially, while this would improve poor working conditions considerably. Christopherson and Lillie (2005), looking at the sourcing practices and CoCs of Wal-Mart and Ikea, argue that low-cost business models based on extensive subcontracting networks of competing suppliers generally contradict the need of TNCs to depict their business practices as ethical. Against this backdrop, let us now consider how Better Work Indonesia (BWI) aims to simultaneously improve international competitiveness and working conditions in Indonesia's garment industry.

6.1.2 Better Work Indonesia

Given the purported success of BFC, the programme was expanded to other countries under the new name *Better Work*. The first round of expanding Better Work included Jordan in 2008 and Haiti and Vietnam in 2009. Lesotho followed in 2010. Better Work became operational in Indonesia and Nicaragua in 2011. Bangladesh is the most recent expansion of Better Work in 2014 (http://betterwork.org/global/?page_id=300).

The set-up of BWI

In its synthesis reports, BWI states that it "aims to enhance enterprise-level performance and promote competitiveness of the garment industry by improving compliance with Indonesian labour law and ILO core labour standards in garment factories" (BWI 2012, 5). The two goals of promoting competitiveness and improving compliance are here brought into a hierarchy. Promoting competitiveness is the end and improving compliance is the means towards that end, rather than an end in itself. The relationship between the two is conceptualised as mutually reinforcing, rather than contradictory. I argue that this imaginary only works when contentious issues such as living wages are excluded from the range of labour standards under assessment. Raising wages substantially would undermine the competitiveness of a labour-intensive industry where low wages are the main competitive advantage.

Other than BFC, BWI has been completely voluntary from the outset since no quota incentives existed as in TATA. Indonesian factories to participate in the programme are initially suggested by transnational buyers who see the benefits of replacing their own auditing and monitoring programmes with BWI. It is, however, a voluntary exercise for the factory to sign up. Voluntariness is a cornerstone of the programme. Factories will not be penalised for violations of labour rights to push them into better compliance. Especially, brands are not allowed to end contracts with suppliers due to labour right violations except for so called "zero tolerance issues" like child or forced labour. The approach adopted by BWI is, thus, a "proactive approach" as opposed to a "penalty approach" (ILO Interview, November 2011) to effect change in the workplace. Christopherson and Lillie (2005, 1935) argue that the former is more likely to improve conditions than the latter since suppliers are given the chance to implement improvements over time,[12] instead of contracts getting cancelled and jobs being lost. The contradiction between low-cost sourcing and ethical production however remains.

BWI is working closely with the employers' association (APINDO) to convince factory owners and managers of the "business case" for decent work. One ILO respondent put it as follows:

"The expectation or hypothesis is, if we help work with factories to address issues within the workplace, proactively, then they will automatically see the benefits and improve conditions" (ILO Interview, November 2011).

Benefits for Indonesian garment factories—often South Korean-owned—are primarily seen in helping them securing contract relationships with international buyers such as major sports brands like Nike and Adidas. The demands by these buyers to comply with their respective CoC or CSR policy, thus, are the main motivation for the employers to participate in BWI, rather than workers' demands for better working conditions articulated by a strong union presence in the factory.

BWI provides a "service" to the factories wanting to participate by assessing them against a number of criteria derived from Indonesian labour law and international labour standards. The first set of criteria is based on the ILO's core labour standards—child labour, forced labour, discrimination and freedom of association and collective bargaining. The second set is based on national labour law and comprises contracting and human resource management, occupational safety and health, working time and wages (BWI 2012, 6). BWI then offers technical cooperation to help the factories addressing the issues that were found. BWI develops a baseline against which future progress will be measured through these assessments. Advisors working for BWI help setting up employer-employee committees in order to facilitate "social dialogue" within factories and identify workplace issues in need of improvement. Management and management-worker committees will be informed about the findings of the assessments and BWI helps employers and employees working together to improve working conditions.

---

12 Christopherson and Lillie use the terms "strict liability" approach for what the ILO officer has called the "penalty approach" and "social connection" model of liability for the "proacticve approach", drawing on Brown (cited in Christopherson and Lillie 2005, 1935).

Over a 12 to 24 months period, BWI will then produce a number of progress reports on the identified issues. These reports are the property of the supplier factory's management and they decide which buyers or brands they want to show it. Individual factory reports are not disclosed publicly or shared with the unions in that factory. They remain the property of the factory under assessment. They are thus a tool for suppliers to demonstrate to transnational buyers that they comply with national and international labour standards, to present themselves as ethical producers. Factories also remain anonymous in the public synthesis reports issued twice a year, so as to not discourage factories from participating. However, this also means that neither progress reports nor synthesis reports can become viable tools for workers and activists to publicly scandalise abuses and violations by naming-and-shaming tactics.

The actors involved in BWI

The main actors of BWI include its nine team members located at the ILO Jakarta office, the Ministry of Manpower and Transmigration, the Indonesian Employers' Association (APINDO), Indonesian garment industry employers organised in the Indonesian Textile Association, Korean garment industry employers organised in the Korean Garment Association, as well as the four officially recognised trade union federations of the garment industry: GARTEKS from KSBSI, TSK-Kalibata and TSK-Pasar Minggu from the two branches of KSPSI and SPN from KSPI (BWI 2012, 5). Other unions with considerable numbers of members in the garment industry such as GSBI-SBGTS or KASBI but without official government recognition are excluded from BWI. This is, of course, a problem with respect to freedom of association. Trade unions that are known to be employer-friendly or government-sponsored can benefit from BWI's training and capacity building exercises, while more genuinely democratic and independent unions cannot. In CPE terms, BWI thus plays an active role in the *selection* and *retention* of the former's imaginaries and practices at the expense of the latter's.

Looking at the BWI team working at the ILO Jakarta office, the set-up of the personnel confirms that the programme primarily addresses businesses to help them demonstrate ethically sound production practices to international buyers rather than addressing workers and their organisations to help them struggle for better working conditions. Out of the nine

BWI officers, six are "enterprise advisers" primarily working with factory owners and managers, one is a "knowledge management officer" working with the media, one is an administrative assistant and one is the programme manager (http://betterwork.org/indonesia/?page_id=49). Out of the six enterprise advisers, none is primarily working with the trade unions and none has a trade union background. They have all worked in compliance, quality or human resources management for private corporations or for other international organisations before joining BWI. Their expertise thus prioritises the employer's perspective at the expense of the workers' perspective. The only exception is the knowledge management officer who was working for the development NGO Oxfam UK (ibid.) before joining BWI.

From the unions involved in BWI, I was able to interview two leading figures from GARTEKS and SPN on the national level to investigate their perspective on and experience with BWI. Unlike SPN, GARTEKS was also helpful in conducting two group discussions with members from the factory level, but these factories did not (yet) register with BWI, so they cannot be used in the analysis of BWI. TSK-Kalibata and TSK-Pasar Minggu were unfortunately not available for interviews. Also, I was not able to get access to the factory level via the ILO Jakarta office. The following analysis of unions' perceptions of BWI is thus based on two expert interviews with national-level union leaders, complemented by document analysis of synthesis reports and academic papers.

BWI from the unions' perspective

When I met one of the leaders of GARTEKS, in early January 2012, BWI had just started operating and had already conducted a number of factory assessments. The GARTEKS leader was aware of BWI's existence, but criticised the lack of active trade union involvement in its initial set-up:

"It's a great pity, I think, because the ILO has invited us many times and suddenly they're making an evaluation of the factories, but I don't know what's happening in the field. […] The ILO said they will give us information. […] But then, when they make an assessment in the factory, the ILO didn't involve the unions" (Union Interview, January 2012).

Although this account was recorded during an early stage of BWI's implementation, it gives insight into BWI's general approach. Trade unions play no active role in setting the agenda of or suggesting factories for registration with BWI or conducting factory assessments. Rather, BWI approaches trade unions after the programme has been set up and started operations. Trade unions, at least the more moderate and business-friendly unions are included in BWI, but their role is a passive one. Active agency is granted primarily to transnational buyer companies, suggesting their supplier factories for participation in the programme and to local supplier companies, voluntarily participating if they see the benefits of a monitoring project under the auspices of the ILO. Rather than working with the workers and the unions to establish their local priorities with regard to working conditions and empower them to address them from the bottom up, BWI's approach is top-down, working with the employers to help them demonstrate compliance with pre-set minimum labour standards. Workers and their experiences on the ground are employed as passive information providers during assessments, but as in the example of BFC, they are unable to actively track their grievances and assess how they have or have not been responded to. The GARTEKS leader continued to explain:

"As long as the ILO doesn't involve the unions, this is useless. […] Better Work is only a project of the ILO. We are only involved for submitting information. The ILO never asked us to be directly involved in the assessment of the companies. […] The ILO will make all look perfect, the contribution and cooperation with the unions, the findings based on our information, but the ILO decides about everything with this project" (Union Interview, January 2012).

The interviewed SPN officer sees BWI as a project that is generally "good enough", but they too raise concerns about the involvement of their federation. Apparently, the ILO had invited different SPN members on different occasions such as information or evaluation workshops without the clear authorisation of the federation. SPN argued that they need a permanent member on the BWI team who understands fully the details of the project, but "if they're changing the team every time, it will be useless" (Union Interview, January 2012).

This may be interpreted as a technical problem or as a problem in communication, but it nevertheless confirms that the initiative in BWI is with the ILO and the employers rather than the workers and the unions. Both union federations regard BWI as "useless", unless the unions and their members become more actively and more systematically involved.

BWI: decent work from above

BWI, as the first major monitoring project of the ILO in Indonesia, replaces private auditing and monitoring schemes in participating factories. It thus serves to reduce auditing costs for employers while improving the credibility of their codes of conduct and CSR mechanisms by linking them to the ILO system. It thereby ostensibly improves competitiveness and enhances productivity. The "business case" for participating in BWI can thus be made quite easily. Whether there is an independent workers' case for BWI, where labour rights are addressed as human rights rather than as export promotion, is harder to answer.

Although one of the purported goals of BWI is to improve the capacity of trade unions and the livelihoods of workers, the genuinely independent and democratic trade unions that have emerged since 1998 are not the main addressees of BWI. The driving force behind BWI is thus not so much realising labour rights as human rights or fulfilling workers' demands for better working conditions as it is the growing demand for social auditing and certification schemes within transnational supply chains and the trend towards "ethical capitalism" (Barry 2004) more broadly.

The track record of Better Work Indonesia is ambiguous. On the one hand, the working conditions in participating factories have been reported to improve over time, especially in the area of occupational safety and health. BWI staff reported that they mainly focus on the safety and health area, because "it enables both workers and managements to find solutions that benefit both parties" (ILO Interview, January 2012). Non-compliance issues in safety and health are quite easily detected by the monitors. In Indonesia, however, they are not as serious as, for example, in Bangladesh, where factories have burned down and buildings have collapsed, killing thousands of workers (Fink 2014). Less serious safety and health issues that were found in BWI's assessments include monitoring temperature in the factories or ensuring workers' access to clean drinking water.

BWI starts its advisory process with these issues that are relatively easy to address in order to establish cooperative relationships between workers and managements before moving into more complicated issues such as overtime, which require more robust discussions among the stakeholders. Child labour and forced labour reportedly do not pose significant problems in the factories participating in BWI. All BWI factories assessed at the time of research (January 2012) have been reported to provide the legal minimum wage, so wages do not seem to be a problem according to

BWI staff (ILO Interview, January 2012). Freedom of association, according to BWI staff, is a potential problem, but it was not found in the 15 factories they had already assessed at that time. Most factories that are registered with BWI have unions present at the shop floor. More detailed discussions about the problems with freedom of association beyond the mere existence vs. non-existence of an enterprise union have not been part of the factory assessments. Where no such committee exists, BWI will help setting up management-worker committees.

On the other hand, Better Work adopts a very *technical* understanding of labour rights and social standards that obscures some important *political* problems of decent work in Indonesia. For example, BWI assesses wages against the legal requirements only. Although being aware that the legal minimum wage is far below the level of a decent living wage, BWI "cannot force anyone to pay a living wage" (ILO Interview, January 2012). Assessing wages only against the legal minimum wage, however, is not sufficient to measure decent work as the minimum wage in most cases still is below subsistence level. Workers regularly have to take up consumer credits to fulfil their basic needs at the end of the month. Here, the limitation of the decent work agenda of not including "the right to earn a living wage—something that was included in Article 23 of the Universal Declaration of Human Rights" (Elias 2007, 52) is an obvious problem. The ILO has shied away from addressing the living wage issue as part of the decent work agenda, presumably because it is very controversial and likely to undermine the harmonious notion of "social dialogue" if it was pursued. Companies can only afford to pay wages below subsistence level, because they can rely on unpaid domestic, care and subsistence work, mostly performed by women. The lower the wage in the factory, the stronger is the compulsion to work extra hours on rice paddies, as street vendors and in kitchens. As long as decent work in general and Better Work in particular does not address this issue head-on, the positive effects for women's double shift are likely to be limited.

The first BWI baseline report issued by the ILO (2012b), states that more than 80 per cent of the workers in BWI factories show concern for their low wages. Even when the minimum wage is paid, the timely payment of wages, overtime pay and other issues make wages a critical topic to deal with. In its first synthesis report, BWI (2012, 10) found that 2 out of 20 assessed factories did not pay their workers the legal minimum wage (10 per cent) and 10 out of 20 did not pay the correct overtime rate (50 per cent). Half a year later, the second synthesis report (BWI 2013a, 11) finds 11 out of 35 factories in non-compliance with respect to the minimum wage (31 per cent) and 21 out of 35 with respect to overtime pay (60 per cent). These numbers went up again to 15 out of 40 assessed factories not paying the minimum wage (38 per cent) and 31 out of 40 not paying the correct overtime wage (78 per cent) in the third report (BWI 2013b, 12). In its latest synthesis report, BWI (2014, 12) found 25 out of 67 factories to be non-compliant with the minimum wage (37 per cent) and 50 out of 67 to be non-compliant with overtime payment (75 per cent). Even though the reports are organised in such a way that makes it impossible to track individual cases of non-compliance in terms of how they have evolved over time, the bare figures do not suggest that BWI has succeeded in raising the level of compliance with wage regulations substantially within the 3½ years of its existence. The fact that BWI does not address the wage question beyond a narrow assessment against the legal requirements may, thus, reflect the limits of its managerial, technocratic, top-down approach. The question of a living wage standard should be discussed more prominently in the context of decent work in general.

Taking the example of freedom of association, this has been reported by BWI staff not to be a problem in participating factories. All were said to comply with national legislation and international standards at the time of research. Nevertheless, the first synthesis report (BWI 2012, 10) found 5 out of 20 factories not allowing their workers to freely form or join unions (25 per cent) and 1 out of 20 discriminating against a particular union where two unions exist in the factory (5 per cent). The second report (BWI 2013a, 11) found 10 out of 35 factories non-compliant with freedom of association (29 per cent) and 2 out of 35 with non-discrimination against members of a particular union (6 per cent), one of which had already been reported in the first report. Again, the first number went up to 12 out of 40 (30 per cent) and the second remained almost constant (5 per cent) in the third report (BWI 2013b, 12). The latest numbers (BWI 2014, 12) indicate some progress with regard to freedom of association. 11 out of 67 factories do not allow their workers to freely form or join unions or interfere with their operations (16 per cent) and 4 out of 67 discriminate against a particular union (6 per cent).

Figure 7: Level of Non-Compliance with Selected Standards Reported by BWI

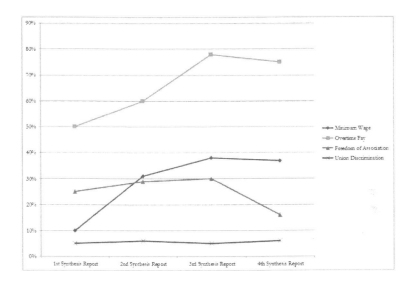

Source: author's compilation

However, primary interview data reveals a major flaw in a narrow measurement of freedom of association against legal requirements only. Indonesia may have ratified ILO conventions No. 87 and No. 98 concerning freedom of association and collective bargaining and translated them into national labour law (Law No. 21/2000 on trade unions), but the mere legal or technical application of this standard obscures the historical and political complexity of this issue in Indonesia, hampers its adequate political discussion and thus reduces political space for addressing it appropriately. A merely technical or legal assessment of freedom of association is not sufficient, because the mere existence of a workplace union does not say anything about the quality and capacity to effectively represent the workers' interests. It does not distinguish whether the union is a "yellow" or a genuinely democratic and independent union.

In many factories, there is more than one union. Employers can easily set up or foster employer-friendly unions and discriminate against progressive unions while claiming overall compliance. Better Work does not help addressing the issue of "union busting" against these newly emerging unions. Even worse, the so-called management-worker committees set up with support from BWI may be seen as competing parallel structures to the unions themselves. If there is an emerging progressive union in that factory, these committees may be used by employers to pre-empt or circumvent independent unionising attempts. Bipartite structures promoted by the ILO, aimed at improving social dialogue and contributing to "sound industrial relations" (ILO 2012a, 17), may thus serve to legitimise and foster employer-friendly union represent-atives while pre-empting or displacing more autonomous, progressive or radical forms of labour organising. This may actually undermine or disempower genuinely democratic and independent trade unions, marginalising their imaginaries, strategies and practices.

This highlights another problem to be considered more broadly in discussions around decent work: the issue of freedom of association in contexts where there are employer-dominated or state-led "yellow" unions has to be addressed more prominently, especially with respect to the question of how to democratically reform these unions and how to prevent discrimination against members of other unions. This question is highly relevant for other countries such as Cambodia and Vietnam as well and it will gain even more relevance for China in the coming years. The "transition from a system of state-led trade union monopoly" has been identified as a challenge to genuine freedom of association by the report of the ILO director-general on freedom of association in practice (ILO 2008b, 11), but it is not addressed in Indonesia's Decent Work Country Program (ILO 2012a).

The next case will show how Indonesian trade unions themselves have realised that effective freedom of association requires more than formal compliance with legal regulations and, supported by international NGOs, have negotiated a private protocol on freedom of association with major sports brands and sportswear producers that exceeds the Indonesian labour law.

6.2 The Play Fair Alliance

The Play Fair Alliance (PFA) is a global campaign coordinated by international trade union federations such as the International Textile,

Garment and Leather Workers' Federation (ITGLWF, today part of IndustriALL) and NGOs such as Oxfam or the Clean Clothes Campaign (CCC). It started campaigning for workers' rights and better working conditions in factories producing goods for major sports brands like Nike and Adidas in 2004, using the Athens Summer Olympics for raising public awareness of and mobilising consumer pressure against sweatshop conditions. The PFA has since organised campaigns around big sports events like the 2008 Beijing Olympics, the 2010 South Africa World Cup and the 2012 London Olympics (Merk 2011b, 9). Globally, it aims at improving working conditions in sportswear manufacturing as well as in infrastructure or stadium building through the main strategy of mobilising consumer pressure. At the same time, it aims at improving organising capacities of trade unions on the ground in order to empower them to struggle for better working conditions in their local contexts.

At first, the PFA lobbied global brands and the International Olympic Committee for industry-wide and cross-country solutions in the form of an international sectoral framework agreement between the global union ITGLWF and the global employers' association World Federation of Sporting Goods Industries. This attempt, however, failed due to resistance from the employers (Merk 2011b, 10). Consequently, the PFA shifted its attention from the global to the national scale. The alliance organised a three-day conference in Hong Kong in 2008 including major sports brands, trade unions and labour NGOs. At this conference, three main issues were identified that need to be addressed as a priority with respect to improving working conditions in the sportswear supply chain: wages, contracts and freedom of association. According to an interviewed unionist, Indonesia was chosen as a pilot country to find solutions on the national level, because "Indonesia's labour condition is known as more dynamic compared to other production countries" (Union Interview, January 2012). Siegmann, Merk and Knorringa (2014, 14), however, argue slightly differently that the reasons for Indonesia as a pilot country were its significant share in global sportswear production and the independence of its trade unions. They do not reflect on the diversity of Indonesian unions and the fact that only some of the Indonesian unions participating in the PFA are genuinely independent and democratic unions while others are formerly state-led "yellow unions" or in the hybrid space in between.

In November 2009, the first PFA workshop in Indonesia was conducted involving Nike, Adidas and other brands, the unions GSBI, SPN,

KASBI, TSK and GARTEKS, major supplier factories such as PT
Panarub and PT Nikomas, as well as representatives from the global PFA
including the ITGLWF, the CCC and Oxfam Australia. The unions had
held their own meeting previous to the workshop. During this meeting, the
unions discussed and agreed on their top priorities ahead of negotiations
with brands and suppliers. From the three main issues identified in Hong
Kong, the unions agreed that freedom of association should be addressed
as a priority, because without freedom of association "the labour unions
will not have power to fight for higher wages or better contracts" (Union
Interview, January 2012). Freedom of association and the right to collective
bargaining are foundational labour rights that enable unions to struggle for
other labour rights and better working conditions. At the November 2009
workshop, the unions and NGOs convinced brands and suppliers to first
start negotiations about a protocol on freedom of association before the
issues of wages and contracts could be addressed in separate protocols.

6.2.1 The Protocol on Freedom of Association

In Indonesia, NGOs involved in the PFA have successfully mediated a
process of discussion and negotiation among major trade unions, major
sports brands as well as major supplier factories that resulted in the signing
of a *Freedom of Association Protocol* (hereinafter FoA Protocol) by these
parties. They have recognised the need for a protocol that stipulates how
freedom of association can be implemented along supply chains in more
detail and beyond the general regulations in Indonesian labour law. This
protocol represents an impressive effort to improve freedom of association
through a private governance framework. The protocol not only stipulates
in more detail what employers must provide with respect to freedom of
association, it also envisages dispute settlement committees to be formed
by the three parties (Gardener 2012, 60). In the Indonesian context, where
there is lack of effective labour inspection, this may improve the situation
of trade unions, but it is not without contestation from labour activists
who believe this is actually the responsibility of public policy, not private
governance.

The FoA Protocol is the result of a careful balancing of the various
interests of the different parties. All agree on the need to improve freedom
of association, but all have their respective agenda and perspective. The
main effort of participating NGOs was to facilitate discussion not only

between brands, suppliers and unions, but first of all between the different unions with their different histories, ideologies and strategies. Although KSPSI initially even blocked the process, the PFA succeeded in convincing them to sign the protocol so as to give as many workplace unions as possible—including those affiliated with KSPSI—access to the instrument. Potentially, the protocol may reach and benefit thousands of workers in Indonesia's sportswear industry, provided that it is implemented as intended. As it is too early in the process to evaluate any outcomes, I want to focus on the substance and the process of the protocol in order to compare it with BWI in the last section of this chapter.

The substance of the protocol

A GSBI union leader has called the preamble "the soul of the protocol" (Union Interview, January 2012). The preamble states that freedom of association is a universal human right, that there are persistent issues with freedom of association in Indonesia and that "a commitment to uphold the right to freedom of association requires transparency and accountability between workers, suppliers and brands, which will in the long run be beneficial to all parties" (FoA Protocol, 1).

Chapter 1 of the protocol defines the parties and other elements as well as the scope of the protocol. It defines workers, unions, suppliers, brands, collective bargaining agreements (CBAs), company regulations and codes of conduct. It also defines the FoA Protocol as "legally binding for those who create it" (ibid., 2). The scope of the protocol is defined as covering Tier 1 factories only that have direct relationships with global brands. Subcontractors, however, shall be encouraged by the suppliers to implement the protocol as well. Thus, at least in its initial phase, the protocol provides support for workers to claim the right to freedom of association and collective bargaining only in those very visible world market factories that have signed the protocol. These are PT Nikomas, a large manufacturer producing shoes for Nike, Adidas and Puma (Siegmann et al. 2014, 15), PT Panarub, the infamous Adidas supplier factory that made it to the headlines globally due to reports about union busting that were circulated and politicised by international NGOs such as Oxfam in the early 2000s (Gardener 2012, 51), PT Tuntex (Nike and Adidas) and PT Adis (Adidas). These factories employ large numbers of mostly female workers and they have been targeted by international NGO campaigns repeatedly. They can also be pressured by brands to comply with core labour standards, because of their direct contract relationship, in contrast to their own sub-contractors. Although Siegmann, Merk and Knorringa argue that the protocol's coverage is wide due to the consolidation of the athletic footwear industry (2014, 15), they admit that the exclusion of Tier 2 factories further down the supply chain remains a serious limitation (2014, 20).

Chapter 2 specifies provisions for implementing freedom of association. Suppliers are obliged to ensure freedom to unionise, not to discriminate against particular unions, not to interfere with union activities, to release union representatives from their work duties for union activities and not to intimidate union leaders and members "in any form whatsoever" (FoA Protocol, 4). It also obliges suppliers to provide meeting space, communication facilities and company vehicles for unions. Trade unions are allowed to display their flags and a signboard to inform members about their activities. Unions are to be given an appropriate space or room within the company's premises. Union activities are to be supported and facilitated by suppliers. CBAs have to be produced "within a time frame of not more than six months after the formation of a union in accordance with applicable legal requirements" (ibid., 5).

Chapter 3 concerns issues of freedom of information so as to ensure the free distribution of information by unions. Chapter 4 specifies how the implementation of the protocol is to be supervised, how disputes are to be resolved and how sanctions may be applied in cases of violations. The parties commit to setting up FoA Protocol Supervision and Dispute Settlement Committees both at the company and the national level. At the time of research, the Standard Operational Procedure for these committees was just being negotiated: "Efforts should be made to resolve violations via consensus building deliberations" (FoA Protocol, 7). Only if these fail, can the matter be brought to the court.

The process behind the protocol

Before negotiations began, the first draft of the protocol was made by the unions themselves, because "the unions have the practice and the experience with union busting" (Union Interview, January 2012). Between November 2009 and June 2011, when the protocol was first signed by the parties, this draft was negotiated directly between unions, brands and suppliers, with NGOs playing a mediating and facilitating role. Adidas took on the leading role for the brands. In the middle of April 2010, negotiations reached a deadlock when suppliers disagreed with particular provisions suggested by the unions. This deadlock could only be broken through intense pressure applied locally by the unions organising demonstrations and globally by the NGOs campaigning with tactics of naming-and-shaming. Negotiations resumed in September 2010 and a deadline for the signing of the protocol was set at June 2011. When the parties met for a two-day meeting on 6 and 7 June 2011, the brands appeared to be willing to postpone the agreement on the first day for legal reasons. However, the "labour unions pressured the brands that, if they don't sign the agreement until June 7th, then there wouldn't be any kind of discussion on protocols anymore" (Union Interview, January 2012). Due to the twin pressure from the local and the global level, the parties finally agreed to sign the protocol on the second day.

Interviewees from human rights NGOs participating in Play Fair were careful to argue that they did not want to be seen as the process leaders although they acknowledged being important facilitators. The CCC, for instance, had experienced that international campaigns for labour solidarity can suffer from being perceived as driven by NGOs, which is what happened to the Asia Floor Wage campaign (see Chapter 3.6). For their conceptual understanding of the FoA Protocol process, it is important to view it as one driven and "owned" by the unions aiming at improving the power balance between workers and employers in the factories by locally applying global pressure. International NGOs utilise their publicity to build up consumer pressure on global brands. These are pushed to respond to these criticisms and most do in the form of voluntary codes of conduct and CSR policies that, in turn, are regularly criticised for failing to improve working conditions in supplier factories.[13] It is vital for sports brands to maintain a positive public image, which is why they increasingly feel the need to push suppliers to better comply with their CoC and/or with national law and international standards. Without this kind of pressure from brands on suppliers, Merk (2011b, 12) argues for instance, it would have been unlikely to convince the major suppliers to sign the FoA Protocol.

---

13 Christopherson and Lillie argue that employers "tend to regard labor rights as 'aspirational', to be implemented when and if they become 'economically sustainable'" (2005, 1922), that is, when and if they become profitable. This underscores the contradiction between low-cost sourcing and ethical production.

These interlinkages between global NGO campaigns and local labour struggles are a good example of what Keck and Sikkink (1998) call the "boomerang effect"—local actors looking beyond their local contexts, searching for allies on a global scale and building transnational networks in order to shift the local balances of power and improve their bargaining position. Most unionists interviewed agree that this kind of strategy is a vital step in regaining some leverage over global capital in times of increasingly transnational supply chains. For them, combining consumer pressure and NGO advocacy in the North with labour activism in the South is a necessary response to globalisation, because traditional worker representation and trade union politics are undermined by the global mobility of capital. Most are confident with their participation and voice in the process and see it as a useful exercise in finding common ground with other unions and overcoming old divisions. The importance of the FoA Protocol, according to one GSBI respondent, is the active involvement of the labour unions in the process of its production, whereas in previous voluntary initiatives such as CoCs and CSR only the brands and suppliers were actively involved (Union Interview, January 2012).

On the other hand, the GSBI unionist also explained that "there aren't any significant changes after the signing of the protocol compared to before" (Union Interview, January 2012). The main problems with freedom of association seem to persist despite the FoA Protocol. The reason given for this is the limited scope of the protocol. Whereas large Tier 1 manufacturers such as PT Nikomas and PT Panarub are covered by the protocol, their main Tier 2 subcontractors such as PT Glostar Indonesia or PT Framas are not. For GSBI, it is important that, if the protocol is to have a lasting impact, it must be implemented along the whole supply chain. These factories are interesting cases for the present study to shed light on the limitations of the FoA Protocol and the dilemma of freedom of association more widely.

6.2.2 The Dilemma of Freedom of Association

PT Panarub is one of the major Tier 1 supplier factories producing footwear for Adidas. It is located in Tangerang, an industrial city forming part of the Greater Jakarta Area called Jabodetabek (Jakarta, Bogor, Depok, Tangerang, Bekasi). As of January 2012, the factory employed a total workforce of 11,300 workers with 75 per cent women. At the time of research, there were three unions present on the factory level. SPN claimed some 6,000 members; SBGTS had 3,800 members and a re-established SPSI workplace union had split-off from SPN with less than 100 members (Worker Group Discussion, January 2012).

PT Panarub had already made it to the international headlines in 2001 when the independent union organiser Ngadinah Binti Abu Mawardi was arrested after organising a strike at PT Panarub over issues such as overtime pay, menstrual leave and meal allowances (Gardener 2012, 51). Ngadinah was one of the leaders of the local PERBUPAS union that would later become part of SBGTS. The majority union SPN in that factory is a direct successor of the Suharto-era SPSI workplace unit (Ford 2013, 230). Ngadinah's arrest alarmed labour rights activists around the globe when it was publicly scandalised by NGOs such as Oxfam and the CCC as well as the ITGLWF. Adidas was pressured to take on their responsibility for ensuring freedom of association in their supplier factory. Observed by international NGOs, the charges against Ngadinah were eventually dropped and she had to be reinstated. After Ngadinah had been reinstated, she was transferred from the production line to the human resources department against her wish so as to stop her from organising union activities on the shop floor (Kühl 2006, 196).

PT Panarub has been under international observation ever since. PERBUPAS and later SBGTS had already good relationships with the CCC, which was helpful in making the case public. As a result of local labour struggles supported by international solidarity campaigns, working conditions in that factory have improved in some important ways. For example, as of January 2012, there were only permanent workers employed in the core business, the production of shoes, making it compliant with Indonesian labour law in this regard. Nevertheless, problems remain, especially with freedom of association. In 2005, 33 SBGTS leaders were fired after a one-day strike, again prompting an international solidarity campaign for their reinstatement (Gardener 2012, 58). Today, PT Panarub is party to the protocol on freedom of association.

Although it is too early to make final judgments, the right to freedom of association, collective bargaining and especially the right to strike seem to continue to be denied or undermined by management and "yellow" unions after the signing of the FoA Protocol. Management continues to discriminate against SBGTS in favour of SPN, intimidate workers wishing to join SBGTS and push them to join SPN instead. One of the SBGTS leaders, for example, has been offered a 120,000,000 Rupiah (about 9,000 US Dollar) bribe to leave the union. SBGTS members receive "warning letters" from management. The SPN leadership, in turn, prohibit their members to participate in demonstrations that are being organised by other unions at the end of each year at the occasion of minimum wage negotiations. SBGTS members, therefore, continue to see the SPN and SPSI units in their factory as "yellow unions". At the time of research, PT Panarub workers organised in SBGTS reported that the FoA Protocol had brought about "only little to none progress" (Worker Group Discussion, January 2012). As this was only seven months after the signing of the protocol and it had not yet been incorporated into the CBA, they still hoped that improvements could be achieved in the long run.

The limitations of the FoA Protocol

During negotiations about the protocol, participants deliberately ignored the differences and conflicts between authoritarian, reformed, progressive and radical trade unions. Setting aside inter-union conflict was necessary to facilitate dialogue among them and reaching a consensus about the protocol. Confronting this sensitive issue possibly would have precluded an agreement. The protocol potentially empowers independent unions if implemented into CBAs and respected on the shop floor. This strategy, however, is risky, because it also empowers "yellow" unions and adds to their legitimacy vis-à-vis the workers. Treating non-equals equally reproduces their inequality. The FoA Protocol does not specifically support independent unions to address the particular problems with freedom of association and union busting they experience on a daily basis. Rather, it supports all the unions from the left to the right end of the spectrum without any differentiation. It therefore glosses over the contradictions inherent in Indonesia's fragmented labour movement rather than helping to overcome them.

Siegmann, Merk and Knorringa's overly optimistic argument, thus, has to be qualified. They argue that the "Indonesian union movement's internal fissures were bridged through joint engagement in the international Play Fair campaign" and that "the labour movement's internal divisions [were] overcome" (2014, 16). Although it is true that there is more collaboration between the different unions, especially on the local level, evidence from my own research suggests that the internal divisions were *not* actually overcome in practice, but only rhetorically. KASBI trade unionists have argued that SPN and SPSI continue to be "yellow" unions, at least on the level of national leadership. For them, signing the protocol is not evidence of divisions already overcome, but a "tactic" (Union Interview, February 2012) that may help them organising plant-level unions *against* their management-sponsored rivals at SPN and SPSI. Harmony and unity among the different unions in Indonesia is thus part of the PFA's economic and political *imaginary*, rather than a material outcome of the negotiating process. Ideological and political differences, personal animosities and power struggles, suspicion and distrust between Indonesian trade unions on the national level continue to render this imaginary's prospects for translation into material practice rather remote. I argue below that the PFA's intervention into labour politics in Indonesia has in some ways even contributed to *new* divisions within the trade union movement.

Another limitation of the protocol has already been mentioned: it only covers the big Tier 1 factories. An episode from PT Nikomas and one of their subcontractors may help to understand that the situation of freedom of association in these factories is in great need of substantial improvement, but the situation further down the supply chain is even worse. At PT Nikomas, a large Taiwanese-owned supplier factory for Nike, around 4,500 workers had been forced to work overtime for two hours a day, six days a week. This forced overtime had not been paid as required by law. The enterprise majority union at PT Nikomas is affiliated with SPN, but workers found it hard to pursue their interests through SPN. Reportedly, the local SPN leadership at that time was close to management and they simply denied the allegations of unpaid overtime (NGO Interview, December 2011). SPN members regularly consulted GSBI instead of their own national federation (Union Interview, January 2012) and they sought international support by the US labour NGO *Educating for Justice*, run by former US athlete Jim Keady (Jakarta Globe, 12 January 2012). Keady lobbied Nike, the Taiwanese owner of PT Nikomas and the factory's management itself for several months. In January 2012, an agreement was reached that nearly 1 million US Dollar worth of overtime pay will be distributed to the workers. Although SPN attributed this victory to their own activities, interview respondents from other unions argued that it was largely due to the international pressure mounted by Jim Keady's solidarity campaign (Union Interviews, January 2012). Initially, SPN denied the allegations and blocked the complaint process. During the process, however, the leadership of SPN in the factory was replaced and rank and file members sought to transform their union into a genuine body representing their interests. This shows that there are sometimes big gaps between the leadership of "yellow" unions and their members and that struggles are underway within them to transform them into genuine unions. These intra-union struggles for more intra-union democracy have important implications for freedom of association, but the FoA Protocol does not in any way support or even mention them.

PT Glostar is another example of "yellow" unionism. It is a Tier 2 subcontractor for PT Nikomas. On 14 July 2011, Associated Press reported that workers from PT Glostar "say supervisors throw shoes at them, slap them in the face and call them dogs and pigs". They had interviewed dozens of workers and recorded testimonies of labour rights abuses that were thought to have vanished since the late Suharto-era. Outright violence against workers is generally said to be a thing of the past in Indonesia. This was also the enterprise union leader's opinion: "As far as I'm concerned, we haven't seen such abuses for a long time now", he said (Jakarta Globe, 21 July 2011). The plant-level union at PT Glostar is affiliated with SPSI-TSK. Their denial of the allegations made it hard for workers to air their grievances and seek redress. Evidence from interviews suggests that such cases are not exceptional. They occur seldom in the big Tier 1 factories that are regularly being monitored and audited, but more regularly further down the supply chain where labour right violations are less visible (NGO Interviews, December 2011).

Another example can be taken from PT Framas, another Tier 2 factory that is located one step down the supply chain and thus less visible to transnational NGO networks and less likely to draw attention from brands fearing for their reputation. It is a supplier factory for PT Nikomas and PT Panarub, producing the outsoles for Nike and Adidas sports shoes. Whereas PT Panarub has eliminated contract workers from their core business, 470 out of 850 workers at PT Framas are employed on a temporary contract. Some workers have not seen a contract at all. There is a minority SBGTS union with 70 members in that factory affiliated with GSBI. The majority union affiliated with SPSI has about 700 members (Worker Group Discussion, January 2012). SBGTS members continue to face a whole range of union busting strategies by management. Union organisers on the production lines have been moved to other segments such as cleaning services in order to undermine their unionising activities.

The SPSI unit at PT Framas is seen as a "yellow union" siding with the employers against their independent rivals at SBGTS. New workers hired by that factory have been registered with SPSI without their consent. Management refuses to negotiate with SBGTS and, together with SPSI, continues to discriminate against the leaders and members of SBGTS. There is a strong sense of being disempowered among SBGTS members at PT Framas due to their limited organisational power and the stiff competition provided by SPSI. They have expressed hope that signing the FoA Protocol could change their situation (Worker Group Discussion, January 2012). The protocol stipulates that all unions present in a factory have the right to be included in bipartite negotiations, provided office space and not being interfered with by management. This could improve SBGTS's capacity for organising considerably. Unfortunately, the protocol only vaguely incorporates the prospect for extending the scope of the protocol further down the supply chain. Most unionists interviewed tend to be sceptical about these prospects, arguing that it will very hard to convince subcontractors to sign, because they cannot be pressured by brands or targeted by transnational NGO networks to the same extent as Tier 1 suppliers can. Lacking institutionalised forms of international solidarity from which they can draw resources and support, the local power base of these unions becomes all the more important.

Bianca Kühl argues that the boomerang effect applied through transnational networking played the key role in cases such as Ngadinah's arrest at PT Panarub and "so far no alternative to it seems to be available" (2006, 222). While she may have slightly overstated the role of Western NGO networks and underestimated the importance of the unions' local power base, the case of PT Nikomas shows that transnational boomeranging can have positive effects on the local balance of power. At PT Glostar and PT Framas, where such transnational strategies were less available, progress on labour rights and working conditions is much harder to achieve. It constitutes a major limitation of the FoA Protocol that it initially only targets Tier 1 factories, where some progress has already been achieved through local struggles with international support, but falls short of improving freedom of association further down the supply chain where it would be needed the most.

More protocols to come?

It has been noted that the PFA identified freedom of association, wages and contracts as the three priority issues to be addressed in three separate protocols. The FoA Protocol was thus the first attempt to create a voluntary, yet binding agreement among stakeholders in Indonesia's sportswear industry that, if signed and implemented, should prepare the ground for negotiations about additional protocols on short-term contracts and living wages. Whereas the concrete measures stipulated in the FoA Protocol such as office space and signboards for enterprise unions are relatively cheap, banning short-term contracts and providing living wages could be very costly. What do the activists involved in the negotiation of the FoA Protocol think about the prospects of the remaining protocols?

Most interview respondents were cautiously optimistic with respect to contracts, but rather pessimistic with regard to wages. For the NGOs, the experience with drafting and negotiating the FoA Protocol was generally very positive. They expected that negotiations about temporary contracts should not be too difficult since major brands such as Nike and Adidas already had committed to permanent contracts in their supplier factories. We have seen that PT Panarub, for example, already employs permanent workers only in the core business. If the protocol on contracts, provided it will be negotiated and signed at all, will also address these large Tier 1 factories only, it may be relatively easy to reach a consensus, but the effects for limiting short-term contracts further down the supply chain will be little to none. They may even be negative if the potential protocol will lead to additional subcontracting and outsourcing of parts of the production process. If the protocol will address Tier 2 and 3 factories to the same extent as Tier 1, its potential effects will be much more substantial for precarious workers, but negotiating and reaching a consensus will be much harder. This is one of the dilemmas of consensus-oriented strategies, acknowledged by Oxfam, for example:

"Actually, we want to cover the whole supply chain down to home workers. When you look at the problems of the subcontractors down to home workers, the conditions are much worse than in Tier 1 factories. The problems are in there, not so much in Tier 1 but, as you know, negotiations must give and take, so this is a compromise" (NGO Interview, December 2011).

Wages, on the other hand, are expected to be the most challenging issue by all parties. One of the reasons is that the methodology for calculating a decent living wage is highly contested as can be seen in the debates around the different concepts of the KHL, the UMP/UMK, the AFW proposal and other proposals suggested by Indonesian unions themselves such as the National Decent Wage (ULN, see Chapter 7.1). The main reason behind these technical difficulties, however, is the fundamental contradiction between capital and labour encapsulated in the wage form and the antagonistic interests of employers and workers. A representative of Adidas explained that they are willing "to see whether or not we can come up with an agreement, but the positions are very far opposite" (Brand Interview, January 2012). NGOs and trade unions expressed a similar scepticism towards the feasibility of a future protocol on living wages.

Living in a dream?

It is interesting to note that Jeroen Merk of the CCC, who was personally involved in the PFA and the events leading up to the signing of the FoA Protocol (Gardener 2012, 54), argues that the protocol addresses a situation, where "workers' struggles often escalate before even an attempt at finding a resolution can be mounted" (Siegmann et al. 2014, 13). In the context of labour militancy in Indonesia, he argues that the protocol "allows actors in the athletic footwear industry in Indonesia to move from a situation of confrontation to one that has the potential to catalyse cooperation" (ibid., 19). While improving freedom of association is the main goal of the FoA Protocol, there seems to be another aspect that is less openly articulated: pacifying the labour movement. This is also the reason why Adidas, the only brand that was available for an interview, decided to support the PFA. They hope that through the signing of the FoA Protocol, there will be fewer industrial actions (Brand Interview, January 2012). Here, we see the dilemma of freedom of association:

"Historically, unions when integrated into the industrial relations machinery of the state have, in most instances, proven to be effective organisations for institutionalising and therefore placing acceptable limits upon working class action" (Lambert 1997, 95).

This form of institutionalisation and pacification, however, only works effectively when freedom of association and the right to collective bargaining are genuinely guaranteed. Otherwise, unions may be seen as illegitimate or not representative of workers' interests, leading to renewed labour unrest where a deal between employers, the state and "yellow" unions had already been struck, as was the case with the different minimum wage negotiations mentioned above. Granting genuine freedom of association to radical trade unions such as KASBI, however, potentially endangers business interests, at least in the minds of employers, because it would empower them and potentially give thrust to their explicit anti-capitalist and anti-imperialist agenda.

The FoA Protocol is the ideal solution to this dilemma. It simultaneously adds to the legitimacy of former state-led unions such as SPN and TSK and to the institutionalisation of progressive and radical unions such as GSBI and KASBI by incorporating both into an industrial relations system that, in contrast to Lambert's argument, is private and voluntary in nature. This raises several questions: What is the main effect of the PFA and the protocol? Is it helping workers to exercise their right to freedom of association and collective bargaining? Or is it helping employers to curb labour unrest and militancy? If both effects are sought by the NGOs facilitating the FoA Protocol process, their idea is a win-win-situation, in this regard not dissimilar to BWI. The problem with this idea, however, is that it glosses over the huge power imbalance between capital and labour in Indonesia, invokes the illusion of a level playing field, while silencing voices that hold on to the importance of adversarial bargaining and industrial action.[14] One activist had a nice way of putting this:

"They want to establish a harmonious relationship based on partnership between unions and employers. That requires first an equal position. With a big gap between unions and employers, you cannot negotiate. They live in a dream. They think they are already equal and they want to negotiate. If you really look at the genuine union leaders, it doesn't mean that they don't want to negotiate, they do want to negotiate after their position is better, at least a smaller gap. We cannot live in a dream" (NGO Interview, December 2011).

Another activist criticised the idea of "social dialogue", which is part and parcel of the ILO's decent work agenda but also one of the strategies of multi-stakeholder initiatives such as the PFA. She argued that "social dialogue" relates to a situation where "everybody pretends to be happy, but actually there is no win-win-solution in that sense" (NGO Interview,

---

14 The economic imaginary of a harmonious relationship between capital and labour, brought about by social dialogue and partnership and enabling win-win-solutions, bears a noteworthy resemblance to the above-mentioned Pancasila Industrial Relations (see Chapter 5.2), glossing over the class antagonism of capitalism and displacing class conflict.

November 2011). Treating a situation of doubled power imbalances, both between capital and labour and between "yellow" and independent unions, as if there already was a level playing field, only serves to gloss over and thus reproduce these power imbalances. Treating a situation where confrontational and militant union strategies have the best chances of changing these power imbalances as if genuine dialogue was already possible, only works towards delegitimising the most promising union strategies. Therefore, the difference between an *imaginary* (or "dream" in the activist's terminology) of genuine dialogue on a level playing field and the actual material practice of such, as theoretically sensitised by CPE, is key to understanding the limitations of the FoA Protocol.

6.3 Decent Work from Above and Below

Having gone into some empirical detail in these concrete case studies, the next step of the CGT process takes these back to a higher level of abstraction in order to construct a critical grounded theory about decent work and alternative strategies in Indonesia. I start with comparing the two cases in terms of their associated economic imaginaries, their main actors, goals, strategies and practices, the type of trade union involvement as well as the general direction of their operations. This discussion is taken up in the next chapter and connected to a case study of recovered imaginaries beyond decent work.

Decent work from above

Better Work Indonesia, to recap, is a monitoring project of the ILO and the IFC targeting the Indonesian garment industry. It aims to "promote competitiveness of the garment industry by improving compliance with Indonesian labour law and ILO core labour standards in garment factories" (BWI 2012, 5) in the Jabodetabek area. Promoting competitiveness by improving compliance is presented as a win-win-solution to the problem of downward harmonisation of labour rights and social standards in the highly competitive environment of neoliberal globalisation. To this end, transnational buyers can suggest their supplier factories to sign up for BWI, but their participation is voluntary. Factories will then be assessed and their compliance reported on by BWI, identifying workplace issues in need of improvement such as occupational safety and health issues. Since individual factory reports remain the property of management and public synthesis reports only contain aggregated, anonymised data, I have argued that these reports are tools for supplier factories to demonstrate labour law compliance to transnational buyers, rather than viable tools for labour activists helping them to campaign against labour rights violations.

Looking at the actors involved in BWI, the inclusion of formerly government-sponsored "yellow" unions and the exclusion of more genuinely democratic and independent unions can be conceptualised as contributing to the *selection* and *retention* of moderate and business-friendly trade union strategies at the expense of other, more radical and militant strategies. Evidence from my own research revealed that even the unions involved in BWI criticise the lack of active trade union participation in setting up the project, suggesting factories or conducting assessments. Workers form part of the BWI structure, but their role is reduced to that of passive information providers, while companies' managements are addressed as the primary active agents of this programme. The main initiative in BWI is with the ILO and the employers rather than the workers and the unions.

BWI primarily addresses occupational safety and health issues since these are seen as providing an easy way towards win-win-solutions. Monitoring temperature, for example, can improve working conditions for workers while being relatively cheap for management. In Indonesia, however, these issues are relatively minor compared to countries such as Bangladesh. Other issues that were reported by trade unionists to be major, such as wages and freedom of association, are assessed against the legal requirements only, that is, against formal minimum standards obscuring some important political implications. For example, BWI assesses the payment of wages against the legal minimum wage only that, in most cases, is below the level of a decent living wage. Many participating companies, however, continue to fail to pay even this legal minimum wage. BWI also assesses freedom of association in terms of the mere existence of a workplace union without regard to it being a "yellow" or a genuinely democratic, independent union. Management-worker committees set up with support from BWI may even undermine or disempower genuinely democratic and independent unionising attempts.

We can conclude that the ILO's approach towards improving labour conditions in Indonesia's garment industry, in the case of Better Work Indonesia, is a (semi-)private top-down approach primarily driven by corporate needs. Global brands feel the need to improve the credibility of their codes of conduct and CSR policies, because purely private company codes have been criticised for failing to deliver on the promise of better working conditions. Public image is a core asset for these transnational corporations and so they are keen to reduce the risk of being targeted by naming-and-shaming campaigns by linking their CSR management to the ILO. Supplier factories likewise feel the need to credibly demonstrate to buyers that they comply with core labour standards in order to maintain orders and contracts. From the CPE perspective adopted for this study, BWI represents a *hegemonic "decent work from above" imaginary*. This hegemonic version of the decent work discourse is dominated by the ILO and transnational corporations, centres around Corporate Social Responsibility, primarily addresses the employers making the "business case" for decent work and foregrounds the technical language of compliance. Unions are involved but only as passive participants and information givers. The content of decent work here is limited to the core labour standards, thus only providing a minimum definition of decent work. It is closely linked to matters of productivity and competitiveness.

This mirrors one of the major tensions within the decent work agenda: From the perspective of competitiveness, higher wages, for example, may appear as detrimental to employment creation, whereas from the workers' perspective, increasing wages is the single most important step towards decent work. It also mirrors a fundamental problem in relation to the transnational supply chains in the global garment and textile industry, because it is highly questionable whether low-cost production can ever be made compatible with ethical labour standards, as Christopherson and Lillie (2005) point out. BWI excludes the contentious issue of living wages presumably because win-win-solutions are obviously very hard to find. The discourse of competitiveness is one of the hegemonic codes of neoliberal globalisation. Improving industry competitiveness by promoting compliance with minimum labour standard, therefore, serves to re-inforce the hegemony of neoliberalism. Better Work underpins a technical understanding of the problem of labour conditions and workers' rights and has a depoliticising effect on trade union strategies and activities or may even undermine the unions' capacities to organise autonomously and independently. It does not empower those suffering from the neoliberal development paradigm to effectively challenge its hegemony.

With regard to informal labour, I have argued that workers suffer from neoliberal production practices more, the further down the supply chain they are located. BWI, like BFC, only covers those Tier 1 factories that maintain direct contractual relationships to transnational buyers. Subcontractors and home workers remain below the waterline and are thus invisible to Better Work. It therefore lacks capacity to address sub-standard working conditions further down the supply chain, much like other instruments of soft-law labour regulation. Feminist hopes for the decent work agenda to progressively address informalised, feminised labour rest on its potential to re-regulate the informal economy. In the case of Better Work, understood as part of the decent work agenda, these hopes are frustrated since it only assesses Tier 1 factories and overlooks the rest of the supply chain down to the level of home workers, where working conditions are worst and the most vulnerable women workers are concentrated. Better Work, therefore, exemplifies the "business case" for decent work rather than materialising the feminist imaginary of decent work.

Decent work from below

The approach of the Play Fair Alliance, in contrast, is much more deliberative and bottom-up as it brings brands, suppliers and unions together to negotiate a protocol on freedom of association that is believed to benefit all three parties. Although the initial impulse came from outside—the global Play Fair campaign—the negotiation process was driven by local needs. After negotiations of an international framework agreement in the global sportswear sector failed, Indonesia was chosen as a pilot country for negotiating voluntary, yet binding protocols on freedom of association, wages and contracts on the national level.

The Indonesian unions themselves were actively involved and supposed to lead the process and set the agenda of this multi-stakeholder initiative. Unions' ownership was seen as vitally important by international NGOs involved in the PFA. These NGOs, however, played a facilitating and supporting role in the negotiations. When negotiations reached a deadlock, for example, they assisted the unions in applying global pressure locally, forcing the employers back to the table. The unions involved in negotiating the FoA Protocol mostly welcomed the facilitating role of international NGOs such as Oxfam. For them, combining global consumer campaigns of NGOs with local labour struggles of trade unions provides a useful way to apply the boomerang effect to the Indonesian context.

The role of international NGOs in the PFA, however, is seen by some other union activists as undue outside intervention that diminishes the self-organising capacities of trade unions. The participation of KASBI in "soft campaigns" like the PFA, facilitated by Oxfam Australia, was one factor contributing to its division and the emergence of KSN (see Chapter 7). The price of strengthening social dialogue among moderate trade unions has been weakening more radical, autonomous labour activism, because integration of left-wing unions into multi-stakeholder negotiations forces them to speak the appropriate language specific to that arena and adopt more moderate strategies. The societal context in Indonesia, however, has not changed the situation of trade unions substantially and the more militant strategies may continue to be more effective.

The participating unions, nevertheless, mostly appreciated the opportunity to establish new forms of communication and cooperation among the different union confederations that had hitherto positioned themselves in fierce competition to one another. On the one hand, the PFA has thus succeeded in fostering cooperation and discussion among different unions and NGOs and reduce fragmentation in a certain spectrum of the Indonesian trade union movement. Even though practical improvements on shop floors were not registered at the time of research, many unionists valued these new forms of inter-union communication as a positive effect of the negotiation process in its own right. I have also argued, however, that the PFA deliberately de-thematises the power imbalances and conflicts between formerly "yellow" and genuinely independent trade unions—a risky strategy that may serve to gloss over the contradictions inherent in Indonesia's trade union landscape rather than helping to actually overcome fragmentations and divisions.

On the other hand, unionists reported "only little to none progress" (Worker Group Discussion, January 2012) in actual practice after the signing of the FoA Protocol. The cases of PT Panarub and PT Nikomas showed that problems with freedom of association persist even in those large Tier 1 factories that had been in the spotlight of global consumer campaigns since the 1990s, now initially the exclusive targets of the FoA

Protocol. The cases of PT Glostar and PT Framas showed that problems with freedom of association become aggravated further down the supply chain. These Tier 2 factories are initially excluded from the scope of the protocol, but it is here where improvements would be needed the most since they are less visible to consumer campaigns and less likely to be targeted by global brands' CSR efforts. The boomerang effect is thus less easily applied and improvements are less likely to be achieved by transnational campaigns such as the PFA. The local power base of the unions themselves becomes even more important as a consequence. The initial focus of the protocol on large Tier 1 manufacturers, where working conditions have already been improved in some limited but significant ways due to global consumer pressure on brands and the exclusion of production sites further down the supply chain, where conditions still are worse, remain serious limitations of the FoA Protocol.

The other prospected protocols on short-term contracts and living wages, if they will be negotiated and signed at all, will most likely reproduce these limitations. In the worst case, this may lead to further subcontracting, because suppliers may seek ways to compensate for higher labour costs by outsourcing more parts of the production process. This, in turn, may produce even more informal and precarious labour, exacerbating the hardships of the most vulnerable women workers at the bottom end of supply chains. The most informalised workers will thus benefit the least from these protocols, questioning the progressive potential of the PFA in terms of the feminist imaginary of decent work.

I have argued that this is related to one of the paradoxes of consensus-oriented strategies. Consensus is much more likely to be achieved where a compromise does not hurt one of the parties considerably more than the other. In cases where a compromise would substantially prioritise some material interests over others, consensus will be much harder to achieve. This is also why the prospects for a voluntary, yet binding protocol on living wages appear rather remote. The fundamental contradiction between capital and labour remains in place despite the PFA's attempts to find win-win-solutions and channel labour conflicts into a private dispute settlement mechanism aiming to replace confrontation with cooperation. Confrontational and adversarial modes of bargaining, backed up by mass demonstrations and large-scale strikes, however continue to be most effective in terms of actually raising minimum wages, for example. The activist's quote from above that Indonesian workers "cannot live in a dream" (NGO

Interview, December 2011) of engaging in a genuine dialogue on a level playing field, when in reality huge power imbalances remain both between employers and unions and between formerly state-led and genuinely independent unions, is very instructive in this regard.

From this perspective, Play Fair represents a *sub-hegemonic "decent work from below" imaginary*. This sub-hegemonic version of the decent work discourse entails more than technical compliance with core labour standards and incorporates stronger political notions of workers' rights and may thus be seen as an alternative appropriation of the ILO discourse. It centres on the notion of fairness, addresses all stakeholders (employers, workers, civil society) and foregrounds social dialogue. The unions participating in this network are very diverse. Nevertheless, the more progressive and radical unions are being integrated into a private governance framework that aims at social dialogue and consensus building and, according to some participants, might have a de-politicising and de-radicalising effect on their strategies and activities in the long run. The dispute settlement committees aim to push unions away from confrontational strategies towards more "cooperative" such. Whether the latter will better serve the interests of marginalised workers than the former, raise poverty wages and end the short-term contract system, is at least doubtful.

Play Fair is conceptualised as "sub-hegemonic" (Sum 2005), because it changes the hegemonic codes of neoliberal labour regulation in some important ways, especially in stressing the importance of ownership and active participation of unions, but it is compatible with the gist of these codes and becomes absorbed by them. Like BWI, it is a private and voluntary initiative, it promotes moderate "social dialogue" strategies and it aims to create win-win-situations. Like BWI, it is initially limited to Tier 1 factories and lacks capacity to effectively improve working conditions further down the supply chain, not to speak of home workers. It thus also replicates BWI's frustration of feminist hopes regarding the progressive potential of "social dialogue" strategies towards decent work.

Unlike BWI, however, it was initiated by trade unions and international NGOs, rather than the ILO and global brands. Thus, there are some similarities between BWI and the PFA, but there are major differences as well. The most important difference is the type of trade union involvement and the operational direction. While BWI is very top-down in its structure and involves the unions only passively, the PFA is much more bottom-up and invites the unions to participate actively. The general thrust of the

PFA, however, aims to introduce more "fairness" into the global garment industry without challenging the fundamentals of neoliberal globalisation. It does not question Indonesia's accumulation regime of low-wage export production in any substantial sense and thus offers little prospect to effectively change the social situation of those marginalised women workers trapped within this regime. As a "flanking mechanism" (Graefe 2006), it therefore helps the hegemonic project of neoliberalism to adapt to societal pressures and flexibly reproduce its hegemony by absorbing alternative codes and thus strengthening the overall consensus in society.

Next, radical alternatives to decent work strategies are explored in terms of their associated actors, imaginaries and practices as well as their counter- and/or sub-hegemonic potential.

7. Recovered Imaginaries Beyond Decent Work

It is important to note that not all unions that are organising garment workers have been part of Play Fair and that part of the reason for their non-participation in the FoA Protocol process is the involvement of international NGOs such as Oxfam. KASBI, until recently the most radical trade union confederation in Indonesia, is in the process of gaining official recognition by the government, meaning that they will be able to participate in tripartite structures (such as the minimum wage committees) on the national, provincial and district/city levels. KASBI is known for staging militant protests and mass actions, seen as radical, progressive and vocal. Not social dialogue, but industrial action and mass mobilisation have been the cornerstones of their overall strategy. It is thus not surprising that discussions about KASBI's involvement in Play Fair have created tensions within the union that ultimately contributed to its division. A more radical fraction wanted to maintain autonomy and independence, rather than engaging in time-consuming negotiations with the employers and the "yellow" unions sponsored by them. They feared that transnational campaigns like Play Fair eventually will lead the unions to become more moderate and less radical, more focused on industrial relations in the narrow sense and less focused on larger political and social issues. This would depoliticise the unions and, thereby, weaken their capacities to effect democratic change not only in the workplace but also in Indonesian society more widely instead of strengthening them (Worker Group Discussion, February 2012). The scepticism of the more radical KASBI fraction towards the PFA can be interpreted as resisting the drive from "social movement unionism" to "business unionism" (Scipes 1992; Moody 1997; Waterman 2004).

Regardless of how one might judge this kind of position, I want to argue, it is important not to overlook or silence it when doing research on trade unions in Indonesia. In the case of Play Fair, KASBI's decision to participate has influenced the radical fraction to disaffiliate from the confederation and found a new one—KSN. The unions affiliated with KSN see more advantage in concentrating on organising mass mobilisations and militant protests and do not want to be "trapped in soft campaigns like Play Fair" (NGO Interview, January 2012). A lesson to be learned from this episode is that labour rights advocates have to reflect their role in the *selection* and *retention* of competing imaginaries. Although with good intentions, the "social dialogue" approach of the PFA in Indonesia was one factor that caused KASBI to split. The more moderate fractions maintained their affiliation with KASBI and joined the PFA, while the more radical fractions left KASBI and formed the new confederation KSN. This means that while the PFA has succeeded in facilitating dialogue between different unions and thus in reducing fragmentation among some trade unions at least around the issue of freedom of association, it has also created ruptures within the trade union movement and produced new fragmentations, de-radicalising and integrating certain fractions while weakening and excluding others. Play Fair has, thus, contributed to a specific discursive order organising the arena of labour conflicts in a certain way that improves social dialogue among moderate trade unions at the expense of more radical trade unions, whose confrontational strategies, discourses and practices are rendered irrational, irresponsible and unrealistic within that order of discourse, although they may continue to be most effective (as in the case of the minimum wage negotiations for 2012, see Chapter 5.4).

This chapter takes a closer look at these actors, who tend to be marginalised within the official decent work discourse and their imaginaries, strategies and practices.

7.1 The National Union Confederation

> *"Buruh berkuasa, rakyat sejahtera!* [With the workers in power, the people will be prosperous!]" (FSBKU members at the end of Worker Group Discussion, February 2012)

In 2007, the owner of the garment factory PT Istana in Northern Jakarta declared bankruptcy and announced the closure of the factory. This is very common in Indonesia's garment industry and usually it is a strategy to undermine the power of organised workers and cut labour costs. For example, the factory may be closed for several weeks or months, only to re-open under a new name with new workers who can be paid less as they are less senior, hired as contract instead of permanent workers and/or are not unionised. Indonesian labour law requires employers to pay severance pay in cases of factory closures. At PT Istana, however, management refused to pay severance pay, which is also very common in such cases. Whereas the usual way to seek redress would be to file a lengthy and costly law suit at the labour court, workers at PT Istana developed a double strategy of following the legal procedures while at the same time occupying the factory and continuing garment production under workers' control (Union Interview, December 2011).

There were about 1,000 workers employed at that garment factory, the vast majority of them women. The workplace union SBKU-Istana, member union of FSBKU (*Federasi Serikat Buruh Karya Utama*, Federation of Main Plant Labour Unions) had organised hundreds of them as their members. FSBKU was affiliated with KASBI at that time; today it is a member of KSN. In order to pressure the employer to pay severance pay according to the law, initially they organised picketing actions. When these failed to take effect, the workers radicalised and decided spontaneously to occupy the factory. FSBKU members assisted and advised the workers since they already had experience with factory occupations in other industries. The workers agreed not to loot the factory, not to take anything or sell the machines to compensate for withheld severance pay. Instead, they decided to guard the machines and continue production under workers' control to raise money and make a living during the law suit. They sought solidarity and support by Indonesian labour NGOs such as PRP and LBH Jakarta (Legal Aid Institute). A PRP member explained that they "came with discussions and played some documentaries from Latin America that show that there is an experience where the factories that were left behind by the owners can be recuperated and run again as a factory occupation" (NGO Interview, December 2011).

A workers' cooperative was set up that would take control of production at PT Istana. Interestingly, some of the workers already had practical experience with running small-scale garment production since they had started a small home-based cooperative a year before the occupation to supplement their meagre income. At the height of the occupation, there were hundreds of workers living, discussing, working and organising in the factory. They decided to set up office in the factory and turn it into their homes. They organised job rotation so as to reduce alienation from dull tasks and maximise opportunities to learn new skills and develop new capacities. They built a public kitchen, so they could share food. They organised their own child day care, because most of the workers were female and many had children. They produced t-shirts with the slogan "100 per cent cooperatively produced" and they connected themselves to *No Chains*, a transnational network of cooperatively operated factories producing sweat-free clothing in Thailand, Argentina and other countries. *No Chains* is marketing these products as "the first global clothing brand free of slave labor" (www.nochains.org). Industrial production, democratic self-organisation, political self-education and social reproduction were all united under the factory roof of PT Istana, at least for a period of time.

Different problems and challenges made it hard and eventually impossible to sustain the experiment at PT Istana. Although the workers won several legal victories in front of the labour court—e.g. the owner was sentenced to one year of prison for not paying severance pay and for bankruptcy fraud—the bankruptcy proceedings also disadvantaged the workers legally. They require that the value of all the assets of the factory must be assessed by a third party and that the assets will then be auctioned. The money raised will then be used first to service bank debts and second to pay other creditors, including workers' severance pay. During the legal dispute, family members of the former owner tried to intimidate the occupying workers, sometime using brute force:

"Several times, they tried to evict the occupiers, those hundreds of FSBKU members. They called in the police and they hired thugs and criminals to force the workers out of the factory, but somehow uniquely, those female workers were able to fight back, so they were able to get rid of the thugs" (Union Interview, December 2011).

Nevertheless, a combination of intimidation, economic hardship and other difficulties pushed many workers to accept subsequent deals with the trustee and look for new jobs. About 300 of them continued the occupation running the factory as a cooperative. They continued producing garments and clothing for the domestic market, while international buyers like Adidas and St. Oliver cancelled their contracts. Financial and technical difficulties made it hard for the cooperative to maintain production on a scale that could sustain all workers. For example, electricity was a problem. The area of North Jakarta where PT Istana is located is often flooded and electricity cannot always be provided. For a while, production was run using diesel engines, but that was not sustainable. One of the lessons of this experience was thus that an isolated factory occupation could not last long if it was not linked up to other struggles in other sectors. PRP activists tried to connect the workers at PT Istana with those in the state-owned electricity company who were resisting privatisation at that time, in order to supply the factory with power. This attempt failed, but later on the idea of linking up private sector workers with those from the strategically important state-owned enterprises would gain currency (see below).

Support from KASBI was also not as intense as the workers at PT Istana had hoped for. Then, a flood in 2008 destroyed most of the machinery and forced the cooperative to leave the factory premises and continue production on a smaller scale from their private homes. Out of the 40 workers who moved production to their homes, today only 15 still continue producing garments as a small home-based garment cooperative. A PRP activist argued that, although cooperative production under workers' control was financially unstable and wages could only be paid irregularly, the empowering experience of collective self-organisation and autonomous production was "like an immaterial substitute" for material gains (NGO Interview, December 2011).

Although the factory occupation at PT Istana can hardly be called a success story of industrial production under workers' control, it clearly shows that there are radical alternatives envisioned and enacted by Indonesian garment workers and their unions. These alternative imaginaries, strategies and practices tend to be silenced in academic discourses about decent work and labour politics in Indonesia today. They are completely absent from the available English literature, which is why my study affords them the analytical space they deserve. Although marginalised and however weak, these radical approaches are far from irrelevant since they provide a repertoire of ideas and experiences counter-hegemonic projects can draw on. Who are the actors producing and circulating the imaginaries underpinning these approaches? Where do they come from? What is their relation to the other imaginaries, strategies and practices of Indonesian trade unions and labour NGOs that have already been discussed above?

7.1.1 Tracing the Emergence of KSN

In 1995, when Suharto was still in power but under domestic and international pressure, a small group of workers at an electronics factory in Tangerang decided to take advantage of the limited labour reform allowing for the formation of enterprise unions where there is no SPSI unit. These non-affiliated factory-level unions were aptly called SPTP (*Serikat Pekerja Tingkat Perusahan*, Enterprise-Level Trade Union). Thirteen workers met clandestinely to prepare the formation of an SPTP at their electronics factory, but their cover was blown and heavy repression followed swiftly. The activists were being interrogated, intimidated and humiliated by management. One of them reported that the factory managers asked him: "Do you know that building a labour union is the act of a communist?" (NGO Interview, January 2012). Then he replied that, in his opinion, building a union on the factory level is actually covered by the reformed labour law. Despite the employer's anti-union repression, the small group continued to meet as a discussion group that would become the embryo of the independent trade union federation FSBKU. Two of them were kidnapped and interrogated by the military in 1996, which had been informed about their organising activities. In order to avoid further repression, they denied the existence of a union at their factory. Instead, they chose to cover themselves as a discussion group named PKU (*Paguyuban Karya Utama*, Main Plant Circle of Friends).

This embryo union expanded quickly to other factories in Tangerang. By 1997, they had some 200 members and decided to hold the first PKU congress in the same year. They saw the necessity for better networking and collaboration among the different SPTPs that had emerged in the late New Order era. They invited other independent factory-level unions to the congress and agreed to set up an SPTP Forum for this purpose. In 1999, after the fall of Suharto, they formally transformed their discussion group into an enterprise union at the electronics factory. By 2000, there were already 18,000 industrial workers from Tangerang linked up to PKU through the SPTP Forum. In 2001, they held their second congress where they officially founded FSBKU as a city-level trade union federation (NGO Interview, January 2012). FSBKU was heavily involved in the Action Committee of Independent Labour Unions (*Komite Aksi Serikat Buruh Independen*, KASBI), founded in 2003 and one of the founding members of KASBI when it was transformed into a national trade union confederation in 2004.

FSBKU activists who were also part of KASBI's national leadership reported that there were three main lessons learned from the KASBI experience: ownership, elitism and bureaucratism (Union Interview, January 2012). First, while KASBI initially was dependent on external support by labour NGOs and intellectuals, they increasingly sought to replace "outsiders" from NGOs with workers. One of them explained that "labour unions tend not to trust the NGOs any longer in Indonesia" (Union Interview, January 2012), because their reliance on foreign funding also makes them less independent with regard to their political agenda. As genuine labour unions grow stronger, there is less need for NGOs as substitute labour unions. Ownership of the unions should be enacted by the workers rather than by "outsiders" from labour NGOs (cf. Ford 2009). This partly explains the scepticism of radical labour activists towards solidarity campaigns that are perceived as driven by NGOs. Second, even in progressive unions putting strong emphasis on intra-union democracy, elitism has been a problem. At the second KASBI congress in 2008, parts of the leadership were re-elected for a second term although the members had decided that they should be replaced in order to prevent the forms of elitism that were common in the bureaucratic SPSI unions. A dispute about the leadership evolved that displayed both growing distance between rank and file members and leaders and growing animosities among leaders where personal conflicts and political differences are not always easily discerned. Third, KASBI's move towards more official recognition and more participation in formal bi- and tripartite structures as well as more informal or private initiatives such as the PFA was perceived by some member federations very critically. For them, this development drives KASBI away from the militant strategies of mass demonstrations and industrial actions that had served them well in the past. The growing amount of red tape and bureaucratism associated with these formal and informal structures, they argue, absorbs important resources and thus diminishes their capacities to organise workers and fight for their interests instead of strengthening them (Union Interview, January 2012).

KASBI's participation in the PFA from 2009 has exacerbated all three of these problems. The FSBKU activists regard the PFA as driven by international NGOs such as Oxfam and the CCC, although the NGOs have been careful to avoid this impression and have also stressed the importance of ownership by the unions. They also regard it as an elitist undertaking, because global brands and supplier factories' managements are sitting at the table with national union leaders, including "yellow" unions, rather than rank and file union members organising themselves. The problem of bureaucratism and red tape is present in the PFA since it is one of the goals of the FoA Protocol to move from militant labour conflict to peaceful dispute resolution through new private governance structures. It is precisely this development of institutionalisation and integration that was seen by some member federations of KASBI as moving the confederation away from their power base, as a form of de-radicalisation and co-optation or as a "trap" (Union Interviews, January 2012).

Tensions within KASBI grew until the third congress in 2010. Then, there was a split in the confederation. In addition to the ongoing quarrel over the leadership, there was a dispute over the direction KASBI would take over the next years. One of the issues was the question of whether or not to integrate workers from state-owned enterprises. Under Suharto, the government-controlled SPSI was reserved for private sector workers: "Employees in state-owned enterprises had hitherto not been unionised" (Ford 2009, 163). Instead, there was a corporatist organisation for the public sector called KORPRI (*Korps Pegawai Republik Indonesia*, Public Employees' Corps of the Republic of Indonesia). *Reformasi* introduced freedom of association for the public sector and quickly enterprise unions in state-owned enterprises such as electricity, oil and telecommunication companies as well as state-owned plantations were set up. In 1999, the Federation of State-Owned Enterprise Workers' Unions (*Federasi Serikat Pekerja - Badan Usaha Milik Negara*, FSP-BUMN) was formed (ibid.). These unions had not been as active in the struggle against Suharto as the clandestine unions of private sector industries and they kept a certain amount of distance to the rest of the trade union movement. Many of their member unions are still dominated by management and close to the state. However, when plans were made to privatise the state-owned enterprises, many of these unions and/or their members became heavily politicised.

In 2008, a coalition of independent trade unions such as KASBI, labour NGOs such as PRP and public sector unions was formed under the name National Solidarity Committee against Privatisation and Union Busting (*Komite Solidaritas Nasional melawan Privatisasi dan Union Busting* or KSN in short). In this coalition, cross-sectoral collaboration between private and public sector unions was good. Within KASBI, suggestions were made to integrate state-owned enterprise unions into the confederation or form a new one together with them. However, "this idea was kind of rejected or wasn't very much welcomed in KASBI, so in the last congress there was some sort of dispute about what will be the direction of KASBI" (Union Interview, December 2011).

Ultimately, the combination of disputes over the leadership, over the participation in "soft campaigns" like the PFA and over the state-owned enterprises led to the division of KASBI at the third congress in 2010. Out of the 20 regional federations affiliated with KASBI, six moved out of the organisation to form the new confederation KSN (*Konfederasi Serikat Nasional*, National Union Confederation), FSBKU among them. This number grew to eleven out of 20 when KSN was officially launched on 11 November 2011 in Bandung, although some federations are claimed by both KASBI and KSN since not all of their member unions joined the new confederation (Union Interviews, December 2011 and February 2012). As with KASBI in the beginning, the founding members of KSN chose to change name but keep the abbreviation that was already well-known. Most of these 11 federations have their main membership base in the garment industry, some in other light manufacturing industries such as electronics and some in the plantation sector. The federations, however, are not organised sectorally but regionally. Two union federations from state-owned enterprises also left FSP-BUMN and joined KSN. The involvement of unions and workers from state-owned and privatised enterprises and plantations also means that the geographical reach of KSN is much greater in comparison with private sector industrial unions. While KASBI is mostly concentrated in the industrial and urban regions on Java, KSN also covers the plantations of North Sumatra and South Sulawesi: "That is a signal of a new frontier or a new base for the trade unions in relation to the capital flow that goes more intensively to Eastern parts of Indonesia" (Union Interview, December 2011) as resource extraction and agribusiness, especially the palm oil industry, expand.

7.1.2 The Strategies of KSN

"What we tried to do with KSN is that KSN should not be trapped in soft campaigns set up by the capitalist system. Campaigns like Fair Trade, the Olympic campaign [the PFA], anti-sweatshop campaigns are soft campaigns in our opinion. In these soft campaigns, the labour unions do not advocate against the capitalist system, but they are trying to make the system look more humane. So, they are integrated in the system, they are trapped within this game of the regime" (NGO Interview, January 2012).

The activists who have left KASBI and formed KSN regard multi-stakeholder initiatives like the PFA as "soft campaigns" they do not want to be "trapped" in. What exactly do they mean by this? Their main argument seems to be that these campaigns are not articulated as counter-hegemonic, anti-capitalist strategies, but as strategies aiming to humanise neoliberal capitalism, integrated into "the system" and co-opted by the "game of the regime". Another argument was that the crucial factor in determining whether a campaign challenges the *status quo* or not is not the question of whether or not it contributes to some incremental improvements of working conditions, but whether these improvements have been achieved through the workers' own struggle and self-organisation or whether they have been implemented from above. Another example may help to explain this argument:

"FSBKU was the first federation that conducted a research on their own. It was about labour market flexibility. They compared the welfare situation and the wages of permanent workers and of contract and outsourced workers. They saw that there are significant differences among those three. The issue got highlighted by the media and there was a buzz about it at the national and the regional level. [...] The research was conducted by the workers themselves; there was no intervention from university researchers" (NGO Interview, January 2012).

FSBKU activists described this experience as very empowering. Not only did they produce critical knowledge about the welfare of Indonesian workers, but they did so without assistance or intervention from outside, e.g. from universities or labour NGOs. They gained insights into the wage system, which they could use for their own concept of and campaign for a decent living wage while simultaneously building their capacities for self-organised research. They investigated the actual consumption patterns of industrial workers and their families on Java to calculate what is really needed for their social reproduction. Based on this research, they developed their own concept of a National Decent Wage (*Upah Layak Nasional*, ULN), which they introduced into a broad labour alliance that was campaigning intensively and successfully against the revision of the Manpower Act in 2005 and 2006. This proposed revision would have produced even more labour market flexibility and job insecurity. The alliance was called ABM (*Aliansi Buruh Menggugat*, Alliance for Workers' Demands) and KASBI's influence was considerable. The second ABM campaign was pushing for the ULN concept, a national cross-sectoral minimum wage that would cover the decent living needs of a family according to the unions' own calculation rather than the KHL.

The ULN campaign was also one of the reasons why the Asia Floor Wage (AFW) campaign had not been picked up by Indonesian unions very well (see Chapter 3.6). They had developed their own decent wage concept, so why would they espouse another concept that, in their perception, was imported from the transnational level by NGOs such as TURC and the CCC? The numbers calculated for the AFW were also well below those calculated for the ULN. For example, in 2006 the ABM had already demanded a national decent wage of 3,270,000 Rupiah while the AFW was calculated at 1,868,650 Rupiah in 2009 (AFW 2009). Due to inflation, the real difference between these numbers is even higher than the nominal difference. The UMK for Jakarta was 1,069,865 Rupiah in 2009 while the government-calculated KHL was 2,446,034 Rupiah (SPN/GARTEKS/AKATIGA 2009). It is not surprising that it was hard for the NGOs involved in the AFW campaign to convince Indonesian unions that they should settle for a minimum wage proposal that was below the government's KHL, which itself was well below their own calculation. The main reason for their non-participation, however, was that the AFW campaign was seen as driven by NGOs rather than the trade unions themselves. Although the ULN campaign was unsuccessful, for the activists involved the empowering experience of being able to conduct necessary research on their own behalf and to build an alliance and launch a campaign based on this research without the intervention of "outsiders" was paramount (NGO Interview, January 2012).

The PFA is seen in a similar vein. The FSBKU activists explained that one of the problems with these kinds of campaigns is that they direct the unions' activities outside rather than inside. They are drawn into negotiations with companies, international NGOs and rival unions. What is needed instead, they argue, is "building capacities and enhancing the skills like building an organisation, supporting the organisation financially independent from outsiders" (NGO Interview, January 2012). Union members would not find these campaigns very empowering. They have to rely on the leaders without being able to improve the conditions of the members themselves. Their criticism towards these campaigns is that the strength of the union is being moderated through them. The union is not in itself strong enough to have a level bargaining position with management, but the unions are being weakened by these campaigns. One activist argued:

"That's one of the major problems in Indonesia for the labour movement in the garment, textile and shoes industry. There are so many interventions from the buyers like Adidas, Nike, Reebok, so many interventions by international NGOs about this issue. I think slowly the unions are getting less strong, because it's a scenario of NGOs and buyers" (NGO Interview, January 2012).

Another added:

"Because what is the role of the union if there are NGOs already facilitating and advocating for the needs of the workers? There is a role switching in this case and this kind of strategy is a systematic effort of the whole system, of the capitalists to de-radicalise the unions" (Union Interview, January 2012).

A "passive revolution" (Gramsci 1971, 194) in the workplace is not empowering for workers, even though it may improve working conditions in some ways.[15] If these improvements are not the result of the workers' own struggle and self-organisation, they do not enhance their capacities and skills for struggling and organising themselves. They will thus help reproducing the hegemonic order by allowing for small adaptations, instead of empowering the subaltern to pursue their own counter-hegemonic project.

7.2 The Indonesian People's Movement Confederation

If workers' capabilities for self-organisation and autonomous action figure so prominently within KSN's strategies, it is not surprising that factory occupations such as the one at PT Istana present to them unique opportunities to develop such capabilities. The case of PT Istana was not the first occupation of a garment factory on Java, but it was the one that

---

15 Gramsci used the term "passive revolution" ambiguously, sometimes referring to a revolution without the participation of the popular masses, sometimes to a "molecular" transformation from above "that accepted a certain part of the demands expressed from below" (Gramsci 1995, 523). I use the term here in the latter sense as suggested by Sum: "'Passive revolution' is a term used by Gramsci (1971) to examine the ways in which a social class maintains its hegemony through gradual, molecular changes that operate through passive consent, the decapitation of resistance movements, and absorption of opposition through compromise and concession" (2010, 76).

was the best politically organised, assisted by the union federation FSBKU and the NGOs PRP and LBH. Interviewees reported several other factory occupations in the Jabodetabek area, all of which had failed after a certain period of time for similar reasons as PT Istana. KSN leaders, therefore, began to systematically think about the factors responsible for the success or failure of recuperated factories. The main lesson drawn from the PT Istana experience was that factory occupations have no chance of survival if they remain isolated from other struggles in other factories and sectors. It has already been mentioned above that activists at PT Istana tried to solve the electricity problem by approaching their colleagues at the state-owned electricity company, at that time to no avail. The idea to link up public and private sector workers, to overcome old divisions among Indonesian wage labourers became, however, one of the two major strategic innovations of KSN vis-à-vis KASBI. The second, perhaps more important innovation relates to the idea of linking urban and rural struggles and therefore connecting workers', peasants' and fishermen's organisations as well as women's and indigenous people's movements.

The newly established radical union confederation KSN is part of a larger multi-sector alliance of Indonesian social movements that was restructured recently for this purpose. The Indonesian People's Movement Confederation (*Konfederasi Pergerakan Rakyat Indonesia* or KPRI) was founded by peasants' and plantation workers' unions as well as KSN labour unions and some progressive NGOs such as women's and indigenous people's organisations as well as environmental groups in 2003. The main *economic imaginary* informing the strategies and activities of KPRI relates to re-organising the production, distribution and consumption of goods beyond the capitalist market by building alternative "closed markets" between recuperated factories and occupied plantations or reclaimed landholdings. Since 1998, peasants' organisations had already begun to reclaim land that had been given to private companies, government officials or military commanders despite being communal land according to customary law. In Indonesia, new rounds of enclosures have dispossessed large numbers of the rural population of access to land that was leased out or sold to agribusiness companies growing cash crops such as palm oil for the global market. The urban labour markets, however, do not have the capacity to absorb these "surplus populations" (Li 2009) and provide them with livelihoods through industrial employment. Reclaiming dispossessed land and cultivating it cooperatively, therefore, has become a central strategy of the rural poor, taken up and systematically promoted by KPRI.

7.2.1 The Economic Imaginary of Alternative Economies

According to KPRI activists, neither factory occupations nor agricultural cooperatives are a novelty in Indonesia, but "the experiment to build a closed market between workers and peasants is a new one. It is an alternative economy, because it is not involved in the liberal markets" (Union Interview, January 2012). The overall discourse of KPRI—its main economic imaginary—is not "decent work" but "alternative economy". The long-term strategic orientation is improving the livelihoods of working people by reclaiming the means for them to sustain their own lives, i.e. reclaiming the means of production and social reproduction. What does "alternative economy" mean on the discursive level?

The idea is that agricultural cooperatives cultivating reclaimed land produce goods such as rice, coffee or rubber while industrial cooperatives working in recuperated factories produce goods such as garments and shoes. Ideally, this would include industrial products necessary for farming like chemical fertilisers or agricultural machinery. Peasants are encouraged to process their raw materials into semi-manufactured products, adding more value to their products and absorbing more labour power, for example pre-processing rubber or roasting coffee. Workers and peasants then exchange these goods on their own "closed markets", thereby bypassing the capitalist markets, cutting the price for the consumers while raising the income of the producers. The above mentioned selling of PT Istana's "100 per cent cooperatively produced" t-shirts via the transnational *No Chains* network indicates that such closed markets can also be established across borders. KPRI has an economic programme consisting of four pillars:

"The first pillar is the production base, the second is the consumption base—how to control both of them is very important for the confederation. The third pillar is collective ownership and the last one is institutionalisation" (Union Interview, February 2012).

Re-organising the production base relates to the just mentioned question of adding more value to the products by integrating more steps of the supply chain under workers' control. Re-organising the consumption base, apart from building autonomous distribution networks, entails a more or less explicit critique of the globalised culture of consumerism. Repeatedly, KPRI activists explaining their economic programme have stressed that a "closed market" could only provide for what a person or family "actually needs" (Union Interview, January 2012). This does not only include the classic "basic needs" for food, clothing and shelter, but also material and immaterial needs such as education, health and communication. It does, however, not necessarily include luxury goods such as "expensive furniture or big plasma TVs" (ibid.), affordable to Indonesian workers only through consumer credits making them dependent on speculative financial markets. This critique of debt-financed consumerism is an interesting parallel to other imaginaries of "alternative" or "solidarity economies" that criticise the present articulation of production and consumption norms as unsustainable and as destructive for both the planet and the people.[16] The consumption pillar of KPRI's programme, however, also relates to the re-organisation of the distribution of goods via "closed markets" itself. Collective ownership refers to the forms of self-organisation and workers' control KPRI is experimenting with such as occupied factories and cooperative farming. Institutionalisation aims to consolidate these experiments over time by building political structures supporting the cooperatives, potentially also including the future formation of a new political party (Union Interview, January 2012).

7.2.2 Practical Experiences with Alternative Economies

In order to get a sense of the chances of this economic imaginary to be *selected* by more social actors or wider social groups and *retained* within actually existing alternatives to neoliberal capitalism, the limited experiences with practical experiments deserve closer attention, even though these are primarily located in the agricultural sector rather than in garment production or other industrial sectors.

A relatively large peasants' union (*Serikat Pertani*) organising landless people is one of the biggest member federations of KPRI. This peasants' union has already reclaimed a total of 500,000 hectares of land on Java, Sumatra, Sulawesi and Nusa Tenggara (Union Interview, March 2013). For

---

16 The "de-growth" imaginary is a case in point (see Brand 2014; Habermann 2012; Jessop 2012).

example, in Yogyakarta they took over a tea and coffee plantation on Suroloyo Mountain and are now producing tea and coffee cooperatively. The coffee from Suroloyo is already being marketed directly to KSN member unions in industrial areas. The local peasants' union at Suroloyo (*Serikat Pertani Kecamatan Samigaluh/ Kabupaten Kulon Progo*, Peasants' Union of the Samigaluh District/Kulon Progo Regency) also has an Independent Women's Union (*Serikat Perampuan Independen*) aiming at training and empowering women to fully participate in the decision-making processes of both the union and the cooperative. Unfortunately, neither the peasant's union nor the women's union were available for interviews at the time of research. One of the KPRI coordinators, however, explained:

> "The plantation used to be run by Gadjah Mada University, but the university sold it to a CEO of some company. After that, it was taken over by the peasants in there. They had to lobby the sultan, because the land is owned by the Yogyakarta sultan. [...] In there, we also have a traditional market, where we can barter, so the people from the mountains don't have to go to the city market anymore" (Union Interview, March 2013).

It is very interesting to note that the "alternative economy" envisioned by KPRI also entails traditional elements of a non-monetary barter economy. Again, we see some parallels to other models of alternative economies such as "local exchange trading systems".[17]

Whereas the sultan was quite supportive of the peasants in Yogyakarta, allowing them to take over the land peacefully, in other places they were less fortunate and had to fight and struggle hard to take over the land. In South Sumatra, for example, in Ogan Ilir there is a sugar plantation named PT Kayumanis. Before Suharto, the land was owned by local peasants, but under Suharto the military took over the land. After Suharto's fall, the peasants reclaimed the land: "They said, this used to be our land; we want to have it back" (ibid.). After that, the military and the police and the company's security guards went to the village and launched heavy repression against the peasants. People were shot dead. KPRI started to advocate on behalf of the peasants; now there are still three people in jail.

---

17 There is a large variety of such "local exchange trading systems". They range from traditional barter economies such as the one at Suroloyo Mountain to modern exchange systems supported by alternative regional currencies. When the Argentinian monetary economy collapsed in 2001, the number of "local exchange trading systems" skyrocketed as a survival strategy in the context of economic crisis and political turmoil (Uriona 2007, 63–65, see Chapter 7.3).

The local leader of the peasants' union, who is also one of the presidents of KPRI, is still in jail. "This shows the tactic of criminalisation of activists" (ibid.), as the KPRI coordinator asserted.

In West Java, the local peasants' union *Serikat Pertani Pasundan* (SPP) has some 90,000 members cultivating a large area of reclaimed land and producing agricultural goods such as rubber, rice, cocoa, vegetables, dairy products and so on. They have built a new village, including an elementary school for children and an educational training centre for adults. The government does not officially recognise these informal structures, but after many years of fighting, at least there is no violent repression anymore (ibid.).

Such land disputes are very common and on the rise in Indonesia. KPRI aims to give them a more coherent organisational framework and to systematically link them up over the huge distances of the Indonesian archipelago. They start with mapping the land and researching the histories of the communal land. Then they investigate the specific legal situation of the case at hand, organise the peasants and campaign for reclaiming the land. Where there is no local peasants' union, they try to help the peasants setting one up. They engage in education, training, exchange and so on to learn from successful examples. Education and training not only refers to skills and knowledge necessary for running plantations under peasants' control, but also to training for social activism such as learning how to build barricades and how to deal with security forces.

After successfully resisting repression, the peasants organised in SPP encountered another problem that illustrates why linking the agricultural and the industrial sectors is so important for KPRI's strategy. The problem is that the prices of their agricultural products are very low since they only sell the raw materials with no added value. For example, there is a reclaimed rubber plantation in West Java but, as a KPRI activist explained, they "need to think about how to set up a communal factory. Now, all factories are still owned by the capitalists" (Union Interview, March 2013). According to this activist, it is very important to gain control over more parts of the production process in order to strengthen the unions of KPRI.

Most practical experiments with building an alternative economy are in stage one of the four pillars of KPRI's economic programme, i.e. re-organising the production base. Coffee production has in some cases moved to stage two, i.e. re-organising distribution and consumption. KPRI still has a long way to go in terms of developing collective forms of ownership, especially with regard to the industrial sector and even more so with regard to building sustainable institutions for the alternative economy: "There is so much potential, but we still can do little practically" (ibid.). In order to raise the prices of the products and thus the income of the producers, one possibility discussed by KPRI includes producing high quality goods. For example, the Suroloyo coffee is deemed to be among the highest quality coffees in Indonesia, second only to the famous Toraja coffee from South Sulawesi. If consumers know that the coffee is of such high quality and that it is cooperatively produced, they may be willing to pay higher prices.

This form of "ethical" production and consumption is fundamentally different from more conventional forms of certification and labelling initiatives such as Fair Trade. The KPRI activist explained that, on the one hand, the two are similar in that both aim to raise prices to the benefit of the peasants but, on the other hand, the Fair Trade market is merely a segment of the normal capitalist market whereas their idea of closed markets strives towards breaking away from it:

"But the normal Fair Trade, all the certification and standardisation, I don't agree with that. I think it's dangerous. It is like our mapping project, but controlled by the capitalists and it's very soft" (Union Interview, March 2013).

In his opinion, the Fair Trade supply chain is controlled by international NGOs and large corporations rather than the peasants' unions and cooperatives themselves. It is interesting to note that the probably most well-known case of "solidarity coffee"—the Zapatista's coffee from Mexico's Chiapas state—is not labelled as Fair Trade and nor is it marketed to European supermarkets either. Instead, they prefer to trust in the Zapatista "label" itself and use autonomous, horizontal ways of distributing their coffee overseas via supporter organisations and a "closed market" of sorts. Unlike the t-shirts from PT Istana that were marketed via the transnational *No Chains* network, the Suroloyo coffee has not yet been exported to other countries, but hopes are high that "closed markets" can also be built across borders.

7.2.3 Radical Imaginaries: Recovered or Travelled?

While in critical research on Latin America these more radical imaginaries of "alternative" or "solidarity economies" are regularly taken up by scientific discourses (on Argentina see Lavaca Collective 2007, Kabat 2011; on Brazil see de Faria and Novaes 2011, Mance 2014; on Venezuela see Azzellini 2011), this remains a task largely to be done for Southeast-Asia.[18] While this is beyond the scope of the present study, I want to contribute to illuminating this often invisible, silenced and marginalised phenomenon in the Indonesian context. Where do these radical imaginaries of cooperative production under workers' control come from? Are there historical links to the imaginaries and practices of Indonesian communists and socialists from the Sukarno era? Did Marxism somehow survive the repression under Suharto underground? Or did the Latin American imaginary "travel" to Indonesia? In other words, is there a specifically Indonesian imaginary at work, or does this imaginary have transnational dimensions?

The limited evidence from my own research pertaining to this question suggests that both are true. It was already mentioned that, at PT Istana, union activists showed documentaries from Latin America to the workers as an inspiration and opportunity to learn especially from the Argentinian experience, but this was connected to the historical experiences of the Indonesian labour movement:

"We took some of the ideas from the Argentina experience, but we also kind of connect it with the history of Indonesian labour struggles, because right after independence the main political agenda or the main struggles of the Indonesian labour movement was to take over companies from the Dutch colonialists and from the British etcetera. So, we kind of mixed it with the idea that it is not only about solidarity but also workers' control" (Union Interview, December 2011).

The historical experiences referred to in this interview are not the focus of my study, but as far as they are relevant for understanding radical imaginaries in the present conjuncture, they are within the remit of the present study. There is very little scholarly literature on these historical experiences with workers' control in Indonesia. Within Indonesia, discussing and reflecting on these experiences today is obstructed by the dictated silence surrounding the events of 1965 and the subsequent mass murder of hundreds of thousands alleged communists.

---

18 A book edited by Denison Jayasooria (2013) is an exception. It collects conceptual reflections and empirical case studies of the "solidarity economy" in Asia. However, the practical examples provided for the most part cover "social enterprises" and "social entrepreneurship", representing something very different from the radical imaginaries that are of interest here. This difference is further elaborated below (see Chapter 7.3).

One publication on this matter that forms an exception is Suryomenggolo (2012). He analyses the emergence of workers' control after independence in 1945. After Japanese and Dutch troops were defeated, he explains, workers began spontaneously to take control over factories, railway stations and plantations. The declaration of independence was signed on 17 August 1945, but the new postcolonial state was still in the making and Japanese troops were still present in key places of public life such as the national railway system and the stations. It was here that workers, motivated by the spirit of national liberation, first started to take away control from the Japanese. In early September 1945, the railway stations of Jakarta were taken over; and by October, all Javanese stations were under workers' control (Suryomenggolo 2012, 268). They quickly implemented an operational system of self-organisation to administer the railway system autonomously. Democratic workers' councils and steering committees were set up to this effect. Suryomenggolo describes a similar process for the worker-controlled plantations formerly owned by Dutch companies or the colonial state:

"The [plantation] workers came to realise that they had the right to the products of their own labour on the plantation. They administered their workplace under their own leadership [and] kept production running. [...] This system of self-administration enabled them to keep their jobs and thus endure the hardship of that time" (2012, 273, my translation).

There were similar experiments with self-administration of industrial factories such as sugar mills. These experiments with workers' control and self-organisation, however, were short-lived. As the new post-colonial state consolidated its power, it increasingly saw workers' control of plantations, factories and stations as a threat to economic and political stability due to their strategic importance. Whereas the nationalist and the labour movements were close allies in the struggle for independence, this alliance broke up when the state started to recapture control over the plantations, factories and stations from early 1946. The government, dominated by nationalists, aimed to integrate and contain the labour movement in the service of national development: "It was vice-president Hatta who criticised the self-organisation of workers publicly as 'syndicalism' in February 1946 at an economic conference in Yogyakarta" (Suryomenggolo 2012, 278, my translation). While he would later become a staunch supporter of a certain, state-controlled model of cooperatives, autonomous self-organisation of workers was lambasted as a "childhood disease" (ibid.,

279).[19] Subsequently, the government moved to regain control over the self-administered plantations, factories and stations by replacing the democratically elected steering committees of the workers' councils with government-appointed officials. Deprived of their self-administrative power in the workplace, the workers' councils began to transform themselves into more conventional, independent trade unions.

Although workers' control and self-organisation lasted for only a couple of months, this episode from Indonesian history shows that the radical imaginaries envisioned by KSN and KPRI have historical forerunners, which they can draw on. This, however, is hampered by the New Order's historiography, silencing and marginalising everything that can even remotely be labelled as "communist". Current debates of Indonesian history are only slowly starting to address this marginalisation and silencing, if at all. How did the economic imaginary of workers' control and self-organisation survive the anti-communist purge and 30 years of victors writing history under Suharto? An activist's response is illuminating:

"It was the students' movement. You cannot just abolish ideas. You cannot repress theories like Marxism. In Indonesia, even though Suharto completely prohibited Marxism and cracked down on communist party members, even after that Marxism still exists in Indonesia. They have survived until today, by means like books well hidden by family members of the PKI members and carefully passed on to others. It survived until today" (Union Interview, January 2012).

The activist making this statement explained that he used to be anti-communist due to Suharto's propaganda but, when he entered college, he got in touch with Marxist theories of class conflict. He came to realise that these theories were forbidden precisely because they could explain the harsh realities of workers' lives in Indonesia and potentially become a powerful weapon in their struggle against capitalist domination and exploitation. According to him, these radical ideas or *imaginaries* survived the New Order underground within families and re-emerged in the struggle against Suharto, recovered by the students' and the workers' movements. In this process, however, the historical imaginary of workers' control in Indonesia came to be re-articulated with the more recent, more transnational imaginary of "alternative" or "solidarity economies", travelling from

---

19 This term goes back to Lenin's critique of "left-wing" communism as an "infantile disorder" (Lenin 1934).

places like Argentina and Venezuela to Indonesia. Currently, KSN and KPRI delegates are planning a prolonged visit to Argentina and Venezuela to exchange experiences and knowledge with worker cooperatives in recuperated factories in these countries. So, there is transnational or trans-local organising around the economic imaginary of an alternative "solidarity economy" that is usually overlooked in mainstream discourses of global labour politics.

7.3 The Solidarity Economy Alternative

We have seen that some trade unions such as the newly emerging KSN, which has split off from KASBI, are critical of multi-stakeholder initiatives like Play Fair. Reasons given for this include the type of trade union strategy they support (social dialogue instead of industrial action), their de-radicalising and de-mobilising effect and the role of international NGOs. They see these initiatives as "soft campaigns" they do not want to be "trapped in" (NGO Interview, January 2012), because they see them as weakening the unions' organising capacities. Instead of investing their resources in time consuming negotiations with employers, brands and rival unions, they prefer to direct them inwards in order to develop their capabilities for self-organisation and autonomous action from the bottom up.

Factory occupations like the one at PT Istana provide opportunities for them to develop such capabilities. Despite its eventual failure, the case of PT Istana shows that Indonesian garment workers, most of them women, have in some instances already begun to envision and enact radical alternatives to moderate decent work strategies. Although the struggle initially was about severance pay, the workers quickly radicalised, occupied their factory and continued production under their own control. Supported by their union federation FSBKU and Indonesian NGOs such as PRP and LBH, they set up a worker cooperative taking control of garment production and organising job rotation. T-shirts produced at PT Istana were marketed transnationally via the cooperative network *No Chains*. The cooperative also organised a public kitchen and a child day care, making this an experiment not only with workers' control of industrial production but also with new collective forms of organising social reproduction. It was thus not a mere economic experiment with cooperative production, but a political experiment with grassroots democracy in the workplace and a cultural experiment with new forms of everyday practices or another way of life as well. This enables new forms of collective identity and subjectivity of women workers that transcend the picture of "Third World women" (Kabeer 2004, 10) helplessly victimised by globalised, neoliberal capitalism and patriarchal gender relations. The "solidarity economy" imaginary may become a weapon for these women to combat victimisation not only by discursively rejecting the Western gaze but through material practices of resistance as well.

The factory occupation at PT Istana ultimately failed and the cooperative had to leave the company premises to continue garment production on a much smaller scale as a home-based cooperative. Nevertheless, the fact that they do continue producing clothing under workers' control shows that strategies and practices underpinned by economic imaginaries such as "alternative economies" or "solidarity economy" are alive in Indonesia. Even though trade unions subscribing to this kind of imaginary are the minority, we cannot dismiss them as irrelevant. To the contrary, we must ask if and how our academic discourses participate in the selection and retention of certain moderate imaginaries at the expense of filtering out and marginalising other, more radical imaginaries. I have argued that these alternative imaginaries, strategies and practices tend to be silenced and made invisible when it comes to Indonesia, whereas in Argentina or Venezuela they are regularly investigated by critical scholars. I hope to contribute to including Indonesian "alternative economies", the actors performing this kind of imaginary and their strategies and practices in these debates. My analysis has, however, mainly identified the existence of these radical imaginaries in Indonesia, rather than providing a deeper ethnographic analysis, which could provide a possible starting point for another round of CPE/CGT research.

I have reconstructed the emergence of the new trade union confederation KSN—an organisational base for such imaginaries, strategies and practices—from clandestine labour resistance against Suharto in the late New Order years, to the development of KASBI from action committee to union confederation, to the split of KASBI and the founding of KSN. Disputes over the leadership, the relationship to public sector workers and the participation in multi-stakeholder initiatives like the PFA have been identified as the main causes of KASBI's division. KASBI's move towards institutionalisation and integration into Indonesia's industrial relations system and private governance structures is seen by KSN activists as a form of de-radicalisation and co-optation, diminishing its power base.

In order to expand its own power base and link urban and rural struggles, KSN has joined the social movement confederation KPRI. I have analysed KPRI's main economic imaginary of "alternative economies" both on the discursive level of how the actors give sense and meaning to it and on the material level of how they have started to put it into practice. KPRI aims to build "closed markets" on the basis of recuperated factories and occupied plantations in order for "surplus populations" (Li 2009) to reclaim the means to sustain their own lives. Discursively, KPRI's economic imaginary entails the stepwise re-organisation of production, distribution and consumption, collective ownership and institutionalisation. Materially, most practical experiences with cooperative production under workers' control are located in the agricultural sector. Most are still engaged in step one, i.e. re-organising the production base, but some have moved to distribution and consumption like the agricultural cooperative at Suroloyo Mountain. The example of the Independent Women's Union at Suroloyo also shows that women's empowerment—in its original transformative sense—forms part of KPRI's strategies and practices.

The historical excursus about workers' control in the early phase of independence indicates that the economic imaginary of cooperative production under workers' control has historical forerunners in Indonesia. Despite the brutal repression against leftist ideas under Suharto, experiences drawn from these short-lived experiments survived the New Order underground. When political space opened up during *Reformasi*, this suppressed imaginary resurfaced and became re-articulated with the more recent imaginary of "alternative" or "solidarity economies" by way of exchange with the experiences of recuperated factories in Latin America. In CPE terms, this is an example of "recovered imaginaries" (Sum and Jessop 2013, 424). These transnational or trans-local radical imaginaries provide a counter-hegemonic alternative to the hegemonic and sub-hegemonic approaches to decent work discussed above.[20]

---

20 Sum and Jessop argue: "Mutualism and cooperation have […] gained greater attention but are still largely confined to the margins of the leading economies as flanking or supporting mechanisms to soften the impact of the GFC [Global Financial Crisis] rather than operating as agents of radical transformation" (2013, 425). In contrast, I argue that it is premature to reduce the recovered "solidarity economy" imaginary to this sub-

Wary of any international campaign that aims at improving labour conditions without questioning the social relations of neoliberal capitalism and being aware of the dangers of social movements to be co-opted, these movements develop their own radical economic imaginaries that tend to be silenced by mainstream discourses of decent work. KPRI and its trade union branch KSN aim at developing radical alternatives to the neoliberal market regime, rather than merely improving working conditions within the neoliberal framework. This social movement confederation taps into discourses like "alternative economies" or "solidarity economy" rather than "decent work", entailing much more than "decent work" in narrowly defined terms—it involves workers' control, self-organisation, building "closed markets" and the vision of a radically democratic transformation of society, including women's empowerment.

Reclaiming the means to sustain their own lives reduces the dependency of marginalised women workers on the informal labour market. The "solidarity economy" not only provides alternative employment opportunities to them, but also new forms of identity and class consciousness. Isolated home workers working individually on a piece-rate basis may become members of a cooperative collectively producing for their common good. In the course of changing their economic circumstances and labour practices, they simultaneously transform their identities and subjectivities. In contrast to BWI and the PFA, which fail to address the whole supply chain, the "solidarity economy" imaginary of KPRI thus potentially offers a way out of marginalisation to the women workers at the bottom end of transnational supply chains.

From a CPE perspective, KPRI thus represents a *counter-hegemonic "alternative economy" imaginary* that goes beyond "decent work". It centres on ideas of autonomous self-organisation and worker's control, addresses the social movements of workers, peasants, fishermen, women and indigenous peoples alike and foregrounds their social emancipation. The economic imaginary of the "alternative economy" may be understood in competition to "decent work", because—as I have argued drawing on the cases of Better Work and Play Fair—decent work strategies may serve to pre-empt, disempower or displace these more radical imaginaries.

hegemonic function. It also carries counter-hegemonic potential, as the Indonesian case and others have shown. This tension is worth being further explored in future CPE/CGT research.

Unlike decent work, however, imaginaries such as "alternative economies" or "solidarity economy" have not been introduced conceptually and/or historically in previous chapters. I have not anticipated their relevance when the research process commenced. They emerged from the empirical data gathered during exploratory and main fieldwork. They have prompted me to revise initial conceptualisations, alter my understanding of decent work and include them in the empirical analysis within the Indonesian context. This openness and flexibility is a methodological principle of CGT. What is left as the final step of this chapter is to return to the global macro-theoretical level and connect the empirical findings from Indonesia to the wider context of the "solidarity economy" alternative and its transformative potential vis-à-vis the deeply entrenched hegemony of the neoliberal project. While an extensive discussion of this topic is beyond the remit of my study since it confronts us with a whole new set of problems, I want to conclude this chapter with an outlook on how the Indonesian case could be contextualised within debates about "alternative economies" or the "solidarity economy".

To this end, the conceptual slippage between "alternative economies" and "solidarity economy" needs to be clarified. Both terms emerged from the data, apparently referring to the same imaginary in the Indonesian context. When asked which term best captures the discursive and material aspects of KPRI's strategy, one activist explained: "It's not really about the label, it's about how you really tackle or solve the question of control and solidarity in the actual practice" (Union Interview, December 2011). The activist clearly thinks of the material "actual practice" as more important than the discursive "label". Nevertheless, from a CPE vantage point, the interplay between both is of central importance and looking at the practice without looking at the discourse is not an option. When peering into other contexts where "alternative economies" or "solidarity economy" are being discussed, both terms seem to be rather indeterminate and elusive with respect to the range of practices, strategies and projects they may refer to. Both are sometimes used interchangeably.

While "the alternative economy is the broad concept" (Union Interview, February 2012) of KPRI, they articulate this concept in their understanding as a "closed market" among agricultural cooperatives and recuperated factories. I have conceptualised this approach as counter-hegemonic. On the other hand, "alternative economy" has been articulated in multiple contexts with diverse meanings. Historically, it has been used to describe the classic cooperative movements in European countries from the 19th century. The classic producer cooperatives, however, have either failed to survive against their capitalist competitors or largely lost their transformative potential by taking on more and more characteristics of capitalist firms (Habermann 2012, 73). In the 1980s, "alternative economy" referred to a new type of cooperatives such as consumer cooperatives, credit unions and agricultural cooperatives that had been set up by social movements looking for a "third way" between capitalism and state socialism. The discussions of these historical experiences are too extensive to be reconstructed for this outlook. Rolf Schwendter (1986a, 1986b) gives an overview of the history, theory, critique, contemporary history and near future of the "alternative economy" imaginary in the German-language debate of the 1980s.

Berlinguer (2014, 111) explains that today in the Italian context the "alternative economy" is understood as comprising for-profit companies such as those engaged in Fair Trade, ethical consumption, organic farming, or eco-tourism. These economic activities, from a CPE perspective, are sub-hegemonic in relation to the neoliberal project, providing material and discursive resources for the social and environmental re-ethicalisation of neoliberalism. In Žižek's terms, they are examples of "cultural capitalism" (2009, 52). KPRI activists have also explicitly distanced themselves from Fair Trade and other labelling initiatives, rejecting strategies that merely serve to humanise neoliberal capitalism and instead stressing the importance of autonomy, self-organisation and workers' control beyond the capitalist market regime. Ranging from "alternatives to capitalism" to "alternative capitalisms", the "alternative economy" may refer to any form of economic activity that is perceived as different from the prevailing mainstream. It is thus too broad a concept for capturing the distinctive imaginaries, strategies and practices of KPRI.

The "solidarity economy" is not necessarily less broad. It has been used to refer to such different experiments as the hippie communes of the 1970s and the new cooperatives of the 1980s (Habermann 2012, 73–74). These examples are very different in nature and have little in common except for their counter-hegemonic self-conceptualisations. The post-1968 communards were determined to delink themselves from the capitalist mainstream as much as possible by producing for subsistence and striving for self-sufficiency. The communes, however, remained isolated experiments that failed to become organically connected and condensed to a viable counter-hegemonic project. Isolationism created a sense of peer pressure among the communards (ibid., 73) that in some cases escalated to forms of sectarianism resembling religious sects. Reactionary practices infused with emancipatory discourses greatly diminished the appeal of the commune imaginary, but successful practical experiments continue to exist until today.

The new cooperatives of the 1980s, similar to the classic cooperatives of the 19th century, have struggled with Franz Oppenheimer's "law of transformation" (Auinger 2009, 12). Oppenheimer had argued that a production cooperative within a capitalist environment cannot possibly take on every worker who wishes to join the cooperative unless it wants to cease to exist economically. A successful cooperative has to block new members from joining but, if it does so, it ceases to exist as a cooperative in the emphatic sense since openness is one of its defining features (Kruck 1992, 6). This law has somewhat mistakenly been understood as arguing that producer cooperatives in capitalist surroundings are theoretically impossible since they either transform themselves into conventional capitalist firms or perish economically. Even if this interpretation of Oppenheimer's law is not entirely in line with his argument, it continues to inform debates within the cooperative movement about the tensions and problems cooperatives generally face. The tendency of being transformed into a capitalist company and thus of becoming co-opted by the capitalist mainstream is a real danger for successful cooperatives today. The alternative they face is to remain "economically unsuccessful and keep on serving as mere self-help organizations" (Auinger 2009, 13). In the former case, cooperatives stop being alternatives to capitalism and become more or less alternative forms of capitalism. In the latter case, cooperatives mainly fulfil self-help functions in contexts of capitalist crises and may be regarded as "one alternative amongst others within the capitalist system that will cushion its dysfunctional effects" (ibid.). In both cases, we are confronted with a basic tension within the cooperative imaginary between the counter-hegemonic intentions of its proponents and the sub-hegemonic effects of many experiments. The experiments of KPRI in Indonesia will in all likelihood not be devoid of this tension.

This tension signals that the solidarity economy imaginary—in this regard not fundamentally different form the decent work imaginary—may initially be articulated as a counter-hegemonic element, but runs the risk of getting co-opted and being transformed into a sub-hegemonic moment of a deepened hegemony of neoliberal capitalism. One discursive strategy to this effect is the re-articulation of the counter-hegemonic "solidarity economy" imaginary with the sub-hegemonic "social economy" imaginary as the new compound "social and solidarity economy". For example, the International Training Centre of the ILO refers to the "social and solidarity economy" as "a concept that refers to enterprises and organizations, in particular cooperatives, mutual benefit societies, associations, foundations and social enterprises, which specifically produce goods, services and knowledge while pursuing economic and social aims and fostering solidarity" (ILO 2011b, vi). Here, cooperatives, non-profit associations and for-profit enterprises are lumped together under a single category. Their differences in terms of their associated imaginaries, strategies and practices are glossed over under the dominance of the "social economy".

The "social economy" usually refers to the classic "third sector", to be distinguished from the public and the private sector (Berlinguer 2014, 101). Traditionally, only non-profit, non-governmental and voluntary organisations were included in this sector. Clubs and societies such as the German *Vereine*, for example, belong to this category since they are neither public institutions nor private businesses. "Social enterprises", on the other hand, are private businesses that produce goods or services for profit, but they also seek additional "social value-added", arguably not the least as a (niche) marketing strategy. The recent shift towards promoting "social entrepreneurship", therefore, signals a shift towards a neoliberal, managerial approach to the social economy in line with market imperatives.

The counter-hegemonic experiments with workers' control and cooperative production I have encountered in Indonesia neither belong to the non-profit nor to the for-profit category of the social economy. The "solidarity economy", in contrast, may refer to "the more radical sectors of the social economy" (Berlinguer 2014, 111), making it a potential category adequate to the Indonesian experiments. Satgar, however, also is careful to argue that the "solidarity economy as part of a counter-hegemonic political economy" (2014, 4) may also be assimilated and co-opted by mainstream "social economy" discourses as exemplified by the ILO's hybrid category "social and solidarity economy" (ILO 2011b). If the ILO integrates the "solidarity economy" imaginary, but directs its resources towards private, for-profit "social economy enterprises", the imaginary's meaning shifts from counter-hegemonic and anti-capitalist to ameliorating and re-legitimising neoliberal capitalism.

On the other hand, CPE's understanding of semiosis implies that there is no necessary relationship between signifier and referent. In that sense, the above-quoted KPRI activist perhaps is correct to argue that the label itself is less important than that which it refers to. Similarly, Satgar argues that "a standard conception or definition of the solidarity economy" is less important than "its actual and potential anti-capitalist practices" (2014, 4). He goes on to explain:

"Unlike the social economy, which can fit into a residual space within capitalism, the solidarity economy determines its own scale, space and positioning; it is an emerging theory and practice that goes beyond capitalism" (ibid., 5).

This understanding is compatible with KPRI's counter-hegemonic project, explicitly championing post-capitalist imaginaries, strategies and practices. It is in this transnational context that I would situate the Indonesian experiments with cooperative production under workers' control.

If we take the principles of autonomy, self-organisation and workers' control as the defining characteristics of a grassroots solidarity economy, understood as alternative economic practices "beyond the capitalist canon" (Santos 2006), we may turn to countries as diverse as Argentina, Brazil, Venezuela, South Africa, Mozambique, Israel, Spain, Greece, Germany, the United States or India. We will find different examples of people taking their matters into their own hands, reclaiming the means to sustain their own lives, developing alternative economic practices, envisioning post-capitalist imaginaries and building solidarity economies everywhere. It is about time to put Indonesia on the map of these struggles as well, both in terms of their local relevance and their global dimension as indicated by the transnational *No Chains* network.

Looking at other countries, Lisa Mittendrein (2013), for example, analyses the emergence of solidarity economies in the context of the recent crisis in Greece. Austerity policies dictated by the Troika (IMF, World Bank and European Union) caused the Greek economy to shrink in an unprecedented manner and pushed many institutions of the Greek welfare state to the brink of collapse. Many people not only lost material income and access to social services but also discursive trust in political institutions. They started to locally organise themselves to provide non-monetary social services to those in need. Social clinics, for instance, were established all over the country, where volunteer collectives provide medical services to those who cannot afford the newly imposed entrance fees for public hospitals, let alone private clinics (Solidarity for All 2014). Similar to the

Argentinian crisis of 2001 (Mittendrein 2013, 44–49), these solidarity economies emerged in response to a financial crisis that escalated into a wider economic and political crisis and, not the least, a crisis of social reproduction.

In Argentina, the neoliberal reforms of the 1990s, including extensive privatisations of public enterprises, lead to rising national debt, unemployment and poverty (Uriona 2007). In 1999, Argentina's economy plunged into recession after Brazil had devalued its currency against the US Dollar in order to recover from its own 1997/1998 crisis. At first, Argentina did not likewise devalue its currency in order to avoid capital flight. When the IMF refused to transfer a 1.3 billion US Dollar credit in November 2001, because Argentina had not met the budgetary goals imposed by the IMF, a massive loss of trust in state institutions and the banking system was the consequence (Wolff 2008, 138). Subsequent large-scale capital flight and currency speculation brought the financial system to the brink of collapse. In December 2001, after the financial crisis had sparked massive social unrest in the streets of Buenos Aires forcing President Fernando de la Rúa to resign, Argentina had to declare bankruptcy. In the economic turmoil that followed, widespread bankruptcies and closures of private companies lead to spontaneous factory occupations and forms of cooperative production under workers' control. These experiments became to be known as "recuperated factories" (*empresas recuperados*). Their number rose from 44 in 2001 to 98 in 2003 to ca. 180 in 2005 (Wolff 2008, 141; Uriona 2007, 65–66). Diego Kravetz, the lawyer and politician who drafted the law that legalised factory occupations by workers and expropriations by the state in 2004, however, is careful to explain: "What I am trying to say is that it was never a utopia of the workers to take over their factories by means of a revolution, but a survival strategy" (Kravetz cited in Uriona 2007, 66, my translation).

Throughout the history of capitalism, cooperatives and other forms of the solidarity economy were often born out of sheer necessity as mere survival strategies and many experiments disappeared as capitalism recovered from crisis (Mittendrein 2013, 42–44). If self-help and survival are the primary motives behind these experiments, they are more likely to become re-absorbed when the crisis appears over than experiments simultaneously envisioning economic imaginaries with transformative, emancipatory potential. Mittendrein concludes:

"Solidarity economy, first, provides the potential of coping with crisis by helping to satisfy material and immaterial needs. Coping with crisis becomes more important for many projects as the crisis intensifies. It often means concrete, collective self-help. Through the collective form and the associated collective identity, coping with crisis however also carries transformative potential" (2013, 185–186, my translation).

In Indonesia, the factory occupation at PT Istana was similarly born out of necessity. Initially, it was developed as a form of self-help to generate income and pressure the former owner to pay severance pay. Over time, however, the transformative potential surfaced as workers radicalised and started aiming to keep the factory running under workers' control. Even though this transformative potential did not unfold to spread to other factories and many workers returned to the formal and informal labour markets after the cooperative had to leave the factory premises, some of them held on to the solidarity economy imaginary and continued to produce clothing collectively as a home-based cooperative. As the analysis has shown, the workers, who are still members of the cooperative, value collective self-organisation very high, even though the cooperative may pay wages only irregularly. Their experience of being able to determine their destiny themselves, to organise a workplace democratically and collectively and to develop a counter-hegemonic imaginary that extends beyond the workplace to envision a radically democratic transformation of society produced collective identities and post-capitalist desires that will continue to spark emancipatory practices.

At PT Istana, another aspect of the transformative potential of the solidarity economy became visible. I have argued that industrial production, democratic self-organisation, political self-education and social reproduction were all united under its factory roof for a limited period of time. The workers not only continued to operate the machines to produce clothing, they also organised their own child day care and public kitchen. While also born out of necessity, this shows the potential of counter-hegemonic practices associated with the solidarity economy imaginary to overcome the division between the production of goods and the social reproduction of people and communities imposed by capitalism. These practices thus underscore the possibility of emancipatorily reconnecting what capitalism has divided: culture, politics and economics as well as productive labour, reproductive care and subsistence work. They can therefore be a reference point for the revitalisation of the global labour movement that also speaks to feminist concerns. CPE, informed by feminist theory and operationalised with CGT, is well placed to further investigate these practices in their cultural, political and economic dimensions.

Whether the practices associated with the solidarity economy imaginary will resist co-optation and tap their transformative potential is an open question. Its answer will partly depend on the ability of the social forces championing these counter-hegemonic imaginaries and practices to further consolidate them into a viable counter-hegemonic project, transforming sporadic and spontaneous elements of counter-hegemonic reactions to capitalist crises (such as the occupation of a factory or a hospital set for closure) into moments of a collective, self-conscious effort to leave behind the impositions of capitalism. In Indonesia and elsewhere, this process is already underway.

8. Conclusion

This final chapter briefly summarises the theoretical, methodological, historical and empirical lines of reasoning of the present study as well as presents some concluding remarks on the paradoxes of decent work.

My study started from the ubiquity of CSR mechanisms in transnational supply chains that have emerged in response to criticisms of sweatshop conditions in world market factories of the Global South, where the bulk of global industrial production was relocated to after the crisis of Fordism. Indonesia was introduced as a critical case for studying the paradoxes of global labour politics in the era of neoliberal globalisation that has created new employment opportunities in the Global South, primarily for young women, but with poverty wages, short-term contracts and denial of fundamental labour rights as their defining features. The ILO was depicted as one of the central nodes of a global multilevel governance network of public and private labour regulation. I argued that transnational corporations fearing for their reputation and brand image sought to link up their CSR mechanisms to the ILO's core labour standards in order to improve the credibility of their codes of conduct that had been criticised for failing to improve working conditions substantially while lending an aura of legitimacy and ethicality to their production practices.

Decent work was initially conceptualised as an inherently ambiguous discourse. On the one hand, it addresses the problem of informal, precarious employment and feminised labour. It thus represents a progressive move away from the male standard employment relationship and may help marginalised groups of workers to struggle for better working and living conditions and challenge the hegemony of the neoliberal project. On the other hand, decent work espouses voluntary initiatives such as CSR and seeks to replace adversarial bargaining and industrial action with "social dialogue". This makes it a soft law approach compatible with neoliberalism, possibly reinforcing its hegemony by appealing to social policy, which becomes a largely symbolical act without materially challenging the neoliberal development paradigm and underlying power relations. Between these two poles, my study sought to empirically investigate the paradoxes of decent work by looking at the ways in which this discourse or "economic imaginary" may be practically used by progressive actors such as trade unions, labour NGOs or social movements in Indonesia in their everyday practices and strategies for better working and living conditions. Additionally, I also wanted to look at alternative discourses, strategies and practices of these actors that may compete with decent work.

This perspective was informed by the theoretical framework of Cultural Political Economy, elaborated in Chapter 2. First, I have introduced CPE's foundation in Regulation Theory and discussed regulationist concepts such as accumulation regime and mode of regulation that would later become important for the historical analysis of the emergence of the decent work discourse in the context of neoliberal globalisation. Social forms were introduced as the physical guises in which people experience their own social relations in alienated, fetishised ways, processing the basic contradictions of the capitalist mode of production. Institutional forms were discussed as more concrete codifications of the abstract social forms, occupying the intermediate level between structure and agency. The wage relation, for example, is an institutional form that makes the contradiction between capital and labour workable in historically and spatially specific ways. The regulationist approach to the state and to hegemony was also briefly reviewed to lay the groundwork for CPE's concepts of hegemony, sub-hegemony and counter-hegemony.

Second, the theoretical move from Regulation Theory to CPE was reconstructed and CPE's conceptual framework introduced. Although notions such as "economic imaginary" and "hegemony, sub-hegemony and counter-hegemony" became more important for my empirical analysis later on, I also discussed the general setup of CPE as a critical theory of society integrating elements from post-structuralist discourse theories but retaining key insights from Marx's critique of political economy. CPE's particular understanding of semiosis and structuration was explained, including a discussion of how CPE endeavoured to integrate Foucauldian concepts such as discourse or dispositive. Most importantly, however, the central concept of economic (and political) imaginaries was clarified that would later become crucially important for my operationalisation of decent work.

This theoretical framework is not only important for the concrete case studies on the micro level, but also to establish the wider macro context of neoliberal globalisation, out of which the decent work discourse emerged, from a critical social theory perspectives that retains key concepts of Marxian theory while aiming to integrate fresh insights from the "cultural turn" in the social sciences.

Building on the framework of CPE, Chapter 3 presented a distinct Critical Grounded Theory methodology (Belfrage and Hauf 2015). First, it reflected on CPE's preferred method of Critical Discourse Analysis and its limitations in terms of analysing the practical use of discourses or imaginaries in people's everyday lives. Second, the necessity of combining discourse analysis with ethnographic fieldwork prompted the exploration of Grounded Theory methods to look for ethnographic tools and techniques serving this purpose. Third, given Grounded Theory's origin in positivist science, these tools and techniques had to be adapted to the critical-realist framework of CPE, enabling a retroductive, spiral movement between theoretical and empirical work as opposed to the inductive, unidirectional movement from empiricism to theorisation of positivist or objectivist Grounded Theory. Against this background, fourth, an abstract model of how the resulting method of Critical Grounded Theory may be employed in research praxis was constructed.

The remainder of the methodological chapter specified the way I have employed CPE to approach the issue of decent work and how I have used CGT to operationalise the research problem. I recounted the concrete steps of the CGT process in terms of approaching the research problem, constructing initial conceptualisations, exploring the field, selecting the cases, revisiting theories, grounding conceptualisations, conducting the main fieldwork and constructing a critical grounded theory. Initially, I conceptualised decent work as potentially functioning as both pro-hegemonic and counter-hegemonic vis-à-vis neoliberalism, depending on which actors appropriate it in which context, for which projects and strategies, with which objectives and interests. This was the result of a review of the scholarly literature on decent work, in which I identified a feminist imaginary of decent work stressing its progressive potential for informalised, marginalised workers and a "business case" imaginary of decent work stressing its re-legitimising function in the context of the crisis of neoliberalism. Between exploratory and main fieldwork, this initial conceptualisation was grounded by putting it into dialogue with empirical findings and participants' own conceptualisations. As a result, it was altered in that I now expected to find counter-hegemonic imaginaries at the edge or beyond the official decent work discourse rather than within. Decent work imaginaries building on the feminist case and other progressive arguments for decent work were re-conceptualised as potentially sub-hegemonic.

Chapters 4 and 5 provided the historical context for the case studies of Chapters 6 and 7. First, I reconstructed a brief history of neoliberalism starting from Fordism and its crisis, including a discussion of Fordism in the periphery and the move from import substitution to export orientation. The neoliberalisation and feminisation of labour and the emergence of transnational supply chains were introduced as central features of neoliberal global restructuring, giving rise to indecent working conditions and propelling a "race to the bottom" in the Global South. Second, a similarly brief history of global labour regulation was presented. The International Labour Organisation was discussed in historical context from the Fordist period to the crisis of Fordism to the age of neoliberal globalisation. The debate about a multilateral "social clause" within the framework of the World Trade Organisation and the emergence of private forms of labour regulation (the "myth" of CSR) were critically reconstructed. The emergence of the decent work agenda itself was analysed in terms of the basic tension between arguments seeing it either as a sign of counter-hegemonic forces inside the ILO or as in line with the neoliberal development paradigm, co-opted by hegemonic forces. The grounded conceptualisation was iterated as the question of whether the feminist imaginary of decent work has the potential to become counter-hegemonic vis-à-vis neoliberalism or whether it remains sub-hegemonic, running the risk of being subsumed, contained and co-opted within hegemonic codes.

In Chapter 5, the specific history of trade unions and labour politics in Indonesia was briefly recounted in order to clarify the particular context in which I have addressed the general research problem. The time between independence and the beginning of Suharto's New Order, the annihilation of the labour movement and the democide against alleged communists were mentioned as historical legacies with continued, albeit silenced, relevance until today. The Pancasila Industrial Relations system of "harmonious" labour relations under Suharto, the single authoritarian state union SPSI, the particularly Indonesian form of Fordism, including an authoritarian developmental state and a state-led industrialisation strategy shifting from import substitution to export orientation were explained. Finally, the reconstruction of the resurgence of the Indonesian labour movement before and during *Reformasi* clarified how the fall of Suharto opened up new democratic spaces to be occupied by newly emerging, genuinely independent labour unions virtually overnight. This opening produced a large amount of variation in the field of trade union politics with newly emerging unions now competing with old authoritarian unions over members and influence. The leadership of the new independent unions also tend to be young women workers, while SPSI's successor organisations are still headed by mostly male members of the old union elites. Intra-union struggles for more internal democracy and independence from the state are underway. Nevertheless, these large bureaucratic organisations continue to be seen as "yellow unions" by many workers and activists. If the progressive potential of the decent work agenda was to play out in the Indonesian context in a meaningful way, the newly emerging, genuinely independent and democratic labour unions should be empowered against their state- and employer-sponsored, "yellow" rivals.

The research problem was further refined to the question of how the three cases analysed in Chapters 6 and 7 contribute to the selection and retention of certain decent work (or alternative) strategies at the expense of filtering out or marginalising others. What kinds of imaginaries do the different projects and initiatives produce and circulate? What kinds of strategies and practices do they enable or restrict? How can these be employed by counter-hegemonic forces to challenge the hegemony of neoliberalism?

Chapter 5 ended with a discussion of the current situation of organised labour in Indonesia in order to provide an idea of the field, of which the three cases form part or intervene in. Poverty wages, subcontracting and outsourcing as well as freedom of association and union busting were identified as the main concerns of most Indonesian trade unions at the time of research. These three factors, together constituting a massive lack of "decent work" in Indonesia, mutually reinforce each other. Raising minimum wages above subsistence level, ending the temporary short-term contract system and defending the right to organise and bargain collectively are thus the main strategic priorities of Indonesian trade unions, shared by most confederations from left to right, at least rhetorically. The time of research was one of intense and militant labour struggles with mass demonstrations and large-scale strikes, blockings of toll roads and sieges of official buildings. I have argued that these radical or confrontational strategies were decisive in pushing political decision makers to agree to substantial wage hikes. In Jakarta, for example, the minimum wage was raised to the level of the government-calculated "decent living needs" (KHL) for the first time after an unprecedented general strike had signalled the power of a new, reawakened labour movement willing to employ militant strategies to fight for workers' rights. Mere "social dialogue" strategies, in contrast, have often failed to fulfil workers' demands. For example, minimum wage negotiations between employer associations and "yellow unions" behind closed doors have repeatedly frustrated the workers, in many cases causing militant mass protests. This is the particular context, in which the three cases aim to intervene.

In Chapter 6, Better Work Indonesia (BWI) was introduced as the first monitoring project of the ILO in Indonesia, initially targeting the garment and textile industry. BWI acknowledges wages, contracts and freedom of association—among other things—as important issues for Indonesian workers. BWI's approach towards improving such issues, however, has been argued to represent a hegemonic "decent work from above" imaginary. It helps transnational corporations to manage their supply chain in terms of labour law compliance and thus to strengthen their relations to increasingly ethically oriented consumers in the Global North: "Better Work supports enterprises in implementing the core labour standards and national labour laws, thereby improving their ability to compete in global markets, as well as enhancing productivity and product quality" (ILO 2008b, 37). The participation in Better Work improves the competitiveness of Indonesian garment factories, given the demand for ethically produced clothing on the world market. It primarily addresses transnational corporations and their supplier factories as active participants, foregrounds their CSR strategies as integral parts of transnational supply chain management and improves the credibility of their codes of conduct while reducing auditing costs and circumventing independent labour unions. It thereby makes the "business case" for decent work, stressing compliance, productivity and competitiveness. The meaning of "decent work" is here limited to an absolute minimum definition, comprising the core labour standards as well as issues such as occupational safety and health. Such issues are the main area where BWI has achieved improvements, since these are more easily addressed by "social dialogue" strategies seeking win-

win-solutions than the level of wages or the permanence of contracts, for example.

BWI thus contributes to the selection and retention of moderate, managerial, top-down strategies towards decent work while filtering out or marginalising more radical and perhaps more effective bottom-up strategies. Better Work is an example of how neoliberal production practices have been re-ethicalised by incorporating and co-opting critique discursively without changing the structural conditions of these practices, thereby serving to reinforce the hegemony of neoliberalism rather than challenging it. Sum has conceptualised this process as the "new ethicalism" referring to the "ethicalized-managerial strategies that seek to reconnect economic policies with (new) moral norms that are dominated by technicalized and managerialized practices" (2010, 68).

The Play Fair Alliance (PFA), in contrast, was discussed as a multistakeholder initiative involving global brands, supplier factories, labour NGOs and trade unions. The PFA identified the three above-mentioned issues of wages, contracts and freedom of association as the main priorities to be addressed by voluntary, yet binding protocols. I have argued that its approach towards improving these issues represents a sub-hegemonic "decent work from below" imaginary. The freedom of association protocol addresses buyers and Tier 1 suppliers to provide certain standards pertaining to the right to organise and bargain collectively. Trade unions are actively involved in drafting the protocol and monitoring its implementation. The process is much more bottom-up, deliberative and inclusive than BWI. Its main goal is fairness, it addresses all stakeholders as active participants and it foregrounds social dialogue. At the same time, however, dispute settlement committees designated for monitoring the implementation of the protocol aim to replace confrontational union strategies with more "cooperative" strategies. The FoA Protocol aims at moderating class conflict in peaceful, social-dialogical ways. The effects sought are less industrial disputes and less labour unrest. These goals are less openly articulated than the official goal of improving unions' organising capacities as a precondition for struggling for other improvements and rights. As I have argued, however, channelling labour conflicts into a private dispute resolution framework may actually weaken the unions in a hostile environment, in which militant working class strategies may continue to be more effective. Confrontational strategies such as mass demonstrations, large-scale strikes, highway blockages or sieges of government buildings have increased the political power of unions, which provides a substitute for the lack of economic power in transnational supply chains.

The PFA therefore contributes to the selection and retention of moderate, bottom-up, social dialogue strategies towards decent work and, not dissimilar to BWI, to filtering out or marginalising more militant and perhaps more effective trade union strategies. The PFA in Indonesia is an example of how the critique of neoliberal production practices, if articulated in sub-hegemonic rather than counter-hegemonic forms, may become absorbed by hegemonic codes and co-opted by hegemonic actors in the service of flexibly reproducing neoliberal hegemony. The fact that some trade unions and labour NGOs actively participate in this process suggests that Sum's (2010) "new ethicalism" has a hegemonic and a sub-hegemonic discourse strand, the former produced and circulated by transnational corporations, business associations and the ILO, the latter produced as a supplement to the former by "business unions" and international NGOs.

If Play Fair represents a sub-hegemonic imaginary of decent work, we must turn elsewhere to find counter-hegemonic projects actually challenging the logic of the neoliberal project rather than amending and flanking it by social policies. Stumbling upon the factory occupation at PT Istana and following the traces of an alternative counter-hegemonic imaginary, my study has brought to light the "solidarity economy alternative" in Indonesia, which is usually silenced and invisible in mainstream discourses of Indonesian labour politics. The absence of "solidarity economy" experiments from these discourses is a good example of CPE's notion of "discursive selectivity" (Sum and Jessop 2013, 215). The mainstream labour discourse on Indonesia selectively prioritises moderate trade union strategies associated with "decent work" and systematically filters out more radical strategies connected to the "solidarity economy" imaginary.

I have analysed the emergence of the new, radical union confederation KSN and the split from KASBI. The latter's participation in multi-stakeholder initiatives like the PFA and path towards more institutionalisation and integration have been identified as factors contributing to its division. KSN activists feared that this path would de-radicalise and de-politicise the union, thereby undermining its own power base. KSN, instead, has joined the social movement confederation KPRI, aiming to build "closed markets" among urban and rural communities and to break away from the neoliberal market regime. I have argued that this approach towards improving the lives of Indonesian workers and peasants by reclaiming the means to sustain their own lives represents a counter-hegemonic "alternative economies" or "solidarity economy" imaginary that goes beyond "decent work". It centres on ideas of autonomous self-organisation and workers' control and foregrounds social emancipation. It has historical forerunners in experiences of workers' control immediately after independence. These experiences were violently suppressed by the Suharto regime and excluded from public discourse, but they survived underground. Resurfacing practices informed by this kind of recovered imaginary such as factory occupations, land reclaimings and other direct actions are already being waged by the autonomous labour movement, the peasant's movement, indigenous people's and women's movements. Previously excluded meanings, identities and desires are re-entering and re-politicising the arena of Indonesian labour discourses and practices. Drawing on the cases of Better Work and Play Fair, I have argued that decent work strategies may serve to pre-empt, disempower or displace these more radical imaginaries and practices that point towards not only post-neoliberal but post-capitalist futures.

In CPE terms, the institutional decent work discourse, thus, actively participates in the *selection* of competing imaginaries informing the strategies and practices of Indonesian trade unions, privileging moderate union strategies of "social dialogue" and filtering out or marginalising more radical union strategies. This reduces the huge amount of *variation* of trade unions' imaginaries after the fall of Suharto and contributes to the *retention* of the service model of "business unionism"—in the Indonesian case converging with "yellow" unionism—at the expense of the organising model of "social movement unionism" (Scipes 1992, Moody 1997, Waterman 2004).

The following table summarises the comparative analysis of the three case studies of BWI, the PFA and KPRI.

Case	Better Work Indonesia	Play Fair Alliance	Indonesian People's Movement Confederation
Economic Imaginary	Decent Work from Above	Decent Work from Below	Alternative/ Solidarity Economy
Main Initiators	ILO, Brands/ Buyers	NGOs, Unions	Unions, Movements
Main Addressees	Employers/ Suppliers	Brands, Suppliers, Unions	Unions, Movements
Main Goal	Company Compliance	Fairness	Workers' Control
Main Strategy	Factory Assessments	Social Dialogue	Closed Markets
Main Practices	Monitoring and Reporting	Negotiating Voluntary Protocols	Factory Occupations, Land Reclaimings
Union Involvement	Passive Participation	Active Participation	Self-Organisation
Direction	Top-Down	Bottom-Up	Horizontal
Position	Hegemonic	Sub-Hegemonic	Counter-Hegemonic

Table 3: Summary of the Comparative Analysis of the Three Case Studies

Decent work may, after all, be conceptualised as part of what Ngai-Ling Sum (2010) has called "new ethicalism", reconnecting neoliberal production practices to moral values without substantially challenging underlying power relations and structural conditions, thus reinforcing neoliberal hegemony by co-opting criticism rather than challenging the neoliberal project. New ethicalism is a "technology of control in which the audit and certification discourses, practices and procedures are used to ward off dangers and gain mastery over social activism" representing a form of a

Gramscian "passive revolution" (Sum 2010, 65). Interestingly, this corresponds to Franco Barchiesi's argument about decent work in the South-African context as "an antidote to radical demands" holding in a "material reality where work is a condition of dignity and decency for a shrinking minority of the population" (2012, 132). Note the difference between "dignity" and "decency", the former referring to the fundamental inviolability of human dignity enshrined in the Universal Declaration of Human Rights and the latter carrying a much weaker meaning of minimum standards.[21]

The Indonesian general strike of October 3, 2012, the first one after 30 years of military dictatorship, after the anti-communist purge under Suharto and after 15 years of wavering democratisation, showed that the material reality referred to by Barchiesi cannot easily be contained in Indonesia. The government responded to the recent upswing in militant labour activism by increasing the minimum wage for Jakarta by 44 per cent. For the first time now, workers in Jakarta are paid a decent living wage according to the KHL, as a result of the general strike and other radical labour struggles. This may show that what determines the level of decency—or, rather, dignity—of workers' lives at the end of the day is the dynamic of social struggles and the local balances of power or relations of social forces. Due to Indonesia's location within transnational supply chains and labour's limited economic power therein, militant labour strategies have successfully exerted political power on local governments, where final decisions about minimum wages are made.

Although transnational advocacy networks and global consumer campaigns have in some cases contributed to shifting the local balance of power to the benefit of the workers, the above-mentioned boomerang effect is limited to transnationally visible Tier 1 factories. The local power base of the unions, rather than the presence of international NGOs, is the decisive factor for the success or failure of local labour struggles. Bianca Kühl (2006), for example, has overstated the role of Western NGOs and transnational campaigns while underestimating the role of unions' local power base in her analysis of labour rights violations in Indonesia. Don

---

21 A Thai cooperative producing clothing in a factory under workers' control that is member of the above-mentioned No Chains network calls itself Dignity Returns and promotes its products as "Sweat-Free Products of Dignified Labor" (www.dignityreturns.org). The notion of "dignified labour" here represents a counter-hegemonic alternative to "decent work".

Wells has rightly argued that this privileging of the Global North within analyses of transnational advocacy networks detracts from the fact that "the Northern dimensions of this transnational labour politics were not the primary variables; instead they were *auxiliary* to what were predominantly *local* struggles by workers and their allies" (2009, 572, emphasis in the original). Northern actors who wish to practice solidarity play a supportive role that can have positive, empowering but also unintended, negative, disempowering effects. It is workers in the Global South and their local allies that play the starring role in this global theatre of local labour struggles.

Simplifying and reducing complexity while sharpening the critical edge of the argument, the problem with decent work seems to be the following: on the one hand, global capital could only restore its profitability after the crisis of Fordism by relocating industrial production to the "periphery", where wages are low, feminised labour supply abundant and legal standards weak. The key point here are low wages, often even below subsistence level, which secretly rely on unpaid reproductive work mostly performed by women. The human misery produced by the neoliberal regime of accumulation, however, has undermined the legitimacy of global capitalism, because the belief that workers are entitled to "fair wages" is an almost universally held belief, a cornerstone of any capitalist imaginary. The strategic function of "decent work" is to restore legitimacy by "re-ethicalising" neoliberal production practices. However, decent work policies cannot tackle the problem at its structural core. They cannot raise misery wages in the Global South substantially because this would undermine the global neoliberal regime of accumulation itself. The "flexibilisation" of labour markets, which is a euphemism for downgrading labour, is structurally coupled with the operations of transnational supply chains. Dignified labour along the whole supply chain in any substantial sense—including living wages, shorter working hours, permanent contracts, social security, workplace democracy and so on—is *incompossible* with neoliberal low-cost production. Only those elements of the decent work discourse that are *compossible* with other elements of the neoliberal framework will pass the moments of variation and selection and become retained in material practices. This includes better occupational safety and health and other incremental improvements as long as they are not too costly.

What "decent work" thus *can* do is to process or to contain temporarily the basic contradiction between capital and labour in its neoliberal guise. It can defer its post-capitalist sublation to the distant future by transforming the political-economic class conflict into a merely technical problem of labour law compliance, but it cannot resolve that contradiction. The current cycle of labour struggles around the world shows how this contradiction recurrently surfaces as conflicts and crises. After all, the right to decent work appears as that "which we cannot not want" (Brown 2000, 231)—we cannot *not* want poor working conditions to be improved, no matter how slow and incremental. However, we must also reflect on how this may serve to flank neoliberalism and to pre-empt, disempower or displace more radical, counter-hegemonic imaginaries and practices.

Works Cited

AFW (2009). *Stitching a Decent Wage Across Borders: The Asia Floor Wage Proposal,* Written by Jeroen Merk of the Clean Clothes Campaign on Behalf of the Asia Floor Wage Campaign. New Delhi: Society for Labour and Development.

Aglietta, Michel (1979). *A Theory of Capitalist Regulation: The US Experience.* London: Verso.

Albo, Gregory (2009). The Crisis of Neoliberalism and the Impasse of the Union Movement. *Development Dialogue,* 51, 119–131.

Alnasseri, Sabah (2004). *Periphere Regulation: Regulationstheoretische Konzepte zur Analyse von Entwicklungsstrategien im arabischen Raum.* Münster: Westfälisches Dampfboot.

Althusser, Louis (1977). Ideologie und ideologische Staatsapparate: Anmerkungen für eine Untersuchung. In Louis Althusser. *Ideologie und ideologische Staatsapparate: Aufsätze zur marxistischen Theorie,* 108–153. Hamburg: VSA.

Anner, Marc (2006). The Paradox of Labour Transnationalism: Trade Union Campaigns for Labour Standards in International Institutions. In Craig Phelan (ed.). *The Future of Organised Labour: Global Perspectives,* 63–90. Oxford: Peter Lang.

Arnold, Dennis and Toh Han Shih (2010). A Fair Model of Globalisation? Labour and Global Production in Cambodia. *Journal of Contemporary Asia,* 40 (3), 401–424.

Auinger, Markus (2009). Introduction: Solidarity Economics—Emancipatory Social Change or Self-Help? *Journal für Entwicklungspolitik,* 25 (3), 4–21.

Azzellini, Dario (2011). Workers' Control under Venezuela's Bolivarian Revolution. In Immanuel Ness and Dario Azzellini (eds.). *Ours to Master and to Own: Workers' Control from the Commune to the Present,* 382–399. Chicago: Haymarket.

Barchiesi, Franco (2012). Imagining the Patriotic Worker: The Idea of "Decent Work" in the ANC's Political Discourse. In Arianna Lissoni et al. (eds.). *One Hundred Years of the ANC: Debating Liberation Histories Today,* 111–135. Johannesburg: Wits University Press.

Barrientos, Stephanie (2007). Gender, Codes of Conduct and Labor Standards in Global Production Systems. In Irene van Staveren et al. (eds.). *The Feminist Economic of Trade,* 239–256. London/New York: Routledge.

Barry, Andrew (2004). Ethical Capitalism. In Wendy Larner and William Walters (eds.). *Global Governmentality: Governing International Spaces,* 195–211. London/ New York: Routledge.

Bartley, Tim and Curtis Child (2014). Shaming the Corporation: The Social Production of Targets and the Anti-Sweatshop Movement. *American Sociological Review,* 79 (4), 653–679.

Belfrage, Claes and Felix Hauf (2015). Operationalising Cultural Political Economy: Towards Critical Grounded Theory. *Journal of Organizational Ethnography,* 4 (3), 324–340.

Becker, Joachim (2002). *Akkumulation, Regulation, Territorium: Zur kritischen Rekonstruktion der französischen Regulationstheorie.* Marburg: Metropolis.

Becker, Joachim (2009). Regulationstheorie. In Joachim Becker et al. (eds.). *Heterodoxe Ökonomie,* 89–116. Marburg: Metropolis.

Behrens, Martin et al. (2006). Conceptualizing Labour Union Revitalization. In Carola M. Frege and John Kelly (eds.). *Varieties of Unionism: Strategies for Union Revitalization in a Globalizing Economy,* 11–29. Oxford: Oxford University Press.

Berlinguer, Marco (2014). The Social Economy in Italy: Limits and Possibilities. In Vishwas Satgar (ed.). *The Solidarity Economy Alternative: Emerging Theory and Practice,* 101–125. Pietermaritzburg: University of KwaZulu Natal Press.

Bhaskar, Roy (1986). *Scientific Realism and Human Emancipation.* London: Verso.

Bonacich, Edna et al. (1994). The Garment Industry in the Restructuring Global Economy. In Edna Bonacich et al. (eds.). *Global Production: The Apparel Industry in the Pacific Rim,* 3–18. Philadelphia: Temple University Press.

Boyer, Robert (1990). *The Regulation School: A Critical Introduction.* New York: Columbia University Press.

Boyer, Robert (2005). How and Why Capitalisms Differ. *Economy and Society,* 34 (4), 509–557.

Boyer, Robert and Yves Saillard (eds.). (2002). *Régulation Theory: The State of the Art.* London/New York: Routledge.

Brand, Ulrich (2014). Kapitalistisches Wachstum und soziale Herrschaft: Motive, Argumente und Schwächen aktueller Wachstumskritik. *Prokla,* 175, 289–306.

Brand, Ulrich and Nicola Sekler (2009). Postneoliberalism: Catch-All Word or Valuable Analytical and Political Concept? Aims of a Beginning Debate. *Development Dialogue,* 51, 5–13.

Brown, Andrew et al. (eds.). (2002). *Critical Realism and Marxism.* London/ New York: Routledge.

Brown, Wendy (2000). Suffering Rights as Paradoxes. *Constellations,* 7 (2), 230–241.

Breuer, Franz (2010). *Reflexive Grounded Theory: Eine Einführung für die Forschungspraxis,* 2. Auflage. Wiesbaden: VS.

Buckel, Sonja (2007). *Subjektivierung und Kohäsion: Zur Rekonstruktion einer materialistischen Theorie des Rechts.* Weilerswist: Velbrück.

Bührmann, Andrea and Werner Schneider (2007). Mehr als nur diskursive Praxis? Konzeptionelle Grundlagen und methodische Aspekte der Dispositivanalyse. *Forum Qualitative Sozialforschung,* 8 (2), Art. 28.

Burawoy, Michael (1998). The Extended Case Method. *Sociological Theory,* 16 (1), 4–33.

Burckhardt, Gisela (ed.). (2011). *Mythos CSR: Unternehmensverantwortung und Regulierungslücken.* Bonn: Horlemann.

BWI (2012). *Better Work Indonesia: Garment Industry 1st Compliance Synthesis Report.* Geneva: ILO.

BWI (2013a). *Better Work Indonesia: Garment Industry 2nd Compliance Synthesis Report.* Geneva: ILO.

BWI (2013b). *Better Work Indonesia: Garment Industry 3rd Compliance Synthesis Report.* Geneva: ILO.

BWI (2014). *Better Work Indonesia: Garment Industry 4th Compliance Synthesis Report.* Geneva: ILO.

Caraway, Terry (2004). Protective Repression, International Pressure and Institutional Design: Explaining Labor Reform in Indonesia. *Studies in Comparative International Development,* 39 (3), 28–49.

Castells, Manuel and Alejandro Portes (1989). World Underneath: The Origins, Dynamics and Effects of the Informal Economy. In Alejandro Portes et al. (eds.). *The Informal Economy: Studies in Advanced and Less Developed Countries,* 11–37. Baltimore/London: Hopkins University Press.

Charmaz, Kathy (2006). *Constructing Grounded Theory: A Practical Guide Through Qualitative Analysis.* Thousand Oaks: Sage.

Chorus, Silke (2013). *Care-Ökonomie im Postfordismus: Perspektiven einer integralen Ökonomie-Theorie.* Münster: Westfälisches Dampfboot.

Chowdhry, Geeta (2004). Postcolonial Interrogations of Child Labour: Human Rights, Carpet Trade and Rugmark in India. In Geeta Chowdhry and Sheila Nair (eds.). *Power, Postcolonialism and International Relations: Reading Race, Gender and Class,* 225–254. London/New York: Routledge.

Christopherson, Susan and Nathan Lillie (2005). Neither Global Nor Standard: Corporate Strategies in the New Era of Labor Standards. *Environment and Planning A,* 37 (11), 1919–1938.

Clarke, Adele E. (2011). Von der Grounded-Theory-Methodologie zur Situationsanalyse. In Günter Mey and Katja Mruck (eds.). *Grounded Theory Reader,* 207–229. Wiesbaden: VS.

Clarke, Adele E. and Carrie Friese (2007). Grounded Theorizing Using Situational Analysis. In Antony Bryant and Kathy Charmaz (eds.). *The SAGE Handbook of Grounded Theory,* 363–397. Thousand Oaks: Sage.

Coe, Neil M. et al. (2008). Global Production Networks: Realizing the Potential. *Journal of Economic Geography,* 8 (3), 271–295.

Collier, Andrew (1994). *Critical Realism: An Introduction to Roy Bhaskar's Philosophy.* London: Verso.

Cox, Robert (1977). Labor and Hegemony. *International Organization,* 31 (1), 385–424.

Dackweiler, Regina (1995). *Ausgegrenzt und eingemeindet: Die neue Frauenbewegung im Blick der Sozialwissenschaften.* Münster: Westfälisches Dampfboot.

de Faria, Maurício S. and Henrique T. Novaes (2011). Brazilian Recovered Factories: The Constraints of Workers' Control. In Immanuel Ness and Dario Azzellini (eds.). *Ours to Master and to Own: Workers' Control from the Commune to the Present,* 400–417. Chicago: Haymarket.

Eagleton, Terry (1993). *Ideologie: Eine Einführung.* Stuttgart: Metzler.

Ebenau, Matthias et al. (2013). Zurück in die Zukunft? Dependenzperspektiven in der Analyse der Diversität des Gegenwartskapitalismus. *Peripherie,* 130/131, 220–242.

Ehmke, Ellen et al. (2009). Internationale Arbeitsstandards im globalen Kapitalismus. In Ellen Ehmke et al. (eds.). *Internationale Arbeitsstandards in einer globalisierten Welt,* 12–42. Wiesbaden: VS.

Elias, Juanita (2007). Women Workers and Labour Standards: The Problem of "Human Rights". *Review of International Studies,* 33 (1), 45–57.

Fairclough, Norman (2005). Peripheral Vision—Discourse Analysis in Organization Studies: The Case for Critical Realism. *Organization Studies,* 26 (6), 915–939.

Fairclough, Norman (2009). A Dialectical-Relational Approach to Critical Discourse Analysis in Social Research. In Ruth Wodak and Michael Meyer (eds.). *Methods of Critical Discourse Analysis,* 2nd Edition, 162–186. Thousand Oaks: Sage.

Fairclough, Norman et al. (2004). Critical Realism and Semiosis. In Jonathan Joseph and John M. Roberts (eds.). *Realism, Discourse and Deconstruction,* 23–42. London/New York: Routledge.

Faubert, Violaine (2011). Learning from the First Globalisation (1870–1914). *Trésor-Economics,* 93. 14 October 2014 https://www.tresor.economie.gouv.fr/File/333672.

Federici, Sylvia (2012). *Aufstand aus der Küche: Reproduktionsarbeit im globalen Kapitalismus und die unvollendete feministische Revolution.* Münster: Edition Assemblage.

Federici, Sylvia (2014). The Reproduction of Labour Power in the Global Economy and the Unfinished Feminist Revolution. In Maurizio Atzeni (ed.). *Workers and Labour in a Globalised Capitalism: Contemporary Themes and Theoretical Issues,* 85–107. Basingstoke: Palgrave Macmillan.

Feministische Autorinnengruppe (2013). Das Theorem der Neuen Landnahme: Eine feministische Rückeroberung. In Hans Baumann et al. (eds.). *Care statt Crash: Sorgeökonomie und die Überwindung des Kapitalismus,* Denknetz Jahrbuch 2013, 99–118. Zürich: Edition 8.

Ferenschild, Sabine (2011). "Better Factories Program" in Kambodscha—ist der Name auch Programm? In Gisela Burckhardt (ed.). *Mythos CSR: Unternehmensverantwortung und Regulierungslücken,* 83–87. Bonn: Horlemann.

Fink, Elisabeth (2014). Trade Unions, NGOs and Transnationalization: Experiences from the Ready-Made Garment Sector in Bangladesh. *ASIEN,* 130, 42–59.

Flyvbjerg, Bent (2006). Five Misunderstandings about Case-Study Research. *Qualitative Inquiry,* 12 (2), 219–245.

FoA Protocol (2011). *Freedom of Association Protocol,* 7 June 2011—English Translation. 19 March 2015 https://www.oxfam.org.au/wp-content/uploads/2011/08/oaus_foaprotocol_7_06_2011_englishtranslation.pdf.

Foucault, Michel (1972). *The Archaeology of Knowledge.* London/New York: Routledge.

Foucault, Michel (1978). *Dispositive der Macht: Über Sexualität, Wissen und Wahrheit.* Berlin: Merve.

Foucault, Michel (1980). *Power/Knowledge: Selected Interviews and Other Writings 1972–1977.* New York: Pantheon.

Foucault, Michel (1983). The Subject and Power. In Hubert L. Dreyfus and Paul Rabinow (eds.). *Michel Foucault: Beyond Structuralism and Hermeneutics,* 208–226. Chicago: University of Chicago Press.

Foucault, Michel (1988). Technologies of the Self. In Luther H. Martin et al. (eds.). *Technologies of the Self: A Seminar with Michel Foucault,* 16–49. Amherst: University of Massachusetts Press.

Ford, Michele (2000). Continuity and Change in Indonesian Labour Relations in the Habibie Interregnum. *Southeast Asian Journal of Social Science,* 28 (2), 59–88.

Ford, Michele (2006). Labour NGOs: An Alternative Form of Labour Organizing in Indonesia, 1991–1998. *Asia Pacific Business Review,* 12 (2), 175–191.

Ford, Michele (2009). *Workers and Intellectuals: NGOs, Trade Unions and the Indonesian Labour Movement.* Honolulu: University of Hawai'i Press.

Ford, Michele (2013). Employer Anti-Unionism in Democratic Indonesia. In Gregor Gall and Tony Dundon (eds.). *Global Anti-Unionism: Nature, Dynamics, Trajectories and Outcomes,* 224–243. Basingstoke: Palgrave Macmillan.

Gardener, Daisy (2012). Workers' Rights and Corporate Accountability: The Move Towards Practical, Worker-Driven Change for Sportswear Workers in Indonesia. *Gender & Development,* 20 (1), 49–65.

Gereffi, Gary and Miguel Korzeniewicz (eds.). (1994). *Commodity Chains and Global Capitalism.* Westport: Praeger.

Gereffi, Gary et al. (2005). The Governance of Global Value Chains. *Review of International Political Economy,* 12 (1), 78–104.

Gibson, Barry (2007). Accommodating Critical Theory. In Antony Bryant and Kathy Charmaz (eds.). *The SAGE Handbook of Grounded Theory,* 436–453. Thousand Oaks: Sage.

Glaser, Barney G. (1992). *Emergence vs. Forcing: Basics of Grounded Theory Analysis.* Mill Valley: Sociology.

Glaser, Barney G. (1998). *Doing Grounded Theory: Issues and Discussions.* Mill Valley: Sociology.

Glaser, Barney G. (2001). *The Grounded Theory Perspective: Conceptualization Contrasted with Description.* Mill Valley: Sociology.

Glaser, Barney G. and Anselm L. Strauss (1967). *The Discovery of Grounded Theory: Strategies for Qualitative Research.* New York: Aldine.

Graefe, Peter (2006). Social Economy Policies as Flanking for Neoliberalism: Transnational Policy Solutions, Emergent Contradictions, Local Alternatives. *Policy and Society,* 25 (3), 69–86.

Gramsci, Antonio (1971). *Selections from the Prison Notebooks.* New York: International Publishers.

Gramsci, Antonio (1992). *Gefängnishefte,* Band 4, Heft 6–7. Hamburg: Argument.

Gramsci, Antonio (1995). *Further Selections from the Prison Notebooks.* London: Lawrence & Wishart.

Habermann, Friederike (2008). *Der homo oeconomicus und das Andere: Hegemonie, Identität und Emanzipation.* Baden-Baden: Nomos.

Habermann, Friederike (2012). Von Post-Development, Postwachstum & Peer-Ecommony: Alternative Lebensweisen als "Abwicklung des Nordens". *Journal für Entwicklungspolitik,* 28 (4), 69–87.

Hadiz, Vedi R. (2000). Retrieving the Past for the Future? Indonesia and the New Order Legacy. *Southeast Asian Journal of Social Science,* 28 (2), 10–33.

Hauf, Felix (2006). *Regulation und Geschlecht: Zur feministischen Erweiterung der Regulationstheorie bei Kohlmorgen.* Diplomarbeit, Goethe-Universität Frankfurt.

Hauf, Felix (2013). Regulationstheorie, Cultural Political Economy und feministische Gesellschaftstheorie. *Femina Politica,* 1/2013, 56–68.

Hauf, Felix (2015). The Paradoxes of Decent Work in Context: A Cultural Political Economy Perspective. *Global Labour Journal,* 4 (3), 324–340.

Hassel, Anke (2008). The Evolution of a Global Labor Governance Regime. *Governance,* 21 (2), 231–251.

Heinrich, Michael (2001). Monetäre Werttheorie: Geld und Krise bei Marx. *Prokla,* 123, 151–176.

Hirsch, Joachim (1995). *Der nationale Wettbewerbsstaat: Staat, Demokratie und Politik im globalen Kapitalismus.* Berlin: Edition ID-Archiv.

Hirsch, Joachim (1998). *Vom Sicherheits- zum nationalen Wettbewerbsstaat.* Berlin: ID.

Hirsch, Joachim (2003). The State's New Clothes: NGOs and the Internationalization of States. *Rethinking Marxism,* 15 (2), 237–262.

Hirsch, Joachim (2005). *Materialistische Staatstheorie: Transformationsprozesse des kapitalistischen Staatensystems.* Hamburg: VSA.

Hughes, Caroline (2007). Transnational Networks, International Organizations and Political Participation in Cambodia: Human Rights, Labour Rights and Common Rights. *Democratization,* 14 (5), 834–852.

Humanity United (n.d.). *Exploitative Labor Practices in the Global Palm Oil Industry,* Prepared by Accenture for Humanity United. 23 May 2014 http://humanityunited.org/pdfs/Modern_Slavery_in_the_Palm_Oil_Industry.pdf.

Hurley, Jennifer and Doug Miller (2005). The Changing Face of the Global Garment Industry. In Angela Hale and Jane Wills (eds.). *Threads of Labour: Garment Industry Supply Chains from the Workers' Perspective*, 16–39. Malden: Blackwell.

ILO (1919). *Constitution of the International Labour Organization.* Versailles: ILO.

ILO (1944). *Declaration Concerning the Aims and Purposes of the International Labour Organisation.* Philadelphia: ILO.

ILO (1948). *Convention Concerning Freedom of Association and Protection of the Right to Organise.* San Francisco: ILO.

ILO (1996). *Convention Concerning Home Work.* Geneva: ILO.

ILO (1998). *Declaration on Fundamental Principles and Rights at Work.* Geneva: ILO.

ILO (1999). *Decent Work: Report of the Director-General,* International Labour Conference, 87th Session. Geneva: ILO.

ILO (2006). *Fixing Minimum Wage Levels in Developing Countries: Common Failures and Remedies.* Jakarta: ILO.

ILO (2008a). *Declaration on Social Justice for a Fair Globalization.* Geneva: ILO.

ILO (2008b). *Freedom of Association in Practice: Lessons Learned.* Geneva: ILO.

ILO (2010). *Global Jobs Pact Country Scan, Indonesia.* Geneva: ILO.

ILO (2011a). *Convention Concerning Decent Work for Domestic Workers.* Geneva: ILO.

ILO (2011b). *Social and Solidarity Economy: Our Common Road Towards Decent Work,* Reader for the Social and Solidarity Economy Academy 2011. Turin: ILO.

ILO (2012a). *Indonesia Decent Work Country Programme 2012–2015,* Geneva: ILO.

ILO (2012b). *Better Work Indonesia Garment Industry Baseline Report: Worker Perspectives from the Factory and Beyond.* Geneva: ILO.

Ives, Peter (2004). *Gramsci's Politics of Language: Engaging the Bakhtin Circle and the Frankfurt School.* Toronto: University of Toronto Press.

Jäger, Siegfried (2001). Dispositiv. In Marcus S. Kleiner (ed.). *Michel Foucault: Eine Einführung in sein Denken,* 72–89. Frankfurt/New York: Campus.

Jäger, Margarete and Siegfried Jäger (2000). *Von der Diskurs- zur Dispositivanalyse: Überlegungen zur Weiterführung eines Stadtteilprojekts,* Vortrag gehalten auf dem Workshop des DISS am 27. Mai 2000 in Freudenberg. 16 October 2013 http://www.diss-duisburg.de/2000/05/von-der-diskurs-zur-dispositivanalyse.

Jäger, Siegfried and Florentine Maier (2009). Theoretical and Methodological Aspects of Foucauldian Critical Discourse Analysis and Dispositive Analysis. In Ruth Wodak and Michael Meyer (eds.). *Methods of Critical Discourse Analysis,* 34–61. Thousand Oaks: Sage.

Jayasooria, Denison (ed.). (2013). *Developments in Solidarity Economy in Asia.* Puchong: JJ Resources.

Jenson, Jane (1997). Die Reinstitutionalisierung der Staatsbürgerschaft: Klasse, Geschlecht und Gleichheit im Fordismus und Postfordismus. In Steffen Becker et al. (eds.). *Jenseits der Nationalökonomie? Weltwirtschaft und Nationalstaat zwischen Globalisierung und Regionalisierung.* Argument-Sonderband, 249, 232–247. Berlin: Argument.

Jessop, Bob (1990). *State Theory: Putting the Capitalist State in Its Place*. Cambridge: Polity.

Jessop, Bob (2002). Capitalism, the Regulation Approach and Critical Realism. In Andrew Brown et al. (eds.). *Critical Realism and Marxism*, 88–115. London/New York: Routledge.

Jessop, Bob (2004). Critical Semiotic Analysis and Cultural Political Economy. *Critical Discourse Studies*, 1 (2), 159–174.

Jessop, Bob (2007). *State Power: A Strategic-Relational Approach*, Cambridge: Polity.

Jessop, Bob (2009a). Vom Regulationsansatz zu kultureller politischer Ökomomie: Geld und Rechte an geistigem Eigentum. In Peter Mooslechner et al. (eds.). *Auf der Suche nach dem Selbst: Finanzmärkte, Individuum und Gesellschaft*, 17–32. Marburg: Metropolis.

Jessop, Bob (2009b). Cultural Political Economy and Critical Policy Studies. *Critical Policy Studies*, 3 (3–4), 336–356.

Jessop, Bob (2012). Economic and Ecological Crises: Green New Deals and No-Growth Economies. *Development*, 55 (1), 17–24.

Jessop, Bob and Stijn Oosterlynck (2008). Cultural Political Economy: On Making the Cultural Turn without Falling into Soft Economic Sociology. *Geoforum*, 39, 1155–1169.

Jessop, Bob and Ngai-Ling Sum (2001). Pre-Disciplinary and Post-Disciplinary Perspectives. *New Political Economy*, 6 (1), 89–101.

Jessop, Bob and Ngai-Ling Sum (2006). Towards a Cultural International Political Economy: Poststructuralism and the Italian School. In Marieke de Goede (ed.). *International Political Economy and Poststructural Politics*, 157–176. Basingstoke: Palgrave Macmillan.

Jessop, Bob and Ngai-Ling Sum (2010). Cultural Political Economy: Logics of Discovery, Epistemic Fallacies, the Complexity of Emergence and the Potential of the Cultural Turn. *New Political Economy*, 15 (3), 445–451.

Jessop, Bob and Ngai-Ling Sum (2012). Cultural Political Economy, Strategic Essentialism and Neoliberalism. In Jenny Künkel and Margit Mayer (eds.). *Neoliberal Urbanism and its Contestations: Crossing Theoretical Boundaries*, 80–96. Basingstoke: Palgrave Macmillan.

John, Matthias (2011). Der Global Compact der Vereinten Nationen—Instrument für mehr verantwortliches Unternehmensverhalten oder doch nur "Blue-washing"? In Gisela Burckhardt (ed.). *Mythos CSR: Unternehmensverantwortung und Regulierungslücken*, 94–97. Bonn: Horlemann.

Kabat, Marina (2011). Argentinian Worker-Taken Factories: Trajectories of Workers' Control under the Economic Crisis. In Immanuel Ness and Dario Azzellini (eds.). *Ours to Master and to Own: Workers' Control from the Commune to the Present*, 365–381. Chicago: Haymarket.

Kabeer, Naila (2004). Globalization, Labor Standards and Women's Rights: Dilemmas of Collective (In)Action in an Interdependent World. *Feminist Economics*, 10 (1), 3–35.

Keck, Margaret E. and Kathryn Sikkink (1998). *Activists Beyond Borders: Transnational Advocacy Networks in International Politics*. Ithaca: Cornell University Press.

Knapp, Gudrun-Axeli (2010). "Intersectional Invisibility": Anknüpfungen und Rückfragen an ein Konzept der Intersektionalitätsforschung. In Helma Lutz et al. (eds.). *Fokus Intersektionalität: Bewegungen und Verortungen eines vielschichtigen Konzeptes*, 223–243. Wiesbaden: VS.

Kohlmorgen, Lars (2004). *Regulation, Klasse, Geschlecht: Die Konstituierung der Sozialstruktur im Fordismus und Postfordismus*. Münster: Westfälisches Dampfboot.

Kruck, Werner (1992). "Transformationsgesetz" und Wirklichkeit der Oppenheimerschen Genossenschaftstheorie. *Zeitschrift für öffentliche und gemeinwirtschaftliche Unternehmen*, 15, 1–16.

Kühl, Bianca (2006). *Protecting Apparel Workers Through Transnational Networks: The Case of Indonesia*. Stuttgart: Ibidem.

Kushner, Kaysi E. and Raymond Morrow (2003). Grounded Theory, Feminist Theory, Critical Theory: Toward Theoretical Triangulation. *Advances in Nursing Science*, 26 (1), 30–43.

La Botz, Dan (2001). *Made in Indonesia: Indonesian Workers since Suharto*. Cambridge: South End.

Laclau, Ernesto (1980). Populist Rupture and Discourse. *Screen Education*, 34, 87–93.

Laclau, Ernesto and Chantal Mouffe (1985). *Hegemony and Socialist Strategy: Towards a Radical Democratic Politics*. London: Verso.

Lambert, Rob (1997). Authoritarian State Unionism in New Order Indonesia. In Rob Lambert (ed.). *State and Labour in New Order Indonesia*, 56–82. Nedlands: University of Western Australia Press

Lavaca Collective (2007). *Sin Patrón: Stories from Argentina's Worker-Run Factories*. Chicago: Haymarket.

Lemke, Thomas (1997). *Eine Kritik der politischen Vernunft: Foucaults Analyse der modernen Gouvernementalität*. Argument-Sonderband, 251. Hamburg: Argument.

Lenin, Vladimir I. (1934). *"Left-Wing" Communism: an Infantile Disorder*. London: Lawrence & Wishart.

Li, Tanja M. (2009). To Make Live or Let Die? Rural Dispossession and the Protection of Surplus Populations. *Antipode*, 41 (S1), 66–93.

Link, Jürgen (2011). Diskursanalyse unter besonderer Berücksichtigung von Interdiskurs und Kollektivsymbolik. In Rainer Keller et al. (eds.). *Handbuch Sozialwissenschaftliche Diskursanalyse*, Band 1: Theorien und Methoden, 3. erweiterte Auflage, 433–458. Wiesbaden: VS.

Lipietz, Alain (1985). Akkumulation, Krisen und Auswege aus der Krise: Einige methodische Überlegungen zum Begriff "Regulation". *Prokla*, 58, 109–137.

Lipietz, Alain (1987). *Mirages and Miracles: The Crisis of Global Fordism*, London: Verso.

Lipietz, Alain (1988). Accumulation, Crises and Ways Out: Some Methodological Reflections on the Concept of "Regulation". *International Journal of Political Economy*, 18 (2), 10–43.

Lipietz, Alain (1992). Vom Althusserismus zur "Theorie der Regulation". In Alex Demirovic et al. (eds.). *Hegemonie und Staat: Kapitalistische Regulation als Projekt und Prozess*, 9–54. Münster: Westfälisches Dampfboot.

Lutz, Helma (2001). Die neue Dienstmädchenfrage im Zeitalter der Globalisierung. In Mathias Fechter (ed.). *Gesellschaftliche Perspektiven—Wissenschaft—Globalisierung: Jahrbuch der Hessischen Gesellschaft für Demokratie und Ökologie*, 114–135. Essen: Klartext.

Lutz, Helma (2005). Der Privathaushalt als Weltmarkt für weibliche Arbeitskräfte. *Peripherie*, 97/98, 65–87.

MacDonald, Marjorie (2001). Finding a Critical Perspective in Grounded Theory. In Rita S. Schreiber and Phyllis N. Stern (eds.). *Using Grounded Theory in Nursing*, 113–157. New York: Springer.

McNay, Lois (1994). *Foucault: A Critical Introduction*. Cambridge: Polity.

Mance, Euclides (2014). The Solidarity Economy in Brazil. In Vishwas Satgar, (ed.). *The Solidarity Economy Alternative: Emerging Theory and Practice*, 150–176. Pietermaritzburg: University of KwaZulu Natal Press.

Marsden, Richard (1999). *The Nature of Capital: Marx After Foucault*. London/New York: Routledge.

Marx, Karl (1890). *Das Kapital: Kritik der politischen Ökonomie*, Erster Band, Marx-Engels-Werke, Band 23. Berlin: Dietz.

Marx, Karl (1893). *Das Kapital: Kritik der politischen Ökonomie*, Zweiter Band, Marx-Engels-Werke, Band 24. Berlin: Dietz.

Marx, Karl (1894). *Das Kapital: Kritik der politischen Ökonomie*, Dritter Band, Marx-Engels-Werke, Band 25. Berlin: Dietz.

Maupain, Francis (2013). *The Future of the International Labour Organization in the Global Economy*. Oxford/Portland: Hart.

Mayring, Philipp (2008). *Qualitative Inhaltsanalyse: Grundlagen und Techniken*. Weinheim: Beltz.

Merk, Jeroen (2008). The Private Regulation of Labour Standards: The Case of the Apparel and Footwear Industries. In Jean-Christophe Graz and Andreas Nölke (eds.). *Transnational Private Governance and its Limits*, 115–126. London/New York: Routledge.

Merk, Jeroen (2009). Jumping Scale and Bridging Space in the Era of Corporate Social Responsibility: Cross-Border Labour Struggles in the Global Garment Industry. *Third World Quarterly*, 30 (3), 599–615.

Merk, Jeroen (2011a). Cross-Border Wage Struggles in the Global Garment Industry: The Campaign for an Asia Floor Wage. In Andreas Bieler and Ingemar Lindberg (eds.). *Global Restructuring, Labour and the Challenges for Transnational Solidarity*, 116–130. London/New York: Routledge.

Merk, Jeroen (2011b). *Cross-Border Anti-Sweatshop Campaigns and Local Bargaining in the Sportswear Industry: Negotiating a Protocol on Freedom of Association in Indonesia.* Paper Presented at the Workshop: Transnational Private Regulation in the Areas of Health, Environment, Social and Labor Rights: Theoretical Approaches and Empirical Studies, 28–29 January 2011, Free University Berlin.

Merk, Jeroen (2012). *10 Years of the Better Factories Cambodia Project: A Critical Evaluation,* Report for the Community Legal Education Centre and the Clean Clothes Campaign. Amsterdam: Clean Clothes Campaign.

Meuser, Michael and Ulrike Nagel (2005). ExpertInneninterviews—vielfach erprobt, wenig bedacht: Ein Beitrag zur qualitativen Methodendiskussion. In Alexander Bogner et al. (eds.). *Das Experteninterview: Theorie, Methode, Anwendung,* 2. Auflage, 71–93. Wiesbaden: VS.

Mittendrein, Lisa (2013). *Solidarität ist alles, was uns bleibt: Solidarische Ökonomie in der griechischen Krise.* Neu-Ulm: AG Spak.

Moody, Kim (1997). Towards an International Social-Movement Unionism. *New Left Review,* 225, 52–72.

Nadel, Henri (2002). Regulation and Marx. In Robert Boyer and Yves Saillard (eds.). *Régulation Theory: The State of the Art,* 28–35. London/New York: Routledge.

Nike (n.d.). *Nike Better World Manifesto.* 5 July 2012 http://www.nikebetterworld.com.

Parnreiter, Christof et al. (1999). Globalisierung und Peripherie. In Christof Parnreiter et al. (eds.). *Globalisierung und Peripherie: Umstrukturierung in Lateinamerika, Afrika und Asien,* 9–33. Frankfurt: Brandes & Apsel.

Offe, Claus (1974). Structural Problems of the Capitalist State: Class Rule and the Political System. On the Selectiveness of Political Institutions. In Klaus von Beyme (ed.). *German Political Studies,* Volume 1, 31–57. Thousand Oaks: Sage.

Oliver, Carolyn (2012). Critical Realist Grounded Theory: A New Approach for Social Work Research. *British Journal of Social Work,* 42 (2), 371–387.

Parente, Robert (2009). *Dismantling a Developmental State: Indonesia's Historical Shift from Keynesianism to Neoliberalism.* Major Paper in Support of the Masters in Public and International Affairs, Virginia Polytechnic Institute and State University, Blacksburg.

Pauker, Guy J. (1969). *The Rise and Fall of the Communist Party of Indonesia.* Memorandum Prepared for the United States Air Force under Project RAND. Santa Monica: The RAND Corporation.

Peck, Jamie and Adam Tickell (2002). Neoliberalizing Space. *Antipode,* 34 (3), 380–404.

Pfau-Effinger, Birgit (2004). Socio-Historical Paths of the Male Breadwinner Model: An Explanation of Cross-National Differences. *The British Journal of Sociology,* 55 (3), 377–399.

Polanyi, Karl (1944). *The Great Transformation: The Political and Economic Origins of Our Time.* New York: Farrar & Rinehart.

Poulantzas, Nicos (1978). *Staatstheorie: Politischer Überbau, Ideologie, Sozialistische Demokratie.* Hamburg: VSA.

Poulantzas, Nicos (2002). *Staatstheorie: Politischer Überbau, Ideologie, Autoritärer Etatismus.* Hamburg: VSA.

Prugl, Elisabeth (1999). *The Global Construction of Gender: Home-Based Work in the Political Economy of the 20th Century.* New York: Columbia University Press.

Przyborski, Aglaja and Monika Wohlrab-Sahr (2008). *Qualitative Sozialforschung: Ein Arbeitsbuch.* München: Oldenbourg.

Roosa, John (2006). *Pretext for Mass Murder: The September 30th Movement and Suharto's Coup d'État in Indonesia.* Madison: University of Wisconsin Press.

Ruddick, Susan (1992). Das Gesellschaftliche konstruieren: Armut, Geschlechterverhältnisse und Familie im Goldenen Zeitalter. In Alex Demirovic et al. (eds.). *Hegemonie und Staat: Kapitalistische Regulation als Projekt und Prozess,* 290–315. Münster: Westfälisches Dampfboot.

Rutherford, Donald (1998). *Leibniz and the Rational Order of Nature.* Cambridge: Cambridge University Press.

Sablowski, Thomas (1994). Zum Status des Hegemoniebegriffs in der Regulationstheorie. In Josef Esser et al. (eds.). *Politik, Institutionen und Staat: Zur Kritik der Regulationstheorie,* 133–156. Hamburg: VSA.

Salzinger, Leslie (2004). From Gender as Object to Gender as Verb: Rethinking How Global Restructuring Happens. *Critical Sociology,* 30 (1), 43–62.

Santos, Boaventura de Sousa (ed.). (2006). *Another Production is Possible: Beyond the Capitalist Canon.* London: Verso.

Satgar, Vishwas (2014). The Crises of Global Capitalism and the Solidarity Economy Alternative. In Vishwas Satgar (ed.). *The Solidarity Economy Alternative: Emerging Theory and Practice,* 1–34. Pietermaritzburg: University of KwaZulu Natal Press.

Scherrer, Christoph (1995). Eine diskursanalytische Kritik der Regulationstheorie. *Prokla,* 100, 457–482.

Scherrer, Christoph (2011). Reproducing Hegemony: US Finance Capital and the 2008 Crisis. *Critical Policy Studies,* 5 (3), 219–246.

Scherrer, Christoph and Thomas Greven (2001). *Global Rules for Trade: Codes of Conduct, Social Labeling, Worker's Rights Clauses.* Münster: Westfälisches Dampfboot.

Schwendter, Rolf (1986a). *Die Mühen der Berge: Grundlegungen zur alternativen Ökonomie—Teil 1.* München: AG Spak.

Schwendter, Rolf (1986b). *Die Mühen der Ebenen: Grundlegungen zur alternativen Ökonomie—Teil 2.* München: AG Spak.

Schwenken, Helen (2012). Vom "Dienstmädchen" zur "Arbeiterin": Die Konvention Nr. 189 der Internationalen Arbeitsorganisation "Menschenwürdige Arbeit für Hausangestellte". In Andrea Jung and Felix Hauf (eds. for EPN Hessen) *Gute Arbeit weltweit? Entwicklungspolitik, Gewerkschaften und Wissen-*

schaft zu globalen Arbeitsrechten und Sozialstandards, 37–40. Frankfurt: Entwicklungspolitisches Netzwerk Hessen.

Scipes, Kim (1992). Understanding the New Labor Movements in the "Third World": The Emergence of Social Movement Unionism. *Critical Sociology*, 19 (2), 81–101.

Sibbel, Lejo and Petra Borrmann (2007). Linking Trade with Labor Rights: The ILO Better Factories Cambodia Project. *Arizona Journal of International and Comparative Law*, 24 (1), 235–249.

Siegmann, Karin A. et al. (2014). Voluntary Initiatives in Global Value Chains: Towards Labour-Led Social Upgrading? *ISS Working Paper*, 586, 1–24. The Hague: Institute of Social Studies.

Solidarity for All (2014). *Solidarity is People's Power: Towards an International Campaign of Solidarity to the Greek People*. 4 March 2015 http:// www.solidarity4all.gr.

Sparke, Matthew (2013). *Introducing Globalization: Ties, Tensions and Uneven Integration*. Hoboken: Wiley-Blackwell.

SPN/GARTEKS/AKATIGA (2009). *Upah Layak untuk Sektor Tekstil dan Garmen di Indonesia* [Decent Wages in Indonesia's Textile and Garment Industry]. 18 December 2014 http://www.indotextiles.com/download/ Kajian%20Upah%20Layak%20Industri%20TPT.pdf.

Standing, Guy (1989). Global Feminization through Flexible Labour. *World Development*, 17 (7), 1077–1098.

Standing, Guy (1999). Global Feminization through Flexible Labour: A Theme Revisited. *World Development*, 27 (3), 583–602.

Standing, Guy (2008). The ILO: An Agency for Globalization? *Development and Change*, 39 (3), 355–384.

Strauss, Anselm L. and Juliet Corbin (1990). *Basics of Qualitative Research: Grounded Theory Procedures and Techniques*. Thousand Oaks: Sage.

Suddaby, Roy (2006). From the Editors: What Grounded Theory is Not. *Academy of Management Journal*, 49 (4), 633–642.

Sum, Ngai-Ling (1997). Ostasiatischer "Exportismus" und global-regional-lokale Dynamiken: Von der Regulation zur (Geo-)Governance von Zeit und Raum. In Becker, Steffen et al. (eds.). *Jenseits der Nationalökonomie? Weltwirtschaft und Nationalstaat zwischen Globalisierung und Regionalisierung*. Argument-Sonderband, 249, 167–213. Berlin: Argument.

Sum, Ngai-Ling (2005). From "Integral State" to "Integral World Economic Order": Towards a Neo-Gramscian Cultural International Political Economy. *Cultural Political Economy Working Paper*, 7. Lancaster: Cultural Political Economy Research Centre.

Sum, Ngai-Ling (2006). Towards a Cultural Political Economy: Discourses, Material Power and (Counter-)Hegemony. *Demologos Spot Paper*, Lancaster: Cultural Political Economy Research Centre.

Sum, Ngai-Ling (2010). Wal-Martization and CSR-ization in Developing Countries. In Peter Utting and José C. Marques (eds.). *Corporate Social Responsibility and Regulatory Governance*, 50–76. Basingstoke: Palgrave Macmillan.

Sum, Ngai-Ling and Bob Jessop (2013). *Towards a Cultural Political Economy: Putting Culture in its Place in Political Economy*, Cheltenham: Edward Elgar.

Summers, Clyde (2001). The Battle in Seattle: Free Trade, Labor Rights and Societal Values. *University of Pennsylvania Journal of International Economic Law*, 22 (1), 61–90.

Suryomenggolo, Jafar (2012). Indonesien: Arbeiterkontrolle in Java 1945/1946. In Dario Azzellini and Immanuel Ness (eds.). *"Die endlich entdeckte politische Form": Fabrikräte und Selbstverwaltung von der Russischen Revolution bis heute*, 262–283. Köln/Karlsruhe: ISP.

Tambunan, Rita (2010). *Workers and Trade Unions in Indonesia: Some Facts & Reflections*. Pointers for a Discussion at IG Metall Headquarters, Frankfurt (unpublished).

Tjandraningsih, Indrasari and Hari Nugroho (2008). The Flexibility Regime and Organised Labour in Indonesia. *Labour and Management in Development*, Volume 9, 1–14.

Ulbricht, Christian (2012). Entzauberung eines Mythos? Kritik und Rechtfertigung am Beispiel von Nike. *Peripherie*, 32 (128), 445–470.

Uriona, Viviana I. (2007). *Solidarische Ökonomie in Argentinien nach der Krise von 2001: Strategische Debatten und praktische Erfahrungen*. Kassel: Kassel University Press.

Uwiyono, Aloysius (2007). Indonesian Labor Law Reform since 1998. In Naoyuki Sakumoto and Hikmahanto Juwana (eds.). *Reforming Laws and Institutions in Indonesia: An Assessment*, 187–203. Chiba Shi: Institute of Developing Economies.

Vosko, Leah F. (2002). "Decent Work": The Shifting Role of the ILO and the Struggle for Global Social Justice. *Global Social Policy*, 2 (1), 19–46.

Vosko, Leah F. (2004). Standard-Setting at the ILO: The Case of Precarious Employment. In John J. Kirton and Michael J. Trebilcock (eds.). *Hard Choices, Soft Law: Voluntary Standards in Global Trade, Environment and Social Governance*, 134–152. Aldershot: Ashgate.

Wallerstein, Immanuel M. (2004). *World-Systems Analysis: An Introduction*. Durham: Duke University Press.

Waterman, Peter (2004). Adventures of Emancipatory Labour Strategy as the New Global Movement Challenges International Unionism. *Journal of World-Systems Research*, 10 (1), 217–253.

Wetterer, Angelika (2003). Rhetorische Modernisierung: Das Verschwinden der Ungleichheit aus dem zeitgenössischen Differenzwissen. In Gudrun-Axeli Knapp and Angelika Wetterer (eds.). *Achsen der Differenz: Gesellschaftstheorie und feministische Kritik II*, 286–319. Münster: Westfälisches Dampfboot.

Wells, Don (2009). Local Worker Struggles in the Global South: Reconsidering Northern Impacts on International Labour Standards. *Third World Quarterly*, 30 (3), 567–579.

Wick, Ingeborg (2005). *Nähen für den Weltmarkt: Frauenarbeit in Freien Exportzonen und der Schattenwirtschaft*. Siegburg: Südwind.

Wilkinson, Rorden (2002). Peripheralizing Labour: The ILO, WTO and the Completion of the Bretton Woods Project. In Jeffrey Harrod and Robert O´Brien (eds.). *Global Unions? Theory and Strategies of Organized Labour in the Global Political Economy*, 204–220. London/New York: Routledge.

Williams, Elena (2007). *Transnational Feminism and Labour Organising: The Case of Gabungan Serikat Buruh Indonesia*. BA Thesis, University of Sydney.

Wolff, Jonas (2008). *Turbulente Stabilität: Die Demokratie in Südamerika diesseits ferner Ideale*. Baden-Baden: Nomos.

Wright, Erik O. (2000). Working-Class Power, Capitalist-Class Interests and Class-Compromise. *American Journal of Sociology*, 105 (4), 957–1002.

Žižek, Slavoy (2009). *First As Tragedy, Then As Farce*. London: Verso.

Index